BOSTON

Pictorial Research by Sharlene Voogd Cochrane
"Partners in Progress" by Mary M. Whelan

Produced in cooperation with the
Greater Boston Chamber of Commerce
Windsor Publications, Inc.
Woodland Hills, California

BOSTON

CITY

ON A

HILL

An Illustrated History by

Andrew Buni and Alan Rogers

"For Boston, for Boston..."

Windsor Publications Inc.
History Books Division
Publisher: John M. Phillips
Editorial Director, Corporate Biographies: Karen Story
Senior Picture Editor: Teri Davis Greenberg
Design Director: Alex D'Anca
Marketing Director: Ellen Kettenbeil
Sales Coordinator: Joan Baker

Staff for *Boston: City on a Hill*
Senior Editors: Annette Igra, Jim Mather
Picture Editor: Nancy Evans
Assistant Director, Corporate Biographies: Phyllis Gray
Corporate Biographies Editor: Judith Hunter
Editorial Assistants: Kathy Brown, Patricia Buzard, Gail Koffman,
    Lonnie Pham, Pat Pittman
Sales Manager: Ruth Burton, Michele Sylvestro
Sales Representative: Mary Whelan
Layout Artist: Karen McBride

Library of Congress Cataloging in Publication Data

Buni, Andrew.
    Boston, a city on a hill.

    Bibliography: p. 235
    Includes index.
    1. Boston (Mass.) —History. 2. Boston (Mass.) —Description.
3. Boston (Mass.) —Industries. I. Rogers, Alan, 1936-   . II. Title.
F73.3.B96   1984   974.4'61   84-21977
ISBN 0-89781-090-2

Contents

Foreword

The history of Boston is unique because of the remarkable persistence of a theme first articulated in 1630 by its Puritan founders. The Puritans conceived of themselves as free, disciplined individuals whose pursuit of their own self-interest had to be joined by a commitment to serve the community. "See what there is to be done," urged the Reverend Richard Baxter, "and do it with all your might." The character of the city and its people has been shaped by this dynamic charge.

Boston was intended to be a "City on a Hill," a shining example of how men and women motivated by a commitment to hard work and to personal, religious, and civic reform might change the course of history. Guided by this ideal, the people of the city

have, at times, acted nobly. Boston proudly
boasted that it was "Freedom's Birthplace,"
the "Athens of America," and the "hub of the
cosmos," and that its citizens were a chosen
people whose special mission was to lead the
way to a better America. To be sure,
narrowmindedness, racism, and political
corruption have sometimes dimmed the beacon
light. But the ideals of reform and hard work
have persisted.

These ideals were initially the preserve of a
unified, homogeneous Yankee population. The
Irish, Italians, Jews, and other immigrant
groups challenged this claim. Beginning in the
1880s the Irish took control of the city's
political life. "Honey Fitzgerald" and James
Michael Curley replaced Josiah Quincy and
James Jackson Storrow. At the same time the
city divided into ethnic neighborhoods, each
within walking distance of the other but
separate nevertheless. Most recently racial
conflict has ripped at the heart of Boston.

This divisiveness has caused some to decry
the death of the city. Certainly pessimists
have held center stage before. In the 1840s
and 1880s some prophets of doom predicted

the demise of the idealistic republican dream. It was impossible, they predicted mournfully, to assimilate millions of immigrants. The city and its ancient values would be destroyed.

There have been vast and countless changes—new land, peoples, buildings, ideas, and leaders have transformed Boston. Rather than braking these developments, however, the old principles have provided a rich historical legacy that has allowed Boston not only to survive a succession of crises but also, in the recent words of Mayor Kevin H. White, to stand poised for flight into the 21st century.

I
City on a Hill

Boston's history may be said to have begun at that moment in 1534 when King Henry VIII turned his back on the Pope. Henry knew, of course, that his bold act would have sharp repercussions, but it was easy for the king to be optimistic. He and his new bride, Anne Boleyn, were happy—for the moment—and thousands of Englishmen applauded Henry's decision to leave the Catholic Church. They believed it would now be possible to purify England's churches, making them truly Protestant.

But Henry VIII and his immediate successors, who after the break with Rome headed the Church of England, resisted the efforts of those militant Protestant reformers called Puritans. Still the number of Puritans increased. When Henry's daughter, Mary

Tudor, tried to return England to the Pope she was scorned publicly. Privately some Puritans called for her head. She survived, however, and the Puritans paid a heavy price for their impetuousness.

In 1558 Elizabeth I succeeded her sister Mary. The Puritans were both pleased and dismayed by the policies Elizabeth pursued. They were delighted that she defied the Pope and made England a bulwark of Protestantism against the Catholic power of Spain. She even made a few Puritans part of her inner circle of advisors. Yet Elizabeth also insisted that the Anglican Church be administered by archbishops and bishops and that all Englishmen agree to a bundle of moderate statements of faith—the Thirty-Nine Articles. For zealous Puritan reformers these measures smacked of Catholicism, but they told themselves, comfortingly, that the country was moving their way.

The Puritan way was a hard road to follow. To begin with, the Puritans adhered to the Calvinist idea that God had predestined those who were to be saved and those who were to be eternally damned before they were born. Man could do nothing. No amount of prayer and contemplation nor good behavior would alter God's plan. Puritanism required that man face this fact unblinkingly, but at the same time commit himself to a lifelong struggle to achieve salvation. Puritanism demanded that man do good, but told him he was a hopeless sinner. According to Puritan belief God commanded that the world be totally reformed, although He admitted that evil was incurable. Puritans were required to work long and hard and successfully at a job to which God had "called" them, while at the same time fixing their complete attention on God. Puritans were to live in this world but not be of it.

The anxiety caused by these contradictory commands could be overpowering. A young English tailor's apprentice, for example, made some halfhearted attempts to reform his life but fell far short of the goal of perfection demanded by Puritan preachers. He was paralyzed. "I knew not what to do, thinking God now had utterly forsaken me," he wrote years later when he was living in Boston. "And when I had cried so long that I could cry no longer, I rose up in a forlorn condition." Eventually this young man joined in the "great coming to New England," settling first in Roxbury.

The inner tension felt by those who would be Puritans might also, however, stimulate activity, a relentless drive to achieve God's grace and to fulfill His purpose. Those men and women who seemingly had been predestined by God were the "elect," saints in a sinful world struggling to make everything right. Of course no one could—or should—be certain that they were one of God's elect for God's ways were mysterious and man's reasoning weak. But doubt did not lessen the Puritan's obligation to reform religion and the world. "See what is to be done, and do it with all your might," the Reverend Richard Baxter told his congregation early in the 17th century.

The Puritans expected the Church of England and the English government to help them. The state and the churches were to work together to root out sin and corruption. Anglican churchmen believed that the Church of England provided the means to bring man to a state of grace. The Puritans disagreed. Priests and rituals interfered with a man's search for salvation, they argued. The essence of religious experience, according to the Puritans, consisted of two simple interlocking elements: a struggle by man to bring his open and willing soul into direct contact with God; and a commitment to learn as much as possible about God's plan by reading the Bible.

One other important difference divided Anglicans from Puritans. Anglicans felt that it was impossible to determine who had achieved a state of grace and who was still a sinner. Therefore orthodox clergymen argued that everyone should be a member of the church. In short the Church of England was a national church to which all Englishmen belonged by birthright. The Puritans disagreed vehemently with this position. They thought it was possible—if difficult—to determine if a person was one of God's elect by administering the proper exams and by correctly interpreting the signs of favor. This meant it was possible—and, according to zealous Puritans, desirable—to restrict church membership only to those who were thought to be saints. A Puritan congregation was an exclusive gathering of the elect, not an inclusive national church.

These differences were not mere empty theoretical squabbling—how many angels can dance on the head of a pin? Gaining entrance into a church was the central event in a 17th-century Englishman's life. When, for example, one distraught young man came to the dark conclusion that he was a hopeless sinner, he decided "it was a greater evil to live and to sin against God than to kill myself." So he slung his gun over his shoulder and walked out into the woods. Then, he tells us, "I cocked my gun, and set it on the ground, and put the muzzle under my throat, and took up my foot to let it off." Happily he had second thoughts. In fact he "thought that God's blessedness might belong to me, and it much supported my spirit." Not all Puritans were so intense, but all of them yearned to be counted among God's company of saints.

People's fears and aspirations were not allayed completely even if they were convinced that God had chosen them. Every nation, the Puritans believed, had a convenant with God. If a people abided by His laws, He would treat them well. The chief function of government, therefore, was to ensure good behavior, to stamp out sinfulness. If the government failed to do its job satisfactorily, the people were obligated to overthrow it, replacing the corrupt rulers with better ones. If they did not, God's wrath would destroy the nation.

Gradually the Puritans came to the conclusion that they were living in "evil and declining times" and that they had to act quickly to save themselves and England. Increasingly they were

John Winthrop was an English gentleman, a Puritan, and the first governor of the New World Puritan Commonwealth. (TBS)

persecuted, chased from chapel, thrown into prison, fined, and berated. Archbishop William Laud, appointed by King Charles I in the 1620s, believed the Puritans were dangerous revolutionaries. The archbishop once shouted at the Rev. Thomas Shepard that he belonged to "a company of seditious, factious, bedlams" and forbade Shepard to exercise any ministerial functions. Shepard's Puritan congregation promptly disregarded the ban.

Other Puritans were prompted to act because of their declining economic situation. Englishmen believed that they were threatened by the country's rapidly increasing population. Based on the assumption that there was a fixed and limited amount of wealth to be distributed, men worried, as one Elizabethan official put it, that "our land has not milk sufficient in the breast thereof to nourish all those children which it hath brought forth."

Puritans such as John Winthrop, a country squire forced by economic necessity to increase his law practice in order to expand his shrinking resources, were convinced that corruption and sin lay at the root of England's economic woes. Therefore their preachers called for reform. But increasingly the way to change seemed to be blocked. Lawmakers,

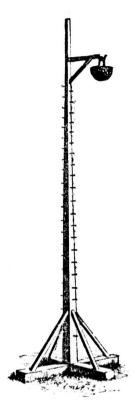

The original Beacon Hill beacon alerted the country to invasion. It was a tall mast with an iron frame projecting 65 feet from the base, holding a barrel of tar. When fired, the light could be seen for a great distance. Winds blew the beacon down in 1789. From King's Handbook of Boston, Moses King, 1883

members of Parliament sympathetic to the Puritans, were frustrated by King Charles II's incompetence and angered by his softness on the issue of Catholicism. When in 1629 Parliament balked at the means by which Charles II demanded money be raised for a foreign adventure, he dissolved Parliament and made it plain that he did not intend to call another.

While some Puritans began to whisper to one another about revolution, others—such as squire John Winthrop and the distraught young tailor's apprentice who once had contemplated suicide—thought about creating a "new" England. In 1628 a small group of dissenters had put together a land company and sent out an advance party to settle on Cape Ann, north of Boston. A year later the Crown granted a charter to the Massachusetts Bay Company, permitting it not only to trade and to settle in New England but also "to govern and rule all His Majesty's subjects that reside within the limits of our plantation." By chance the charter omitted any reference to the place that the company should hold its meetings.

Winthrop and 11 other Puritan leaders met in Cambridge in the summer of 1629 and decided to take advantage of the Crown's mistake. They boldly and unanimously agreed that "the government and patent should be settled in New England." Pushed by the conviction that England would soon suffer God's wrath and pulled by the prospect of establishing a prosperous Bible Commonwealth, the Puritans prepared to leave Old England for New in the spring of 1630.

John Winthrop was elected governor, the company choosing him over John Humfrey, Isaac Johnson, and Sir Richard Saltonstall. Six months of hectic preparation followed. Clergymen, of course, but also skilled workmen were especially recruited for the new colony. Not all those who won Winthrop's approval to sign on were Puritans. Not all those who were chosen were able to pay their own way. Winthrop and some other leaders, therefore, paid the fares of some

men and women in exchange for their services for a specified number of years.

Clearly the group that set sail from Southampton in April 1630 was not a homogeneous community. Some were religious dissenters—Puritans—others were not; some were wealthy, some were poor. They jammed into 17 ships, more than a thousand men and women in search of a new life. It was an exciting adventure, though tinged with sadness. "We cannot part from our native Country," they declared in a published statement, "without much sadness of heart and many tears in our eyes."

Heavy seas, a sparse diet, and the long voyage across the North Atlantic took a toll. By June of 1630, when Cape Ann was sighted, many among Winthrop's company were sick and dying. Still, Winthrop and the other leaders decided almost immediately that "Salem, where we landed, pleased us not," and they cruised up and down the coast, poking in and around the small islands and rivers that marked the shoreline, looking for a better place to settle. After some controversy and a couple of false starts, the hilly, tadpole-shaped peninsula that the Indians called Shawmut (crossing place) was the spot chosen for the colony's central community.

Dorchester was a group of rural villages until well into the 19th century. This was the view from a small park at the summit of Mt. Bowdoin in the center of Dorchester (now near Bowdoin and Bullard streets). Painting by H. Knacht. (TBS)

Boston—a name selected earlier to commemorate the English town where the Rev. John Cotton had given the farewell sermon to the settlers—was chosen primarily because it had an excellent source of clear spring water. (Dozens of settlers had sickened and died after they had come ashore at Salem, and the cause was believed to have been the water they drank.) At first glance the site seemed to have little else to recommend it. To begin with the Shawmut peninsula was almost an island. Roughly two miles long and no more than a mile wide, it was connected on the south with the Puritan settlement at Roxbury by the narrowest neck of land. To the west of the neck were large mud flats and marshes, and beyond was the Charles River that flowed into Boston Harbor and separated the peninsula from Charlestown. A deep cove carved out of the eastern side of the peninsula divided Boston into North and South ends, each dominated by a small, steep hill. Between Fort Hill in the South End and Windmill or Copp's Hill in the North End, there was a ridge, or as William Wood described it in 1634, "a high Mountain with three little rising Hills on the top of it, wherefore it is called the Tramount." The three peaks were Cotton Hill on the east, West Hill on the Charles River side,

and in the center, Beacon Hill—so-called because the government ordered in 1634 that "there shall be. . .a beacon set on the. . .hill at Boston, to give notice to the country of any danger."

By August Winthrop's group had established itself just below Cotton Hill and along a line leading to Town Cove. In the waning days of summer, children scrambled about the hills picking berries, and at low tide they jumped from rock to rock searching for mussels. The adults, meanwhile, prepared as best they could for the approaching winter. There was too little wood on the peninsula and too little time before winter to build proper houses, so the people of Boston dug in, scooping caves into the hills or digging cellars to be covered over with planks.

While the settlers were digging in, Winthrop sent a ship to England with instructions to buy provisions and return to Boston as soon as possible. At the same time the governor sent men along the coast to trade for corn with those Indians who were willing to sell. Winthrop himself sought to make contacts with local Indian tribes for the same purpose.

These efforts met with some success—one boat brought 100 bushels of corn from Cape Cod—but the winter of 1630-1631 was harsh and long and marked by death. By the time the relief ship sailed into Boston Harbor in February, 200 men and women had died. A like number decided they had had enough and returned to England.

The morale of those who survived and stayed was surprisingly good. The coming of spring boosted people's spirits and released their energies. "The winter's frost being extracted forth the earth," wrote Edward Johnson, an artisan who lived through the winter of 1630, the people "fell to tearing up the roots and bushes with their hoes; even such men as scarce ever set hand to labor before...readily rush through all difficulties." Gardens were planted in the fields of Boston, and on the mainland large farms were cut out of the wilderness. Winthrop, for example, set his servants to work clearing 600 acres of rich land along the Mystic River. Gradually houses began to take shape. One group of settlers clustered around Town Cove, another just to the south, where the marketplace would be built. Before long Samuel and Anne Cole opened a part of their newly built house as a tavern. Not far away a meetinghouse for both civic and religious purposes was built.

While a great deal remained to be done—there were in Winthrop's words, "All things to do as in the beginning of the world"—it was evident by 1632 that Boston would survive. By the end of the decade, farmers around Boston were producing an agricultural surplus. Dorchester was noted for its orchards, Roxbury for its cattle, and Boston's gardens and smaller fields yielded an abundance of corn, peas, barley, and oats.

The town's future, however, did not lie with agriculture. During the first 10 years of its existence Boston was sustained, and indeed prospered, because thousands of immigrants arrived in the colony each year. Between 15,000 and 20,000 newcomers swelled the population of Massachusetts Bay from 1630 to 1640. The ships on which they arrived brought a variety of manufactured goods—axes, guns and gunpowder, clothing, nails, and

pots and kettles—that were quickly sold to old settlers. At the same time the newcomers needed lumber and food, which local merchants were happy to sell. The demand for goods was so great that merchants soon adopted the practice of rowing out to meet an incoming ship as soon as it entered Boston Harbor, shouting bids, and buying goods before the ship docked at Town Cove.

The Puritan governors were embarrassed by these chaotic scenes and passed several laws designed to control Boston's burgeoning commercial life. But mere laws could not hedge the enterprising spirit. Gradually the town's economic activity was made more orderly by the merchants who came to dominate the trade. Men such as Robert Keayne, the Hutchinsons, and the Tyngs, who had family ties or friendships in London, were able to place orders for the goods they needed and so insure that their potential customers would have an adequate stock. Furthermore, these early Boston merchant families began to dominate the inland trade, acting as middlemen for merchants in the outlying towns. By the 1640s, therefore, Boston was the hub of a complex external and internal trade network, extending from England to the Caribbean and from Long Island Sound to Springfield.

"It hath pleased God," boasted a group of prosperous Bostonians in 1648, "that our Town chiefly consists of Trade .. a mart to the Country." Not everyone agreed that prosperity was a blessing. Speaking for the colony's political elite, the Massachusetts General Court expressed its shock at the social consequences of commerce. The assembly declared:

Its utter detestation and dislike, that men or women of mean condition should take upon them the garb of gentlemen, by wearing gold or silver lace, or buttons...or to walk in great boots, or women of the same rank to wear silk or tiffany hoods or scarves which, though allowable to persons of greater estates or more liberal education, yet we cannot but judge it

Dorchester was settled in June 1630, some weeks before Boston. An early resident, Robert Pierce, built this house in 1640. (TBS)

intolerable in persons of such like condition.

Fashion was merely the tip of the iceberg. The colony's leaders felt a pervasive sense of disorder.

The Puritans had come to Boston, after all, to build a new kind of community. It was to be a covenanted community, existing under a commission from God. Winthrop had laid out a blueprint while still on board the *Arbella.* It was God's intention, Winthrop declared, that "every man might have need of other, and from hence they might all be knit more nearly together in the bonds of brotherly affection." If the Puritans adhered to the buiding principle of "brotherly affection," if they all worked together, they would fulfill the terms of God's special commission and He would favor the community. But if the people were selfish "the Lord will surely break out in wrath against us," Winthrop warned.

The success or failure of the Bible Commonwealth would have worldwide and historic consequences. "For we must consider," Winthrop said, "that we shall be as a city on a hill, the eyes of all people are on us." The people of Boston were expected, in other words, to look forward to the final establishment of a utopian Christian community. Every individual was bound in this special compact with God and each other. The ties extended vertically, uniting classes and the society. The individual had to be concerned, therefore, not only with his own behavior but also with that of the total community. An individual's shortcomings imperiled the group. So too did attacks on authority.

Fully mindful of this danger, a group of rebels nevertheless openly and militantly challenged the spiritual and secular authorities of Boston in 1636. The dissidents were led by Ms. Anne Hutchinson, a remarkably witty, aggressive, and intelligent woman. She had come to Boston from England in 1634, as many Puritans had, in order to achieve salvation as a member of the Reverend John Cotton's church. Cotton was a brilliant theologian who articulated a position that placed him and his followers into opposition with Puritan

This gravestone for Jerome Topliff, who died in 1640, is located in the Old Burying Ground in Dorchester at the corner of Stoughton Street and Boston (now Columbia) Road. (TBS)

orthodoxy. Cotton minimized the importance of individual action, or preparation, and emphasized the belief that salvation could be demonstrated only by the individual's feeling God's grace within. He directed his Boston congregation "not to be afraid of the word Revelation."

While the majority of Puritans condemned Cotton's doctrine as smacking too much of the heresy known as Antinomianism, Anne Hutchinson and many others were attracted to his ideas. Indeed Ms. Hutchinson began to hold weekly meetings in her home in which the sermon of the previous Sunday furnished the starting point for a religious discussion. She soon went beyond Cotton's careful distinctions and argued instead for a doctrine that posited a mystic relationship between God and an individual in which a consciousness of the Holy Spirit's presence within a person was the only acceptable sign of salvation. Moreover Ms. Hutchinson declared that only those people within whom the Holy Spirit dwelt, were able to recognize others who were saints.

From the orthodox point of view,

Hutchinson's ideas were extremely dangerous, a frontal assault on the structure of Puritan society. Puritan ministers stressed the importance of the Bible, of their preaching, and of membership in a congregation. Ms. Hutchinson talked about an individual's feelings. Puritan magistrates believed that their most important job was to use their authority to hold together a stratified, hierarchical community. To the contrary Ms. Hutchinson emphasized the autonomous individual. In short Ms. Hutchinson's doctrines saw ministers and magistrates as obstacles to salvation and to equal opportunity and treatment.

Given the very limited role women were expected to play in society, Ms. Hutchinson's ideas were especially appealing to the women of Boston. A woman was supposed to be weak, submissive, and modest; she was urged to avoid books and in church to follow the apostle Paul's dictum that women were not "to teach, nor to usurp authority over the man, but to be in silence."

Ms. Hutchinson was neither silent nor submissive, and under her leadership female resistance to male authority figures and to narrowly defined social norms became more defiant. She and her followers charged that the orthodox clergymen were unfit to preach. They demonstrated their disdain by walking out of the Boston church en masse when the Rev. John Wilson rose to preach. And Ms. Hutchinson encouraged the men in her group to provoke religious debates in town meetings, within the militia, and even on the floor of the General Court.

By the winter of 1636, Boston and many of the outlying towns were divided into hostile camps. The annual elections were hotly contested. With Ms. Hutchinson's movement clearly in mind, Winthrop moaned that "All things are turned upside down among us" and asked voters to restore order by reelecting him. Because, among other reasons, women could not participate in politics, Winthrop was returned to office, and within a few months he moved to crush the opposition by attacking Ms. Hutchinson.

She was brought to trial—such as it was—in November 1636 charged with three civil offenses: that she had encouraged people to sign petitions; that she had held meetings for women and men in her home, which was not "comely" nor "fitting" for a woman to do; and that she had violated the Fifth Commandment by disobeying her "parents," the magistrates. There was no jury and no apparent procedure. Questions and accusations were flung angrily at Ms. Hutchinson and her answers brusquely pushed aside when they didn't suit the magistrates. It was obvious they were determined to get rid of her. When they were unable to best her on theological grounds, the magistrates fell back on denigrating Ms. Hutchinson as a woman. She and her female followers were accused simultaneously of usurping their husbands' authority and of encouraging "foul, gross, filthy and abominable" sexual promiscuity. Even her onetime friend, the Reverend Cotton, resorted to using the technique of guilt by sexual innuendo. "Though I have not heard, neither do I think, you have been unfaithful to your Husband in his Marriage Covenant, yet," he added disingenuously, "that will follow."

Despite this and other slurs on her character, Ms. Hutchinson was winning the debate when, in an unguarded moment, she blurted out that God would punish her accusers. Asked how she knew this, she explained, "by an immediate revelation." This was heresy. It required only the briefest deliberation for the court to agree that Ms. Hutchinson's declaration was cause for banishment from the colony.

A few months later the Boston church excommunicated Anne Hutchinson. The Reverend Wilson commanded her "as a Leper to withdraw yourself out of the congregation." Anne rose, accepted the hand of her friend, Mary Dyer, and walked out. (Twenty-two years later, Dyer returned to Boston and was hanged as a Quaker.) Together with a few others

Anne Hutchinson was tried by the magistrates in 1636 and, convicted of heresy, she was banished to Rhode Island. From Scribner's Popular History of the United States, *1897. Courtesy, Rhode Island Historical Society*

they joined a settlement in Newport, Rhode Island, where they lived until 1642. Fearing that the Massachusetts' authorities would seize the settlement, Anne fled to Long Island. In August 1643 she and five of her children were killed by Indians.

Boston's clergymen rejoiced, claiming that the "American Jezebel" had been destroyed by God, and the magistrates heaved a sigh of relief thinking they had guaranteed their unqualified hold on power. But the freemen of the colony had their own ideas. In 1634 they had won the right to elect deputies to the General Court, which was to meet four times every year to make laws. While this process was disrupted somewhat during the dispute with Anne Hutchinson, the freemen were not willing to bow to Governor Winthrop's argument that a benevolent despotism was the best form of government. The representatives who sat in the General Court disagreed with Winthrop and did their best to enlarge their role. The House and the governor fought over the issue of whether a piece of legislation could become law over the veto of the governor and his assistants in

One spiritual threat
perceived by the new
Puritan Commonwealth
was the "inner light"
faith of the Quakers.
Threatened with death
twice for preaching in
Boston, Mary Dyer
returned a third time
and was hanged. Her
statue, created by Sylvia
Shaw Judson,
stands before the
Massachusetts State
House. Courtesy,
Massachusetts State
House

MARY DYER

QUAKER

WITNESS FOR RELIGIOUS FREEDOM

HANGED ON BOSTON COMMON 1660

"MY LIFE NOT AVAILETH ME
IN COMPARISON TO THE
LIBERTY OF THE TRUTH"

the upper House. When Isreal Stoughton,
a freeman from Dorchester, drew up a list
of arguments against Winthrop's position,
the governor branded him "a troubler of
Isreal" and demanded that the House
burn Stoughton's article and bar him from
office for three years. Winthrop still had
enough prestige to force his will on the
House, but his vindictiveness caused the
voters to turn him out of office in 1637
and again in 1641.

With Winthrop out of the way, the
members of the General Court were able
to press forward with their project to
articulate the general principles of
government. The Body of Liberties,
drafted by Nathaniel Ward of Ipswich,
did not describe in detail the machinery
of government in the Bible
Commonwealth, but it defined and
protected the people's civil rights and
gave the sanction of law to the unique
form of town government that had
emerged in Boston and the other towns.
The freemen of every town, the Body of
Liberties stated, had the right to choose

each year "select persons" who would
make bylaws.

Just how firmly the people were
committed to the new code was illustrated
in 1645. A political squabble broke out in
Hingham between contending candidates
for a militia command. Winthrop
intervened citing one faction for contempt,
but the lower house of the General Court
impeached him for having exceeded the
powers of his office and for having
violated fundamental law. Although
Winthrop was acquitted and the
representatives, therefore, were forced to
listen to his "victory" speech in which he
defined liberty as obedience to authority,
it was clear that absolute control had
slipped from his hands. Social order in
Boston was not destroyed by the struggle
between the governor and the freemen for
political power, nor by the controversy
that swirled around Anne Hutchinson, nor
was the Puritan world transformed. But
everywhere—in all aspects of
society—there were uncertainties and
changes. Some were apparent to the eye.
Boston had become by mid-century "the
Center Town and Metropolis," with
shipyards crowded in the North End and
businesses of all sorts clustered around
the dock and market areas. Commerce
was clearly the lifeblood of Boston.

A new group of merchants had surged
to the top with the town's growth spurt
during the second half of the 17th
century. These men had not brought
wealth with them from England, but had
made their fortunes in Boston. And unlike
the older elite whose wealth was in
farmland, the new group owned town lots
and houses, invested in shipping, or
owned businesses. John Mylam, for
example, arrived in Boston in 1635 and
bought 14 acres of land at Muddy River
(Brookline) that he exchanged in a few
years for several town lots in Boston,
which he sold later for a considerable
profit; this capital he used to launch a
trading partnership with William Tyng.
Thomas Leverett, another of Boston's
nouveau riche, gradually put together a
large commercial farm that was worked

for him by laborers and tenants. In the 1650s he was one of 14 investors who built a wharf and warehouses at Town Cove. One of Leverett's partners, Thomas Clarke, was elected a constable of Boston shortly after the completion of the waterfront development.

Not everyone succeeded, of course. Some failed and some men moved on to other towns. Nor were the results of Boston's new commercial prosperity an unmixed blessing. Puritan ministers thought too many men showed "an over-eager desire after the world." Likewise, the General Court was deeply concerned in 1650 by the "many and great miscarriages...committed by sailors" swaggering through the streets of Boston. And one snowy evening in November 1685, Samuel Sewall, one of the new group of merchants, reported matter-of-factly that a newborn baby boy had been left at the door of Shaw's tobacco shop.

But this side of Boston's burgeoning society should not be overemphasized. The townspeople were moral, God-fearing men and women who sought salvation first and prosperity and pleasure second. A *New England* was emerging, but the changes had not yet settled into permanent new forms. A crisis—the outbreak of an Indian war in the summer of 1675—accelerated the process of change and in its aftermath a new order was plainly evident.

While New Englanders' relationship with the neighboring Indian tribes had been pockmarked by sporadic violence since 1637 when the Pequot War ended, it was the pressure of population growth and the land hunger that accompanied it that caused the long and bloody conflict known as King Philip's War. Between 1650 and 1675 the Anglo-American population in the greater Boston area doubled and both speculators and the government were eager to push westward and southward onto the lands occupied by the Naragansetts and the Wampanoags. Metacom, or King Philip as the English called him, sachem of the Wampanoags, was forced by the New England

Confederation to accept one humiliation after another. The worst came in 1671 when he was compelled to surrender a large stock of guns and to accept government control of his tribal lands. From that time on, it would seem, Metacom began building a league of Indian resistance.

The incident that ignited the league's fury was the trial of three Wampanoags for the murder of John Sassamon, a Christian and Harvard-educated Indian who had warned leaders in Plymouth that the Wampanoags were planning an all-out attack on the Anglo-American settlements. A jury of 12 Englishmen and a smaller auxiliary jury composed of Indians found the Wampanoags guilty. The three men were hanged June 8, 1675. There were immediate outbreaks of burning and looting, and before the month ended Metacom's warriors swooped down on the frontier towns of Swansea and Mattapoiset, killing nine men. Meeting in Boston, the New England Confederation created a special war committee that selected Captain Daniel Henchman to command a company of 100 men drafted from the militia companies of Boston and

The Townhouse, built in 1657, was the institutional center of colonial Boston. Residents sold products in the marketplace, received punishments at the stocks and whipping post, and met here for formal governmental sessions and informal citizen gatherings. This structure burned in 1711 and was replaced by the brick State House which still occupies the site. Courtesy, Boston Athenaeum

This weathervane of molded copper, representing the Massachusetts and Wampanoag Indians, was fashioned by Shem Drowne for the cupola of the Province House, home of the colony's royal governors. Courtesy, Massachusetts Historical Society

several surrounding towns. On the night of June 26th, drums beat for volunteers. Within hours Captain Samuel Moseley, a hard-bitten adventurer who had sailed into Boston Harbor only a few weeks earlier towing a captured pirate ship, signed up nearly 100 more men.

Boston's soldiers were soon joined by men from throughout New England. Although they were well armed and supplied and determined to fight, the troops were unable to pin down the highly mobile Indian warriors. Several sweeps of the Mount Hope peninsula, where Metacom was reported to be hiding, yielded nothing. Indeed while Captain Henchman's men slowly searched the swampy ground along the Acushnet River, Rehoboth, Taunton, and Dartmouth were attacked. The Reverend John Eliot, who had spent his life attempting to Christianize the Indians, summed up the frustration and the danger of fighting such an elusive enemy. "We were too ready to think that we could easily suppress that flea," he commented, "but now we find that all the craft is in catching of them and that in the mean while they give us many a sore nip."

Buoyed by Metacom's successful hit-and-run attacks, tribe after tribe joined the Wampanoags. By the time of the first snowfall in November 1675, the entire upper Connecticut Valley had been laid waste by Indian forays and a score of frontier towns destroyed. By March Metacom's warriors were attacking Medfield and Weymouth, less than 20 miles from Boston.

Thoughts of English superiority were gone, replaced by fear and apprehension. Resistance to the draft became a serious problem by the spring of 1676, and refugees from frontier towns poured into Boston. "Many people in these parts are souls distracted, running hither and thither for shelter, and no where at ease," wrote Samuel Gorton. The selectmen were sympathetic, but they grumbled about the cost of feeding and housing the refugees and worried about what to do with all the young unmarried people who were

footloose and fancy-free in Boston.

In the late spring of 1676, the Indian offensive began to wane. The Indians had difficulty in obtaining food and weapons; they were losing the war of attrition. First a few warriors, then groups of half-starved men, women, and children began to surrender. In July 180 Nipmucks voluntarily surrendered to Boston authorities. Among them was the sachem, Matoonas, who was identified as a leader of the first attack on a Massachusetts town. He immediately was marched to Boston Common, tied to a tree, and shot. The others were tied together by a rope around their necks, dragged through the streets, and finally imprisoned on Deer Island in Boston Harbor. Those Indians who were not executed (records indicate 14 men were either shot or hanged) or held captive (there were more than 450 prisoners on Deer Island) were sold into slavery.

Finally on August 12, 1676, Captain Benjamin Church's men launched a surprise attack on a Wampanoag village near Bridgewater. Afterwards the soldiers discovered that one of the Indians they had killed was Metacom. Church ordered the body decapitated and quartered, and he and his men proudly displayed the head on their triumphant march back to Boston. Several thousand other Indians and about as many Englishmen were killed during this bloody, bitter war. Of some 90 Puritan settlements, 52 had been attacked and 12 destroyed. Many Indian villages were devastated. For the Indians of New England it was the last gasp.

There were important and far-reaching consequences for the people of Boston as well. The war accelerated the process of change already in motion, and the result was the clear emergence of new forms and values. First of all the war legitimized the merchants' claim to elite status. Boston merchants had provided vital support to the government during the war. When the New England Confederation needed money and supplies, it turned to the merchant community, to men who had capital and connections and know-how.

And no one asked if these men were members of a Puritan church. Some were; some were not. Those merchants who were not saints were honored nevertheless by the town for their contribution to the colony's war effort. Those merchants who had been accepted as saints before the war were viewed with much less suspicion afterwards. This meant that wealthy merchants were able to break through the old social barriers. A recent immigrant to New England was astonished, for example, to discover that Boston merchants "will marry their children to those whom they will not admit to baptism, if they be rich."

Merchants thought better of themselves. Samuel Sewall, a third-generation Boston merchant who kept a diary most of his adult life, reflects the passing of rigid Puritanism. In all outward ways Sewall kept the faith. But the intensity of his spiritual life slackened as the years passed. He simply was not interested in brooding introspection; he was a genial man who succeeded in trade and lived a full, honorable life as a merchant-gentleman.

The second major change stimulated by King Philip's War was the tendency to explain events by reason, rather than by divine intervention. After the war there was a debate about the causes of the conflict and how future trouble with the Indians might be avoided. In a pamphlet published in 1676 as a part of a complete history of the war, the Reverend Increase Mather, minister of Boston's North Church, argued that the war had been punishment for the sins committed by the people of Massachusetts. The Indians were the agents of Satan. In order to avoid new calamities, Mather prescribed prayer, fasting, and a strict adherence to "the Laws which are founded upon the word of God."

William Hubbard, a member of Harvard's first graduating class and a reluctant minister, disagreed. He bluntly told the General Court in his election-day sermon that the war was not God's doing, but "can be imputed to nothing more

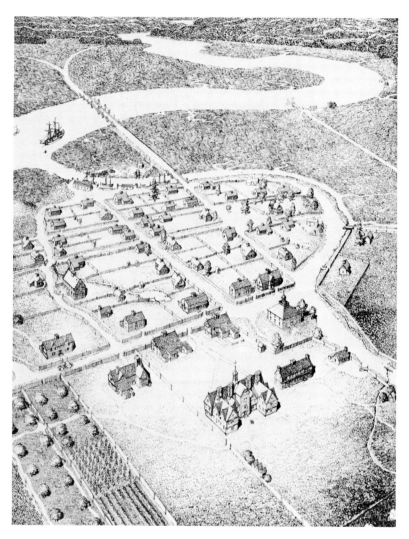

than to the contempt of our enemies, or overweening thoughts of our own skill and courage." Hubbard recommended legislation that would control the business activities of greedy land speculators, men who "easily swallow down hundreds of acres of land and are not satisfied."

Clearly the social groupings and values of the Founders were crumbling. The people of Boston had emerged from the war with a new consciousness: they were more comfortable with material success and with worldly explanations. Bostonians believed they were in control of their own destiny. When, in the next century, England threatened Boston's sense of community, there followed a series of political upheavals and ultimately a revolution.

Nathaniel Shurtleff created this conjectural view of Harvard College for Samuel Eliot Morison's Harvard College in the Seventeenth Century, *published in 1936. The large building in the foreground is probably at a right angle to the present site of Matthews Hall, while the Charles River winds through the background. Courtesy, Harvard University Archives*

II
The Cradle of Liberty

The leaders, ideas, and events that sparked the American Revolution were Boston's before they were America's. Eighteenth-century Boston was a unique political community, so intensely concentrated, homogeneous, and self-conscious in culture that its influence reached far beyond its borders. Boston's political leaders did not set out to foment a revolution. But their deep commitment to liberty—stemming in part from the Puritan idea that America had a special place in God's plan—put them on a collision course with British politicians who sought to tighten their control over imperial trade and politics.

Before the 1750s the American colonists had been loyal, if somewhat factious and uncooperative subjects of the British Crown. For more than three generations Bostonians

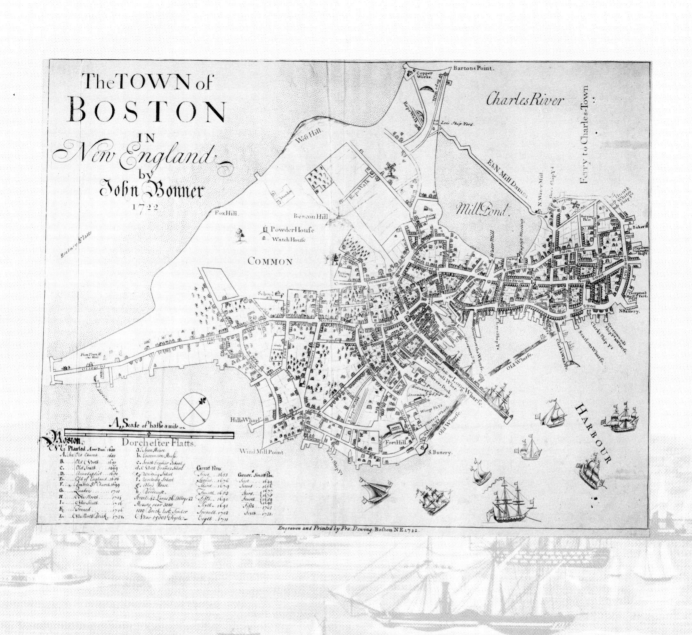

The TOWN of
BOSTON
IN
New England
by
John Bonner
1722

Previous page: The most well-known map of colonial Boston, Captain John Bonner's rendition of the town indicates that Boston's population was clustered about the one-half mile Long Wharf in marked contrast to the open western lands, where the rope walks and Boston Common were located. Courtesy, New York Public Library

Above: One hundred years after settlement Boston was still a walking city, only two miles long and one mile wide. Shipping and sea commerce employed the majority of workers, and the biggest trading customer was England. This photograph is part of an engraving by I. Carwitham. (TBS)

had accepted the restrictions imposed on their commercial activities by the Laws of Trade and Navigation. Based on the assumption that the colonies were in an inferior and dependent relationship to the mother country, the Navigation Acts stipulated that all American goods were to be monopolized by British merchants and shippers. England alone, it was decreed in 1660, would enjoy the profits of shipping and reexporting colonial goods. A second parliamentary act passed a few years later stated that no European goods could be shipped directly to America; all goods from Europe first had to be sent to England, unloaded there, and reshipped to the colonies.

Largely because this economic system was inefficiently and laxly administered, Boston prospered during the 17th and early 18th centuries. In fact Boston was the first American city to experience the leavening effects of trade, because it was the hub of a transatlantic trade network. Boston merchants exported molasses, rum, lumber, fish, livestock, hay, and flour to the West Indies and imported sugar from the islands. New Englanders also carried black slaves from the Ivory Coast to the West Indies. This Atlantic trade generated bills of credit drawn on English merchant houses that were used by Boston merchants to purchase manufactured goods.

While the triangle trade system was far-flung and potentially very lucrative, it was relatively flexible and easy to enter. Thomas Hancock, for example, came to Boston from Lexington at the age of 14 years as an apprentice to a bookseller. Within two decades Hancock's hard work and a "good marriage" enabled him to accumulate enough capital to finance several commercial ventures. He traded molasses from the West Indies for fish in Newfoundland and imported Dutch tea from the West Indies to Boston. By the late 1730s Hancock owned his own fleet of ships and had built a splendid mansion on Beacon Hill, complete with orchards and formal gardens. Peter Faneuil was another merchant who profited handsomely from the Caribbean trade. To show his gratitude to the city that had made possible his wealth, he gave Boston a "large brick building. . .for the use of a market" in 1742. Located near Town Dock, the building had market stalls on the ground floor and offices and a sizeable hall on the second floor. Designed by Jonathan Smibert, a portrait painter, Faneuil Hall centralized business activities, freeing other sections of the city from the noise and refuse created by unregulated commerce. Between Faneuil Hall and Long Wharf—which stretched 2,000 feet into the harbor-and along Merchants Row, other commercial structures were built during the 1730s to meet the needs of Boston's busy merchants.

About the same time, but far from the hustle and bustle of the North End, where most merchants still worked and lived, a new Congregational church was built. The Old West Church was meant to be an inducement to the development of a new residential area. Simon and Samuel Lynde subdivided their pasture land in 1737 in the hope of luring prosperous families to a life-style characterized by open space and a homogeneous neighborhood. A number of Boston's younger, wealthy merchants and professionals quickly took advantage of the opportunity. Certainly other Boston churches had members who were involved in commerce, but the Old West was noted for its "genteel congregation" and the "high dress" of the women who attended.

While it was most obvious at the Old West, conspicuous consumption, and its economic and social opposite, poverty, came increasingly to characterize Boston society. Wealth was less equitably distributed in the 1770s than it had been at the turn of the century. An assessment carried out by the town in 1774 revealed that the top 5 percent of Boston's taxpayers controlled 49 percent of the taxable assets of the community, whereas the economic elite previously had held only 30 percent. At the same time poverty scarred the lives of a growing number of Bostonians.

During the first half of the 18th century the percentage of poor people—defined as adult white males who were neither property owners nor dependents of taxpayers—more than doubled. And, most alarming to the town fathers, the lower middle class was hardest hit by the economic changes. Boston's selectmen lamented in 1757 that "besides a great Number of Poor...who are either wholly or in part maintained by the Town, and so are exempt from being Taxed, there are many who are Rateable according to Law...who are in such poor circumstances that considering how little business there is to be done in Boston they can scarcely procure from day to day daily Bread for themselves and Families." The fact was that the average carpenter, baker, or tavern keeper who died in Boston around 1760 had less to show for a lifetime's work than his ancestor of a century before.

The difficult situation in which the growing number of poor found themselves was made worse, according to Boston's clergymen, because the wealthy had become too selfish and materialistic and too little concerned about "relieving the wants of the Indigent and Distressed." There was a lack of public-spiritedness; the interdependency of man that the Puritan founders had emphasized had fallen victim to the individualistic pursuit of wealth. Therefore there was a greater need for charity. Sermons designed to promote acts of charity appealed to self-interest. Wealthy men commonly were portrayed as the agents of an enterprising deity, making wise investments in poor relief on His behalf. The Reverend Joseph

This was Faneuil Hall as it looked during the Revolutionary War, before being enlarged by Charles Bulfinch. This print is from an engraving by C.B. Hall, first published in Massachusetts Magazine in 1789. Courtesy, Boston Public Library (BPL)

Allin, for example, told his congregation that "the Great Benefactor" would "highly recompense" the charity of liberal men. Another earthly benefit of charity, according to Cotton Mather's sermon titled *Durable Riches,* was that it helped maintain a stable, hierarchical society. Charity would affirm publicly the distinction between rich and poor. "Doing good," Mather declared, "would assert the superiority of one man above another," underscoring his claim to honor and deference. Despite repeated appeals and warnings of this sort, Boston's elite did not give enough to sustain the growing number of poor. Therefore the city's taxpayers had to shoulder a larger share of the welfare burdens. In the 1720s and 1730s, the overseers of the poor expended 25 pounds per thousand inhabitants; but per capita costs doubled in the 1740s and 1750s and doubled again in the following two decades.

While the number of those who received poor relief increased, there is no evidence of mass destitution. Poverty in Boston never approached the level that characterized England, where poverty was the most serious and most controversial social problem of the 18th century. At times one-third of the population was impoverished; in London the poor overwhelmed the charitable institutions. But even in the worst times after 1760, poor relief involved no more than 5 percent of Boston's population.

Still resentment and anxiety were endemic to mid-18th-century Boston. Although neither the poor nor the well-to-do could measure precisely their economic situations, they could easily discern the general trend. Few working men doubted that the rich merchants were amassing fortunes. At the same time the wealthy elite was deeply anxious about the social consequences of poverty.

Occasionally these hostile feelings just below the surface exploded. An incident that took place at a ferry dock along the Charles River following the Harvard commencement of 1755 reveals how potentially volatile Boston society was:

Notwithstanding the two Constables that placed themselves there, two Gentlemen's Servants were thrown over, and not less than 20 of our poor Slaves (Male and Female) were thus injuriously served that evening. The most astonishing Cursing and Swearing was continually sounding in my Ears. Women as they left the boat, were indecently talked to, and some of them most immodestly handled. That part of the Town was in the utmost Disorder and this effected by a Rabble that consisted of at least 200.

The turbulence caused by the economic tensions was moderate compared to that which developed in religion. Since American culture was still largely religious in its orientation, these tensions lay at the heart of the revival that swept through the colonies in the 1740s. The Great Awakening, as the revival was called, did not begin all at once. There were stirrings in western Massachusetts and elsewhere in the colonies in the 1730s. But when George Whitefield, the brilliant English preacher, toured the colonies in 1740 he carried the torch of evangelicalism with which he set the colonies ablaze with religious fervor for nearly four years.

Whitefield began his spectacular tour in Newport, Rhode Island, where he declared that "the word of the Lord is. . .sharper than a two-edged sword." In late September he moved on to Boston, where his effect was stupendous. At first he preached to hundreds who jammed into the churches. Then when the crowds overflowed the churches, Whitefield held open-air meetings. On October 12, 1740, he preached to an audience of 30,000, nearly twice the population of the city, that packed Boston Common to hear him. Sara Edwards was there. She later described Whitefield as "a born orator. . .with a deep-toned, yet clear and melodious voice. It is wonderful to see what a spell he casts over an audience by proclaiming the simplest truths of the Bible." "I have seen," she wrote, "thousands of people hang on his words with breathless silence,

broken only by an occasional
half-suppressed sob."

Although his style was
revolutionary—because he appealed
primarily to his listeners'
emotions—Whitefield's doctrines were not
new. He stressed the need for an
emotional conversion experience and
downplayed the importance of reason and
good works, or "preparation," in achieving
salvation. In fact the evangelicals claimed
to be doing nothing more than revising
the standards of true Puritanism. Thomas
Prince, copastor of the Old South Church,
for example, insisted that Whitefield
preached "the doctrines of the martyrs
and other reformers, which were the same
as our forefathers brought over hither." In
an elaborate set of sermons published in
Boston in 1743, Prince argued that the
Awakening was part of God's plan for His
chosen people. He insisted that no one
knew who was saved, certainly not the
"cold and careless" ministers who were
more concerned with the "Profits,
Pleasures and Preferments of the World"
than with their souls. Prince's support of
the revival and his attack on orthodox
clergymen did not go unanswered.

Charles Chauncy, pastor of the
venerable First Church of Boston, rushed
into print four antirevival tracts before
Prince's final sermon appeared. Chauncy
was a rational man of regular habits. A
friend described his daily routine: "At
twelve o'clock, he took one pinch of snuff,
and only one in twenty-four hours. At one
o'clock, he dined on one dish of plain
wholesome food, and after dinner took one
glass of wine, and one pipe of tobacco,
and only one in twenty-four hours." Not
surprisingly Chauncy found the revival's
emphasis on emotion and enthusiasm to
be repugnant. He believed religion's proof
and strength were derived from an orderly
and optimistic world view. He appealed to
reason, believing that a person's intellect
controlled, or should control, his emotions.
As the Boston pastor saw it, "there is the
religion of the Understanding and
Judgment and Will, as well as the
Affections; and if little account is made of
the former, while great stress is laid upon
the latter...People should run into
disorder."

Chauncy's worst fears were confirmed
by James Davenport's antics. Davenport
was an orthodox minister who came under
Whitefield's spell. He left his own church
to become an evangelist, preaching
wherever and whenever he was able to
find an audience. Speaking without a text,
Davenport sang and prayed and
encouraged those who had "seen the
light" to do the same. He denounced
every establishment minister as a "dead
husk" and stirred crowds into a frenzy.
Thrown out of Boston as a "madman,"
Davenport sponsored a public burning in
New London, Connecticut. He called upon
his audience to burn books written by
those who opposed the Awakening, as well
as "petticoats, silk gowns, short cloaks,
red-heeled shoes, fans, necklaces, gloves
and other such apparel." While hymns
were sung over the pile, Davenport added
his own pants, "a pair of old, wore out,
plush breaches." This, commented an
observer, would have obliged him "to
strut about bare-arsed" had the fire not
gone out.

*The Reverend George
Whitefield (1714-1770)
was the itinerant
English evangelist who
led the "Great
Awakening." From*
Dictionary of American
Portraits, *Dover, 1967*

For an increasing number of Bostonians, Davenport's behavior aroused fears that all social order would be destroyed if the evangelicals had their way. But by the mid-1740s the most intense fires of the Awakening had faded. But American society would never be the same again. At least three areas of social thought were irreversibly affected by the Great Awakening.

First the authority and status of the conservative Boston clergy and those who supported the passive acceptance of the established hierarchy was permanently weakened. "It is an exceedingly difficult, gloomy time with us," wrote one Boston minister. "Such an enthusiastic, factious, censorious Spirit was never known here....Every low-bred, illiterate Person can resolve Cases of Conscience and settle the most difficult Points of Divinity better than the most learned Divines." The corollary of the new anti-authoritarian attitude that the Awakening encouraged was a virulent attack on the wealthy. An anonymous Boston pamphleteer, for example, charged that the rich squeezed their money from the town's poor people. "No wonder such Men can build Ships, Houses, buy Farms, set up their Coaches, Chariots, and live very splendidly," railed the *Centinel*. "Such men," he concluded bitterly, are "Birds of prey...Enemies to all Communities—wherever they live." Finally the revival conditioned men to accept mass meetings as the natural and logical outcome of confrontation, name-calling, and labeling. Certainly it seemed so to thousands of Boston patriots who gathered on the Common in 1773 to hear an oration on the "Beauties of Liberty."

Like all Englishmen, before 1763 Bostonians accepted the antinomy of power and liberty as the central reality of politics. Power meant the rule of some men over others. The essential characteristic of power was its aggressiveness, its unrelenting attack on liberty. As John Adams—the Braintree lawyer who opened his office in Boston in 1768—put it, the political world was divided into two antagonistic spheres: the sphere of power and the sphere of liberty. Power was in the hands of the government and "like the ocean, not easily admitting limits to be fixed in it." Liberty, by contrast, was always weak, always "skulking about in corners...hunted and persecuted in all countries by cruel power." Liberty was not, therefore, as it is for us, the concern of the people and the government alike, but only of the governed.

The chief aim of a good government was to harness these contending forces for the mutual benefit of all. The British constitution—a bundle of institutions, laws, customs, and the basic principles that motivated them—accomplished this extraordinary task by balancing and checking the basic forces within society. It was commonly assumed that British society consisted of three social orders, each of which would be best served by a different form of government: royalty, whose natural form of government was monarchy; the nobility, whose natural form was aristocracy; the commons, or people, whose form was democracy. The functions of the British government were carefully distributed among these three orders so that no one dominated the others. This "mixed constitution" created a framework that insured order and the preservation of the rights and liberty of all men.

Constitutional liberty was neither license, nor the abstract liberty that existed in a state of nature. Political, or civil, liberty was the capacity to exercise "natural rights" within the boundaries of the law. The rights of all Englishmen, including the American colonists, were understood to be those maxims of reason and justice that were inalienable and God-given. But they were not explicitly written down anywhere, not codified. To assert that all rights might be articulated in a comprehensive code was, as James Otis ("the best lawyer in Boston") declared, "the pedantry of a quack, and the nonsense of a pettifogger." For free

Englishmen, rights were not constricted, but expansively expressed in the common law, acts of Parliament, and in the charters of privileges issued by the Crown.

Somehow England's constitution embodied the rights of Englishmen. John Adams argued in 1763 that the English constitution was "the most perfect combination of human powers in society which finite wisdom has yet contrived and reduced to practice for the preservation of liberty and the production of happiness." But there was always danger. The Boston Town Meeting pointed out, in 1772, that "ambition and lust of power above the law are. . .predominant passions in the breasts of most men." These are instincts that have stimulated "the worst projects of the human mind in league against the liberties of mankind," the meeting added.

Without surrendering this general belief, Boston patriots such as John Adams insisted that Americans were different, unique in their sense of virtue. Political virtue, as it was defined by Adams and other political leaders, was related to the Puritan belief that motivated Boston's settlement; namely, that God had chosen the American people to provide an example to the rest of the world of a just political order, where individuals were free to pursue the acquisition of property.

Property, however, was not a goal to be pursued singlemindedly and selfishly. A virtuous citizen eschewed "luxury and extravagance," focusing instead on what would be good for the community. "It would be the glory of this Age," Sam Adams wrote to a friend, "to find Men having no ruling Passion but the Love of their Country, and ready to render her the most arduous and important Services with the Hope of no other Reward in this Life than the Esteem of their virtuous Fellow Citizens."

Sam Adams of Boston was that man. Son of a Boston brewer, he took up a career as a professional politician soon after graduating from Harvard with the class of 1740. Initially an active participant in the Boston Town Meeting,

Adams was first elected to the Massachusetts assembly in 1765. The following year he was chosen clerk of the General Court for which he received a small stipend, the greater part of his income for the 10 years prior to independence. He was simply uninterested in money or possessions. For Adams, poverty was a source of pride. He confessed to his wife, "I glory in being what the world calls a poor Man." When, in 1774, Adams was chosen a delegate to the Continental Congress, his Boston neighbors collected funds to outfit him so that he would not be an embarrassment to Massachusetts.

Although his life was politics, Sam Adams was not an ambitious, opportunistic office-seeker. He was an organizer, a committee man, whose skill was, as Charles Francis Adams observed in the 19th century, "infusing into the scattered efforts of many all the life and energy which belongs to a single will." Long unfairly accused of being the "Boston dictator" whose sly, manipulative backroom deals singlehandedly brought about the American Revolution, or the "master of the mob" whose command caused the "rabble" to initiate violence and destruction in the streets of Boston, Adams' reputation recently was rescued by Pauline Maier. She put it eloquently: Sam Adams was "the American revolutionaries' American revolutionary. . .confident that the ways of his forefathers were winning their rightful place in the history of mankind, and who died looking forward to a great liberation not from this earth but upon it."

To realize his dream Adams, knowing what all other patriots knew, argued that English tyranny—the use of arbitrary power—had to be resisted. When rulers "pervert their powers to tyrannical purposes," Andrew Eliot, minister of the New North Church of Boston, told his congregation in 1765, "submission is a crime." Jonathan Mayhew, Eliot's colleague across town at the Old West Church, was even more explicit. If public officials oppress the people it is

Right: The Green Dragon Tavern, on Union Street, was a gathering place for patriots to discuss their responses to English tyranny. (BPL)

Above: Coffee at the Green Dragon Tavern was served in this urn, which is eighteen inches tall and six inches wide at the base. (TBS)

"warrantable and glorious to disobey the civil power." Indeed, according to Mayhew, it is the people's duty "to break the yoke of tyranny and free themselves and posterity from inglorious servitude and ruin."

The trick, of course, was to figure out at what point government policies became truly oppressive. When should the people rebel? Was English policy deliberately designed to usurp the liberties of the people? Or were the laws passed by Parliament merely the result of ignorance or incompetence? Gradually and reluctantly from 1750 onwards a majority of Bostonians came to the conclusion that English political leaders had secretly formulated a dark plan to strip Americans of all their liberties, to enslave them. The belief that a conspiracy existed—as one recent historian put it—acted as "an inner accelerator to the movement of opposition." Every law passed, every reaction, and every denial confirmed the suspicion of the patriots. Therefore people were urged to act, to rebel, before it was too late. It was from this perspective that Bostonians viewed the actions of the English government.

The first step toward the creation of a

tyranny, everyone knew, was the establishment and misuse of a permanent professional army and navy. Both the royal navy and army relied upon impressment—recruitment by force—to fill their ranks. In England impressment was commonplace and accepted. But in the American colonies the practice was militantly resisted by the lower classes who were the target of recruiters and denounced by local middle-class politicians. Both groups regarded impressment as a violation of their rights as Englishmen.

On the morning of November 17, 1747, Commodore Charles Knowles sent a press gang into Boston to round up sailors for his fleet that was preparing to battle the French navy near the Gulf of St. Lawrence. The gang moved along the waterfront area collaring scores of apprentices, craftsmen, and laborers as well as merchant seamen. The operation came to a stop, however, when a crowd of angry men armed with clubs and cutlasses attacked the press gang, freeing their Boston neighbors and sending the English sailors fleeing to their warships. Later the same morning a larger crowd surged through the city looking for royal naval officers and English property upon which it could vent its anger and frustration.

Four naval officers were seized as hostages as the crowd moved toward the (Old) State House, at the corner of King (State) and Devonshire streets. Once there the now several thousand protestors hurled bricks through the windows, pounded on the doors, and loudly demanded that the governor prosecute the press gang. The governor and several councillors spoke to the crowd from the balcony, urging the men to disperse. Although Bostonians were hostile, they were not bloodthirsty; the governor was allowed to escort the naval officers inside the State House. Frustrated, the crowd returned to the waterfront "to burn a twenty gun ship now building there for His Majesty."

From the safety of Castle William in Boston Harbor, the governor called upon the town to apologize "for insults to His Majesty George II." The town meeting took a dim view of the crowd's militant behavior, but it also insisted that the press gang was at fault. The citizens of Boston, the meeting declared, had been "exposed to the ill usage of arbitrary power." The following Sunday, Governor William Shirley accepted the Boston Town Meeting's carefully worded apology and wisely considered the matter closed.

Yet this was but the beginning. During the next two decades, nearly every aspect of British policy brought to the surface of public controversy a series of conflicts linked to the very structure of imperial relations. Bostonians began to fear that the British empire and American liberty were not compatible.

Some men reached this conclusion before others. John Adams claimed the "child independence was born" in the (Old) State House in February 1761. In the council chamber on the second floor, a dramatic confrontation took place between Chief Justice Thomas Hutchinson and James Otis, Jr., over the legality and use of writs of assistance, general warrants that authorized searches for smuggled goods. Hutchinson, who had been

appointed to the bench only a few months earlier, was 49 years old in 1761. His family had helped found New England, each generation adding a bit more wealth and prestige. Thomas was born in Boston; and entered Harvard at the age of 12, where, like all his ancestors, he prepared himself for a life of commerce. By his marriage to Margaret Sanford of Rhode Island in 1734, he was able to create a vast commercial network, the Hutchinsons controlling the London-Boston link, the Sanfords handling the links to the West Indies and the Wine Islands.

By 1750 Hutchinson had accumulated a fortune. While the average Bostonian's worth was declining, Hutchinson amassed 15 times more cash than his father had possessed. He owned eight houses (including a mansion in Boston and a country house in Milton), commercial lots, two wharves, and 100 acres of land. At the age of 26 Hutchinson entered politics. In 1737 he was elected a representative of Boston to the Massachusetts house. After 10 years in the lower house he was appointed a councillor and then lieutenant governor. In 1760 Governor Francis Bernard named him chief justice of the Superior Court. Although he was not trained in the law, such an appointment was not unusual, especially given Hutchinson's political experience.

Only two people were immediately critical of Hutchinson's appointment to the court. One was a 25-year-old law student and the other an unstable, if brilliant, lawyer who did not have a political following. Within a few years, however—from the time Hutchinson heard the suit brought against the writs of assistance in 1761 to his attempt to implement the Stamp Act in 1765—John Adams and James Otis, Jr., had turned their personal outrage into an all-out public assault that aroused deep political suspicions among a large number of Bostonians.

Described by a contemporary as "plump, round-faced and smoothskinned," Otis was hired by a coalition of 63 Boston merchants to block issuance of the writs of assistance. The merchants feared that the use of general search warrants was part of a plan to enforce imperial trade regulations. That was precisely the purpose. By allowing Thomas Lechmere, surveyor general of the Customs in Boston, "to enter and go into any Vaults, Cellars, Warehouses, shops or other places to search and see whether any Goods. . .shall be there hid or concealed," the Crown hoped to prevent smuggling and to increase its revenue. Boston merchants believed that they would not survive if the regulations were enforced strictly.

For example, if the duty on molasses imported to Boston from non-English sugar-producing islands was collected, the price would increase by a prohibitive 60 percent. Obviously, merchants forced to sell at this inflated price could not hope to compete with those whose molasses came from the English West Indies. Since only about 25 percent of New England's need for molasses was met by the English islands, a great many Boston merchants, including those who sold agricultural goods, fish, and lumber in the Caribbean, would be ruined if the duty was collected.

Clearly the Boston merchant community was motivated primarily by self-interest when it chose to fight the use of general search warrants. But Otis politicized their drive for economic well-being. He argued that the writs were "against the fundamental principles of law. The privilege of house." "A man who is quiet," Otis stated, "is as secure in his house as a prince in his castle." Therefore the parliamentary act that allowed the courts to issue general search warrants was unconstitutional, a violation of the rights of Englishmen.

Young John Adams sat in rapt attention as Otis spun out his powerful political argument. Otis was a "flame of fire" bombarding the five judges, including Hutchinson, "all in their new fresh robes of scarlet English cloth, in their broad bands, and immense judicial wigs," with a "rapid torrent of impetuous eloquence." Adams may have been too romantic when

he concluded: "Every man of an immense crowded audience appeared to me to go away, as I did, ready to take up arms against writs of assistance." Still Adams was essentially right. A legal squabble motivated by personal animosity and economic selfishness had been transformed into a political struggle for principle and in the process had linked the merchant community to radicals like Otis and Adams.

Hutchinson's response failed to address either the Boston merchants' anxiety or the sweeping political issues raised by Otis. He adjourned the proceedings for nine months and waited for an answer from London. The reply was "of course" the writs should be issued.

During the next few years the Boston customs collectors pried and snooped and occasionally caught a smuggler. Otis and Adams kept up their attacks, painting Hutchinson as the tool of a corrupt and oppressive English government. In April 1763, for example, Otis published an article in the Boston *Gazette* that charged Hutchinson with fomenting "animosities and civil wars" among the people. John Adams condemned him for taking "four of the most important offices in the province into his own hands" and spoke with bitterness of Hutchinson's passion for power. "The liberties of this country," Adams remarked, have more to fear from Hutchinson "than from any other man." Not surprisingly, given this barrage of criticism, Hutchinson was the chief target during the Stamp Act uprising in the summer of 1765.

The stamp tax was intended by the English prime minister, George Grenville, to raise revenue in America that would be used to underwrite the cost of running the British empire. Britain was staggering under a huge debt incurred during the Great War for Empire (1755-1763). While the rewards for Britain's military success against France were potentially enormous—India, Canada, and most of North America east of the Mississippi were seized by Britain—the costs of maintaining the vast empire were equally as large. Nevertheless Grenville hoped to raise enough money in America to pay for the expense of stationing troops there.

He assumed, as did nearly all of his colleagues in Parliament, that the tax on attorneys' licenses, cards, dice, newspapers and pamphlets, deeds for land, and the papers used in clearing ships from harbors was perfectly proper, constitutional. Grenville believed that Parliament represented all Englishmen wherever they lived and whether or not they could vote. According to this theory of government, called virtual representation, Americans were said to be virtually, if not actually, represented in Parliament. Therefore their consent to acts of Parliament could be presumed. By contrast, Americans had come to believe that they could be represented only by men for whom they had actually voted.

The most influential and powerful protests against the Stamp Act came from Boston. Otis and John Adams jumped into print, attacking the theoretical underpinning of the tax. Sam Adams and the Loyal Nine, who formed the nucleus of the Boston Sons of Liberty, militantly, and sometimes violently, resisted the act.

Otis' pamphlet, *The Rights of the British Colonists Asserted and Proved,* clearly stated the ideological dilemma: how could Americans justify their opposition to some acts of Parliament without questioning the basis for Parliament's authority over them? On the one hand Otis passionately argued that Americans were entitled to all the rights of Englishmen, including the rights not to be taxed without their consent. On the other hand Otis acknowledged that the power of Parliament was uncontrollable.

John Adams burst into print with a resolution that became *the* rationale for American resistance to England. Adams had every reason to be happy and content in the summer of 1765: he had married Abigail Smith in the fall and their first child was born in July. Yet that same summer he angrily denounced the Stamp Act and the arrogance of British colonial officials. Adams had a radical solution to

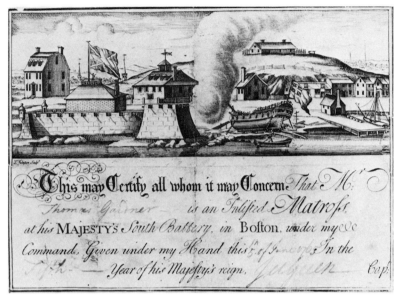

the dilemma posed by Otis. Parliament could make a mistake and when it did it need not be obeyed. The Stamp Act was a mistake, and therefore the law "was utterly void, and of no binding Force upon us, for it is against our Rights as Men and our Privileges as Englishmen."

Thomas Hutchinson flatly disagreed. His position was that American control over its own taxation was an indulgence, not a right. Therefore he publicly counseled his fellow Bostonians to "humbly pray" that as "a matter of favor" Parliament continue the old policy and repeal the new stamp tax. By shrewd, hard politicking Hutchinson won approval in the Massachusetts house for his moderate proposal.

The reaction among the people of Boston was immediate and hostile. It was charged that Hutchinson was not at all opposed to the tax, that he had written secretly to London to encourage the Stamp Act. He was at the head of a cabal, it was rumored, that sought "to advance themselves to posts of honor and profit. . .at the expense of the rights and liberties of the American colonies." When Andrew Oliver, Hutchinson's brother-in-law, was named stamp master for Massachusetts, the people were convinced that his secret motives had been revealed. "Vile serpent," raged John Adams.

South Battery was the fort at Boston Neck which limited land access to Boston. This document with an illustration of the fort certified the bearer as an "enlisted matross," or artillery private, assigned to the installation. Courtesy, Boston Athenaeum

Resistance to the Stamp Act boiled over into the streets of Boston on the morning of August 14, 1765. Organized by the Loyal Nine, a crowd of about 100, composed of people from a wide social and economic spectrum—laborers and artisans, apprentices and small tradesmen—hung an effigy of Andrew Oliver from a tree on Boston Common. That night a group paraded the effigy around the city, tore down a small building belonging to Oliver, and used the wood to make a bonfire on nearby Fort Hill. Oliver's effigy was ceremoniously "stamped," beheaded, and added to the fire. Then the crowd returned to Oliver's house, showered stones through the windows and demolished the garden fence before dispersing for the night.

The following day several gentlemen visited Oliver and persuaded him to resign his position as stamp distributor. One Bostonian happily boasted: "I believe people never were more Universally pleased; not so much as one could I hear say he was sorry, but a smile sat on almost every one's countenance."

Although the immediate political goal of the Boston patriots had been achieved with Oliver's resignation, another crowd action took place on the night of August 26th. This time the target was Hutchinson. Warned that an angry crowd was on its way, Hutchinson and his family fled from their house on Garden Street. The crowd attacked the house in a fury, broke through the doors, swarmed through the rooms, ripped the paneling from the walls, destroyed the furniture and paintings, and smashed the inner walls. Only the heavy brickwork construction of the outer walls prevented their razing the house completely, "though they worked at it till daylight." Hutchinson's trees and gardens were ruined and everything of value carried off. The next day the streets of Boston were littered with money, dinnerware, clothes, and books that had belonged to Hutchinson.

On November 1, 1765, when the Stamp Act was scheduled to go into effect, nothing happened. Nothing, that is, that even suggested that the stamps were going to be used. The day began with the mournful tolling of the city's church bells. Effigies of two English officials were hung on the newly-named Liberty Tree in the South End and a parade of "innumerable people from the Country as well as the Town" marched through the streets shouting "Liberty and No Stamps" and other militant slogans. Governor Bernard fled from the city.

John Adams exalted in Boston's patriotic fervor and its political importance. "The year 1765," Adams wrote, "has been the most remarkable year of my life":

That enormous engine, fabricated by the British Parliament for battering down all the rights and liberties of America, I mean the Stamp Act, has raised and spread throughout the whole continent a spirit that will be recorded to our honor with all future generations. In every colony...the stamp distributors and inspectors have been compelled by the unconquerable rage of the people to renounce their offices.

And Adams realized that politics would never be the same again. "The people, even to the lowest ranks," he noted proudly, "have become more attentive to their liberties...and more determined to defend them....Our presses have groaned, our pulpits have thundered, our legislatures have resolved, our towns voted; the crown officers have everywhere trembled, and all their little tools and creatures been afraid to speak and ashamed to be seen."

The tactics used by Boston's Sons of Liberty were imitated everywhere in the colonies with the same success. "Our brethren in Boston have endeared themselves more than ever to all the colonies in America," claimed a letter in the New York *Gazette* that was widely reprinted. Parliament, under pressure from English merchants as well as an aroused American people, repealed the Stamp Act.

News of the repeal of the Stamp Act was celebrated with parades, pageants, and mass meetings. The Boston Sons of Liberty organized an annual event to be held August 14th, the anniversary of the first militant uprising. In 1769 it was held in Dorchester in a field next to Robinson's Inn (The Sign of the Liberty Tree). Under a huge sailcloth awning, 355 Bostonians heard speeches, sang two versions of the Liberty Song, and drank 45 toasts. (The figure 45 had become a symbol of resistance to England when a radical newspaper, *The North Briton,* No. 45, had been suppressed by the Crown.) Surprisingly John Adams claimed he "did not see one Person intoxicated, or near it." He did notice a growing commitment to the patriot cause. Mass meetings, Adams wrote in his diary that evening, "tinge the Minds of the People, they impregnate them with the sentiments of Liberty. They render the People fond of their Leaders in the Cause, and averse and bitter against all opposers."

After the Stamp Act crisis, American sensitivity to all forms of English taxation was highly aroused. Therefore with the enactment of the Townshend duties in 1768, which levied duties on imports such as paper, glass, and tea, a similar pattern of resistance reappeared. In Boston pamphlets and newspapers again leapt to the defense of liberty, an embargo on English goods was organized by merchants, and crowds surged through the streets threatening and harassing British customs officials.

But now there was an important difference in the patriots' tactics. When John Hancock's sloop *Liberty* was seized for allegedly engaging in smuggling, the leadership of the Sons of Liberty publicly urged Bostonians not to resort to violence. A crowd marching on the house of Benjamin Hallowell, who had ordered the *Liberty* seized, was turned back by Hancock, Adams, and Otis who called out, "No violence, or you'll hurt the cause." Later in the summer the Sons of Liberty moved one of their mass meetings from the Liberty Tree to Faneuil Hall and finally to the Old South Meeting House, so that a proper debate might be carried on. The result was a petition sent to Governor Bernard.

At about the same time the Massachusetts assembly issued a circular letter to the other colonial legislatures denouncing the Townshend duties as unconstitutional violations of the principle of no taxation without representation. The letter called for a united American front and suggested a joint petition of protest to the king. Lord Hillsborough, the first secretary of state for America, ordered the House to rescind its letter. When the House refused by a vote of 92 to 17, Governor Bernard dissolved the assembly. (Paul Revere made a silver punchbowl to commemorate "the glorious NINETY-TWO.") With the legal means for protest closed, unruly crowds once again took to the streets of Boston, intimidating merchants who were thought to be importing English goods contrary to the patriotic boycott.

A confrontation between William Jackson and Theophilus Lille, North End shopowners who insisted upon selling English goods, and a crowd of nearly 2,000 men and boys quickly turned violent. Large painted signs with the word "IMPORTER" were posted and everyone going in or out of the shops was pelted with dirt and garbage. Ebenezer Richardson, a neighbor who made a living as an informant for the customs service, threatened the demonstrators. "I'll make it too hot for you before night," shouted Richardson. Members of the crowd responded by heaving eggs and stones at Richardson's house. In a rage, Richardson stuck a musket out from a second-floor window and fired. He killed 11-year-old Christopher Seider. A group of men rushed the house and dragged Richardson into the street. Although some members of the crowd demanded a hanging then and there, William Molineaux, a leader of the Sons of Liberty, took control of the situation. He had Richardson brought to Faneuil Hall, where a hearing was conducted before four justices of the peace.

When King George repealed the Stamp Act in March 1766, a huge celebration was held throughout Boston. The Liberty Tree, planted at Essex and Washington streets in 1646, was adorned with 150 iron, tin, and glass lanterns, including this one. The tree was among those destroyed by British soldiers for firewood during the winter of 1775. (TBS)

Crispus Attucks, the first black man killed in the Revolutionary War, is featured in this work by W. Champney. The Boston Massacre scene, a lithograph printed by J.H. Bufford, was created in 1856. (TBS)

A massive funeral was held for young Seider. Just two days after a snowstorm on a cold February day, thousands of mourners walked slowly from the Liberty Tree to the Old Granary burial ground. "Young as he was, he died in his Country's Cause," solemnly stated the Boston *Gazette.* When Richardson was found guilty of manslaughter "the Court Room resounded with Expressions of Pleasure," according to Judge Oliver.

Royal officials, believing anarchy existed in Boston, dispatched two regiments of British regulars to restore order. By 1769 there were 4,000 soldiers quartered in the crowded seaport town of 15,000. Their presence confirmed Bostonians' worst fears; the redcoats were a constant reminder of the oppressive power of Great Britain.

Guards stationed on Boston Neck, the entrance to the city, checked everyone going in and out. Patrols marched through the streets day and night, stopping and sometimes harassing people. Military parades were held on Boston Common.

Women were often subjected to coarse insults and rough advances from drunken soldiers. And at a time when unemployment among Boston laborers was high, off-duty redcoats competed for scarce jobs. The atmosphere was charged for an explosion.

On March 2, 1770, workers at Gray's ropeworks brawled with some soldiers who were looking for work. Both sides regarded another clash as inevitable. Three days later on March 5, a crowd assaulted the sentries posted outside the customshouse. Hard-packed snowballs and chunks of ice were hurled at the soldiers, along with scores of insults. The bells of the Old Brick Church rang out and men shouting "Fire, Fire," poured into King Street, adding to the crowd and the confusion. Afraid, goaded beyond endurance, first one and then another soldier leveled his musket and fired into the crowd. Captain Thomas Preston shouted, "Stop firing! Do not fire!" and he rushed in front of the ragged line of soldiers pushing up their muskets with his arm.

Eight men were wounded. Five lay dead. Blood stained the snow on King Street. A massacre, "a horrid, bloody massacre," the Boston *Gazette* labeled it. Dead were: Crispus Attucks, a black man in his forties who had refused to leave the scene even when the soldiers taunted him: "You black rascal," one shouted, "what have you to do with white people's quarrels?"; Samuel Gray, who rushed into King Street because he thought there was a fire; Samuel Maverick, a 17-year-old apprentice who left his half-eaten meal to join the crowd surging through the streets; James Caldwell, a young man who spent his days learning the art of navigation and his evenings courting a young woman; and Patrick Carr, a recent immigrant from Ireland, who lived with his employer in nearby Queen (Court) Street.

The following day a mass meeting was held in the Old South. Sam Adams was instructed by the meeting to demand that the soldiers be withdrawn from the city. When he delivered his ultimatum to Lt. Governor Hutchinson, Adams later recalled, "If Fancy deceived me not, I observed his Knees to tremble. I thought I saw his face grow pale (and I enjoyed the Sight)." Hutchinson capitulated. The troops were ordered into the barracks on Castle William.

Along with six soldiers, Captain Preston was brought to trial in late October 1770. Although a few radical patriots were upset by their decision, John Adams and Josiah Quincy defended the accused men. All but two were acquitted, and those convicted were released after they were branded on the thumb. Still, Adams had the last word: "Soldiers quartered in a populous

Paul Revere's drawing of the massacre scene has a different emphasis, with no distinguishable black victim. Revere felt that the identity of those killed was less important than the concerted fashion in which the British soldiers made the attack. (TBS)

Polly Summer purchased this doll, imported from England, a few days before the Boston Tea Party in 1773. It remained in her family for four generations, and is shown in the arms of Mary P. Langley, Polly's great-great-granddaughter. The doll become well-known in 1893 when New England Magazine *published a story that described Boston through the doll's experiences. (TBS)*

town," he told the jury during his summation, "will always occasion two mobs where they prevent one. They are wretched conservators of the peace."

For more than two years after the Boston Massacre, there was a superficial calm throughout the American colonies. In early November 1772, however, voters at a Boston Town Meeting established a Committee of Correspondence to publicize the Crown's decision to pay governors and judges from customs revenue rather than allowing colonial legislatures to appropriate salaries. As head of the committee, Sam Adams was charged to "state the rights of the colonists," to list the "Infringements and Violations thereof that have been made," and to send copies to other towns in Massachusetts. Boston also asked of rural towns "a free communication of their Sentiments on this Subject."

The pamphlet issued by the committee minced no words. Americans' rights were boldly stated, and the list of grievances against Great Britain unapologetically presented. It was clear that Boston had

come to the conclusion that American liberty was far more important than loyalty to Parliament. It was also clear, from the responses that poured into Adams' committee from small towns throughout Massachusetts during the spring of 1773, that Boston's views had become widely accepted. Nearly all praised Boston's courage and resolve in defense of liberty. Nearly all agreed with Boston's assessment of the current state of affairs. Nearly all stated their belief that resistance to tyranny was "the first and highest social Duty of this people." Buoyed by this show of support, Boston newspapers were talking openly about independence by the summer of 1773. At the same time the British government announced its intention to uphold the authority of Parliament at any cost. Another crisis seemed unavoidable.

The passage of the Tea Act provoked the final crisis. Parliament intended only to save the East India Company from bankruptcy by granting it the exclusive privilege of selling tea in America. Because there was already a tax on tea, Parliament's move touched every raw political nerve in Boston's body politic. Not only did the act allow Boston radicals to point out once again the unconstitutionality of taxes passed without American representation, but it angered those merchants who were excluded from the monopoly driving them into the arms of the radicals. And the Tea Act raised anew the fear that a dark conspiracy existed to destroy American liberty. Radicals called attention to the creation by the act of a "monied interest," a train of arrogant, corrupt men wholly dependent upon the British government for place and profit. Their accusation gained credence when it was learned that among the merchants consigned to sell the tea in Boston were Lt. Governor Thomas Hutchinson's two sons.

The first of three tea ships, the *Dartmouth,* entered Boston Harbor on November 28, 1773; the *Eleanor* and the brig *Beaver* were subsequently tied up to Griffin's Wharf. Warnings to the tea merchants from the Sons of Liberty not to unload the tea were followed by an order from Hutchinson not to allow the ships to leave the harbor. On December 16, more than 5,000 Bostonians crammed into Old South Church. Chaired by Sam Adams, the meeting made one last attempt to persuade Hutchinson to send the tea back to England. He refused.

When that word reached the meeting it was nearly dark. Sam Adams rose and announced, "This meeting can do nothing further to save this country." As if his statement were a signal, shouts and warwhoops rang out from the crowded hall: "Boston harbor a tea-pot tonight! The Mohawks are come!" Outside a group of about 60 men, crudely disguised as Indians, swept down Milk Street toward Griffin's Wharf, where the three tea ships were anchored. The men were well-organized and disciplined. They worked so knowledgeably and effectively that by 9:00 p.m. their work was done: 342 chests of tea were hoisted onto the deck, broken open with axes, the tea shoveled overboard, and the chests smashed. "This is the most magnificent Movement of all," wrote John Adams in his diary the next day. "This Destruction of the Tea," he exalted, "is so bold, so daring, so firm, intrepid, and inflexible, and it must have so important Consequences and so lasting, that I cannot but consider it as an Epocha in History." The Boston Committee of Correspondence, fearful that patriot leaders would be rounded up and transported to England for trial, circulated a petition pledging its signers "at the hazard of our lives and fortunes to prevent any person from being detained in custody and carry'd out of the province." Paul Revere carried a full report of the Tea Party to New York City, where the news of Boston's "bold blow at tyranny" was greeted with jubilation.

When it learned of the Boston Tea Party, the British government reacted with considerably less enthusiasm. Lord North was outraged. He insisted upon

retribution. Angry members of Parliament passed a series of laws aimed at punishing Boston and at forcing all Americans to accept Parliament's right to legislate for the colonies. Known collectively as the Coercive Acts, the punitive measures closed the port of Boston until the tea was paid for, reorganized Massachusetts government so that the royal governor had more power and the town meetings less, allowed royal officials charged with capital offenses to be tried in England, and authorized the quartering of British soldiers in private homes. One final blow: General Thomas Gage, commander in chief of the British army in America, was made governor of Massachusetts.

The Coercive Acts set in motion a chain of events that led directly to war.

In the colonies, political satirists such as Paul Revere used cartoons to garner support for the radical position. In London political cartoons were also popular. This cartoon suggests the effectiveness of the blockade of Boston Harbor. (BPL)

Everywhere royal authority began to dissolve. The Boston Committee of Correspondence called for aid and urged all the colonies to join in a boycott of British goods. Although mass meetings were held, resolutions of support passed and implemented, and new popular political organizations created, the other provinces were not yet ready to take more drastic steps. Instead they suggested that a general congress of the colonies be convened in Philadelphia in September 1774.

Fifty-five delegates from 12 colonies (Georgia excepted) assembled in Carpenter's Hall for the first session of the Continental Congress. The part that Boston had played in the unfolding drama of the American Revolution was illustrated almost immediately. The Reverend Jacob Duche, an Episcopalian,

opened the congress by asking the delegates and the American people to pray "for America, for the Congress, for the Province of Massachusetts, and especially the town of Boston." Within two weeks this symbolic gesture was followed by a specific political gain initiated by Sam and John Adams. Carried to the congress by Paul Revere, the Suffolk Resolves (from the county in which Boston was located) denounced the Coercive Acts as unconstitutional and recommended that the people begin military training. When the congress unanimously endorsed these principles it was clear that Boston's struggle for liberty had become the nation's.

While congress debated, the British government began to prepare for military action. On April 19, 1775, General Thomas Gage sent his troops out from Boston to

The British attempt to force the colonists away from Breed's Hill in Charlestown led to the misnamed Battle of Bunker Hill on June 17, 1775. This engraving depicts Charlestown ablaze, and does not show the hundreds of British soldiers who were killed and wounded, making their victory a costly one. (BPL)

Concord to destroy a cache of military supplies. Warned of Gage's move by Revere and William Dawes, the militiamen were waiting. By the end of that bloody day, 93 Americans had been killed or wounded, the redcoats had suffered 272 casualties, and the vaunted British army was trapped inside Boston by 20,000 militiamen. For nearly a year the two armies stared at each other. Only once did the redcoats attack their beseigers. On June 17, 1775, 2,500 British soldiers drove the Americans from trenches atop Breed's Hill in Charlestown. The British incurred enormous losses in that misnamed Battle of Bunker Hill: over 800 wounded and 230 killed. The Americans lost less than half that number.

Badly mauled, Gage pulled back inside Boston and settled in for a long winter. Although nearly all of the town's patriots had fled, Boston's population soared to nearly 20,000 during the winter of 1775-1776. Loyalists had swarmed into the town to be protected by 13,000 redcoats. Food and fuel were in short supply. Most of the foodstuffs brought in by the royal navy was consumed by the British troops and there was little left for civilians. Meat and milk were impossible to buy and the price of bread, cheese, and potatoes rose to staggering heights. Over 100 buildings were pulled down and used for firewood; the pulpit and pews of the Old South had been ripped up and burned, as had the steeple of the Old West.

The seige ended when Colonel Henry Knox, former Boston bookseller turned artillery officer, brought heavy cannons from Fort Ticonderoga, occupied Dorchester Heights, and forced the British to evacuate Boston. On March 17, 1776, General George Washington liberated Boston. It was a depressing sight. Trees had been cut down everywhere, including those bordering the Common, fences had been ripped up, and buildings had been razed. Public buildings had been maliciously defaced and private homes looted.

But the shock of war and deprivation did not lessen Boston's enthusiasm for independence. On July 18, 1776, the people of the city gathered at the (Old) State House. Standing on the balcony, Colonel Thomas Crafts read the Declaration of Independence. Harrison Grey Otis, who would be mayor of Boston in 1830, recalled that as a boy he had stood in that crowd. The reading of the declaration drew "the heartfelt homage and electrifying peals of men, women, and children of the whole city." And in the evening, as John Adams had suggested would be appropriate, there was a celebration with "pomp and parade ...shows, games, bells, bonfires and illuminations."

The Revolutionary vision of an independent republic, shaped in large part by Boston's sons and daughters of liberty, was now America's destiny.

This plan of a besieged Boston in 1775 depicts the North and South Batteries, the fortifications at Boston Neck, and Charlestown in ruins following the Bunker Hill battle. Photograph by Richard Merrill. (TBS)

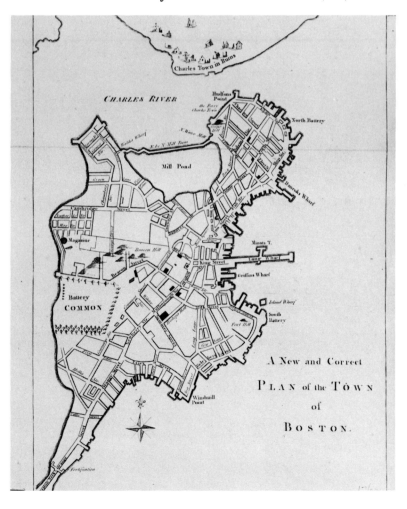

III
Yankee Boston

The Boston ideal burned more brightly after 1783. The Revolution, it seemed, presented Americans with an opportunity to realize a new world, to put the ideals of republicanism into effect, to create an ordered society in which men were free. But something unexpected happened; the ideas that sparked and sustained the Revolution contained within themselves the seed of their own disillusionment and destruction. By 1820 the Boston ideal had been changed, turned upside down.

Before the Revolution it had been argued that Americans were especially virtuous, a people who were naturally committed to civic responsibility. This belief lay at the core of republicanism. For Bostonians in particular republicanism was a secularized version of the

Previous page: Park Street Church, built in 1809, highlights this 1812 oil painting. The artist is unknown; the original painting hangs in the Old State House. (TBS)

This painting, by F.D. Williams, provides an early look at Post Office Square, now the center of Boston's commercial district. Captain James Dalton's house was built in 1758 on the corner of Water and Dalton (later Congress) streets. (BPL)

Puritan's attempt to harness man's selfish and individualistic impulses and to create a political community in which men were linked to one another in harmony and benevolence. More than any other form of government, republics were dependent upon the good, selfless character of their people. "A Citizen," declared Samuel Adams, "owes everything to the Commonwealth." Or as Dr. John Warren, whose brother had died on Bunker Hill, put it in his Fourth of July oration in 1783, "when virtue fails, when luxury and corruption shall undermine the pillars of the state," it will cause "a total loss of liberty and patriotism."

Bostonians' obsession with political virtue was a radical doctrine. It flew in the face of man's natural selfishness. It caused them, therefore, to struggle with a dilemma similar to the one that had confronted their Puritan forebears. John Adams, for example, urged his countrymen to work hard, but at the same time he feared the consequences of prosperity. "Will you tell me how to prevent riches from producing luxury?" he asked Thomas Jefferson. "Will you tell me how to prevent luxury from producing effeminacy, intoxication, extravagance, vice and folly?" As Adams and a cluster of Boston's post-revolutionary leaders saw it, in other words, the development of a manufacturing economy seemed incompatible with virtue.

Unlike his cousin Sam, John did not encourage poverty. He knew that people were anxious to shake off the shackles of economic deprivation. Bostonians loved commerce "with its conveniences and pleasures" too much to put up with privation any longer than necessary. But Adams was deeply troubled by the prospect of a society divided into two competing groups—the rich and well born and the commonality, the haves and the have-nots, the aristocracy and the democracy. While Adams did not always describe the differences between the aristocratic and democratic elements in society in economic terms, he often stated flatly: "It is wealth that produces the inequality of condition." Wealth was the touchstone of social division.

Still, for several decades after the Revolution, politics moderated the distance between rich and poor in Boston. The town meeting brought together men of different economic status and praised those whose eloquence, reason, and character served the community. Boston had a board of selectmen and a variety of other municipal officers who were chosen by the town meeting, where "the meanest citizen ratable at 20 pounds beside the poll, may deliver his sentiments and give suffrage in very important matters, as freely as the greatest Lord in the Land." Dr. Thomas Young, a native of Albany who moved to Boston in the 1760s, added that positions of power were open to "everyone whose capacity, integrity, and diligence in the affairs of his country attracts the public attention." In other words respect, not simply wealth, was an important prerequisite for political power in Boston.

Although Paul Revere held only a few

minor offices, he was a highly regarded political activist during the Revolution whose skills as a silversmith, bell maker, and foundry master made him one of the best-known and successful artisans in Boston. Described by his neighbor, Hannah Mather, as "a man of ingenuity and exertion," Revere "accumulated a handsome property" in the years after the Revolution. Like his fellow artisans Revere worked long and hard from sunup to sundown, but without much feeling of hurry or pressure. The important thing was to do the job well. Revere was, in fact, a superb artist. Before the Revolution his silver pieces—flagons, bowls, and teapots—were ornate and embossed with scrolls, though the purity and simplicity of form that came to characterize his work in the Federal period was always evident.

Following the needs of the young republic, however, Revere made fewer decorative silver pieces after about 1790 and took up, instead, two new crafts—bell casting and the manufacture of sheet copper. His success was astounding. The bell-maker's art called for a thorough knowledge of iron casting, which Revere learned in the years after 1788 when he built his own foundry. But then his stock-in-trade was hardware, stoves, anvils, and forge hammers. To cast a large bell was quite another matter. Nevertheless in 1792 Revere successfully cast his first bell for the Second Church of Boston. Although its sound was "panny, harsh and shrill," Boston and Revere were inordinately proud of the fact that this was an American accomplishment. Indeed, by the following year, Revere justly boasted that "we know we can cast as good bells as can be cast in the world."

Late in 1800 Revere gambled again and won. Although he was 65 years old and well-to-do, he risked $25,000 of his own money to establish a mill for rolling copper into sheets. No one else in America could meet this demand. Within a few years Revere's mill had produced 6,000 feet of copper sheathing for the new State

This silver tankard was crafted by Paul Revere in the late 1700s. After achieving success as a silver craftsman, Revere risked a large part of his fortune to develop the first copper sheeting process in America. Rolled copper from the Revere mill was used to sheath the U.S.S. Constitution. (TBS)

House on Beacon Hill and enough material to copper-bottom the U.S.S. *Constitution* ("Old Ironsides"). On June 26, 1803, Captain Edward Preble wrote in the log of the *Constitution:* "The carpenters gave nine cheers, which were answered by the seamen and calkers, because they had in fourteen days completed coppering the ship with copper made in the United States."

Like Revere, Boston artisans were proud—if not quite so prosperous. They were men who had worked their way up through the craft hierarchy from apprenticeship to ownership of their own shop or business. Their goal was economic independence, defined as ownership of a moderate level of property, not unlimited "accumulation of the *Almighty Dollar.*" According to this view, artisans (or mechanics as they were sometimes called) were one of "three great classes," each representative of a sector of economic activity: the agricultural, the commercial, and the mechanic. Each class performed a special economic function, but depended on the union of all classes to achieve prosperity. "The true interest of one cannot be opposed to the real Interest of either of the others," claimed the

Massachusetts Charitable Mechanic Association, founded in 1795 by Revere and 83 other Boston artisans.

Defining class by economic function also meant that in the artisans' view classes represented vertical not horizontal unities. The commercial class included modest retailers as well as international merchants; the artisan class contained craftsmen at every level—masters, journeymen, and apprentices—and manufacturers. The logo and motto of the Charitable Mechanic Association reflected this conception of society. At the center of their membership certificate, the association placed a scale-beam with packages symbolic of commercial interests suspended from one side and the tools of various crafts hanging from the other. According to the official explanation this design signified "the truth of the maxim contained in the *motto* of the Association, that, equally balanced, the Merchant and Mechanic in being *'Just,'* may *'Fear Not.'"*

Unfortunately the artisans' idealized conception of a just and harmonious society was not a perfect reflection of reality in turn-of-the-century Boston. Many of the town's tradesmen

experienced a relative decline in their economic standing. Bakers, who were among the wealthiest of the town's artisans, had an average assessed wealth of 170 pounds in 1790; barbers were assessed at 65 pounds; and shoemakers averaged 45 pounds. By contrast Boston merchants averaged 1,707 pounds per person. In other words the average merchant was 10 times as wealthy as the average baker, 27 times richer than the barbers, and 37 times wealthier than Boston's average shoemaker. A growing awareness of the economic differences caused the committee organizing a parade honoring President George Washington in 1789 to insist that the artisans march in alphabetical order and not according to wealth or status. Government officials, professionals, and merchants led the triumphal procession through the center of town and thousands of Bostonians cheered as Washington, mounted on an elegant white charger, passed under a huge arch erected in front of the Old State House.

Washington's parade route took him through the richest area of Boston, along State and Cornhill streets. The Massachusetts Bank, the market, professional offices, and various retail shops were located there. Unlike those in the rest of the town, most of the buildings in the center were built of brick. The richest merchants and professional men and almost half the retailers lived here. Generally the further away from State Street a Bostonian lived, the lower his income tended to be.

The South End was mixed, though more than half of the people living in this section had an average assessed worth of 25 pounds or less. Large numbers of leather workers and about a third of Boston's masons, carpenters, and painters lived there. The West End was still sparsely settled in 1790. Some wealthy merchants resided in this section, but so too did most of the town's rope-workers and nearly all of Boston's black people (about 800). The poorest section of town was the North End. More than half of the people living in the two wards furthest

Elizabeth Freeman, shown here in her later years when employed as a children's nurse in Stockbridge, was the first African slave emancipated after passage of the Massachusetts Bill of Rights in 1781. Her nickname, "Mumbet," was probably the children's contraction of "Madam Bet," the name by which people respectfully addressed her. Courtesy, Massachusetts Historical Society

from the center of the town owned no taxable property. Heavily populated by workers, retailers, and sailors who made their living from the sea, the North End grew much more slowly than Boston's other neighborhoods.

Those men and women who were the poorest and least successful often moved out of Boston. There was a floating population at the bottom of society, men who wandered from seaport to seaport looking for work or went to a rural town hoping to live more cheaply. Poor, often unhealthy, and without prospects, they were unwanted. The overseer of the poor in Braintree demanded in 1804 that Boston "remove Stephen Randal belonging to your town. He has been wandering about from place to place," explained the official, before he came to the point—the cost. "About four weeks ago he froze himself very bad in the feet and is at the expense of two dollars and 50 cents per week."

Despite this troubling picture the belief persisted—at least among the wealthier classes—that upward mobility was common. It was possible. A number of Boston's workers improved their relative economic standing during the decades after 1780. Nearly 20 percent of the original members of the Mechanics Association founded in 1795 and open only to master craftsmen, were not on the 1790 tax list. They had either been apprentices or had moved into Boston since that time. Likewise 71 percent of those men owning no property in 1780 who remained in Boston became property owners. Still it was not true, as a local newspaper commented, that "Men succeed or fail. . .not from accident or external surroundings, but from possessing or wanting the elements of success in themselves." The most obvious exception to this belief was black people.

Blacks had lived in Boston since 1638. They had come as "perpetual servants," slaves to wealthy white merchant families. Gradually slaves in Boston acquired a special status. They had the right to own property, to be tried, and to sue in the courts. Yet they were not free. The

Revolution, however, forced Bostonians to confront the issue. The irony of owning slaves while at the same time waging a struggle for freedom from Great Britain became too obvious to ignore. James Otis identified the basic problem in 1764. If according to natural law all people were born free and equal, argued Otis, that meant *all* people, black and white. "Does it follow that 'tis right to enslave a man because he is black?" Otis asked. The same theme was voiced by Boston's black community. A petition was sent to the Massachusetts legislature in 1777, asserting that "in common with all other men," black people had "a natural and inalienable right" to freedom. The legislature responded negatively. But, led by Prince Hall, black Bostonians persisted in their campaign for freedom. Finally in 1783 the Massachusetts courts determined that the clause in the new state constitution declaring "all men are born free and equal, and have certain natural, essential, and unalienable rights" had abolished slavery in the state.

The abolition of slavery, however, did not initiate a trend toward racial equality in Boston. Laws discriminated against free blacks as they had against slaves. Therefore blacks developed their own

Phillis Wheatley was the first published black poet in America. A slave of John Wheatley, whose children taught her to read and write, Phillis began composing poetry before the age of 16 and her work was published in London before the Revolution. (TBS)

The African Meeting House, built in 1806, is the oldest church building still standing in the United States built by black laborers for a black congregation. Located on Beacon Hill, this was the site of the founding meeting of the New England Anti-Slavery Society of William Lloyd Garrison. Courtesy, Society for the Preservation of New England Antiquities (SPNEA)

separate institutions. In 1787 Prince Hall organized the first black masonic lodge in America (African Lodge No. 459); the following year Primus Hall founded a school for black children that met in his home on Beacon Hill; and in 1805 the African Meeting House was built. The successful establishment of these community institutions helped black Bostonians to survive. If they were to prosper, blacks realized they would have to rely on their own efforts rather than the good will of their white neighbors.

Women learned the same lesson. Boston's most famous 18th-century woman, Abigail Adams, prodded John to "Remember the Ladies." She wrote to him on March 31, 1776. "All men would be tyrants if they could," she instructed her husband. "If particular care and attention is not paid to the Ladies we are determined to foment a Rebelion, and will not hold ourselves bound by any Laws in which we have no voice, or Representation."

John Adams didn't take Abigail's

argument seriously. "As to your extraordinary Code of Laws, I cannot but Laugh," he replied two weeks later. But John was worried. He knew—feared—that the revolution he and his colleagues were planning could not easily be limited. "Our struggle has loosened the bonds of Government every where," he noted anxiously. John insisted, however, that women had no reason to complain. "In practice you know We are subjects. We have only the Name of Masters, and rather than give up this, which would completely subject Us to the Despotism of the Petticoat, I hope General Washington and all our brave Heroes would fight."

Abigail did not press for female suffrage, but some of the social bonds that had restricted women's freedom before 1776 were loosened somewhat after American independence was won. The traditional view of marriage, for example, had stressed the subordination of wife to husband. Like their sisters elsewhere, Boston women had expanded their responsibilities during the Revolution, single-handedly managing shops and businesses during their husbands' absences. Women also were involved in boycotts of English goods, in patriotic processions, and, according to one British army officer, "surpassed the Men for Eagerness and Spirit in the Defense of Liberty." One consequence of women's activity during the war was the emergence of a new—republican—definition of marriage. Judith Sargent Murray, who wrote a column published in a Boston magazine, emphasized mutuality as the only acceptable basis for marriage. "Mutual esteem, mutual friendship, mutual confidence, *begirt about by mutual forbearance,*" was how Ms. Murray described the ideal "matrimonial career."

Dissatisfied wives were less willing to remain in unhappy marriages than they had been previously. Divorce petitions in Massachusetts increased sharply after the Revolution. And more wives than husbands sued for divorce, though a greater percentage of men succeeded in gaining favorable action on their petitions.

The reasons for initiating divorce proceedings were varied, of course, but the bulk of the petitions filed in Boston—84 percent of the husbands' and 59 percent of the wives'—included the charge of adultery. These statistics reveal a profound change in social attitude, for only since the 1780s had the law allowed divorce for adultery by either partner.

Official acceptance of male adultery as grounds for a divorce was in part a result of women's willingness to challenge the sexual double standard. In her "Sentiments on Libertinism," published in the *Boston Magazine* in 1784, "Daphne" argued that it was unfair that a single mistake would "forever deprive women of all that renders life valuable," while at the same time "the base betrayer is suffered to triumph in the success of his unmanly arts, and to pass unpunished even by a frown." Equalizing the legal consequences of adultery did not bring about the sexual equality for which "Daphne" called. But the new law did signal to women *and* men that they were

expected to behave like virtuous citizens in both public and private life.

If the young republic was to fulfill its promises, then virtuous families must adhere to strict moral standards. This new attitude had enormous and immediate implications for the status of women. Because the home was perceived as the source of virtue and stability in government, women came to be regarded as the most influential parent. Educated in the principles of republicanism, mothers were chiefly responsible for instructing their children—especially their sons—in the joys of liberty and the benefits of order. Miss P.W. Jackson, a graduating student from Susanna Rowson's Young Ladies Academy, told the *Boston Weekly Magazine* what she had learned. "A woman who is skilled in every useful art, who practices every domestic virtue," she explained in 1803, "may, by her precept and example, inspire her brothers, her husband, or her sons, with such a love of virtue, such just ideas of the true value of civil liberty...that future heroes and

Aqueducts were built to Lake Cochituite when the water supply from Jamaica Plain became inadequate. A great celebration was held when the first water from the new system poured into the Frog Pond in the Boston Common. Bells rang and cannons fired, and an evening fireworks display topped the festivities. (SPNEA)

The Tontine Crescent, designed by Charles Bulfinch in 1793, was a unique building of 16 connected brick houses which curved around a courtyard. The Massachusetts Historical Society and the Boston Public Library were among the occupants before the building was razed in 1858. Courtesy, Mack Lee

statesmen, who arrive at the summit of military or political fame, shall *exaltingly declare, it is to my mother I owe this elevation.*"

Bostonians were very comfortable with the ideology of republicanism. Its demands and promises were well suited to men and women long committed to building a model city. If, however, the ideals were familiar, there was abundant evidence by the early 1800s of a new economic and cultural spirit, of a new Boston.

The town grew dramatically in size and area during the early decades of the 19th century. In 1790 the population of Boston was 18,000; by 1800 it had risen to 25,000; and by 1822 it had jumped to 49,000—an increase of 250% in just 32 years. While the center of the city was still relatively densely populated, people had been gradually moving into the West and South ends. "Where the population was thin," noted a Salem minister, "and there were fields and marshes, are now splendid houses and crowded Streets." Moreover these new neighborhoods were soon linked by bridges to Cambridge and South Boston. The Charles River Bridge (opened with great hoopla on June 17,

1786, the 11th anniversary of the Battle of Bunker Hill) was the first of four bridges built by 1810—that effectively ended Boston's isolation.

A young student traveling in Europe heard the news about the Charles River Bridge with great enthusiasm. Charles Bulfinch, son of Dr. Thomas Bulfinch and a recent Harvard graduate, hoped that when he returned to Boston from his grand tour he would have an opportunity to pursue his "taste for architecture." As it turned out Bulfinch's chosen career was suited perfectly to Boston's needs. He transformed the face of Boston. From 1787 when he submitted plans for the new State House to 1816 when he left Boston to become architect of the capitol, Bulfinch designed a score of mansions, rowhouses, and public buildings. Using a warm, red brick and local granite, his designs reflected the town's love affair with republicanism. Bulfinch pointed the way toward a distinctively American architecture, characterized by economy, symmetry, utility, and simplicity.

A committee of the Boston Town Meeting, headed by Harrison Gray Otis, chose Beacon Hill as the site for the new State House that Bulfinch was hired to design. Understated and beautifully proportioned, his design blended tall windows with inset arches, delicate wooden cornices and balustrades with classical columns. Paul Revere, whose copper sheeting lined the dome, hailed the brick Acropolis as a "safe and secure abode" for liberty.

By the time the State House was completed in 1798, Beacon Hill was well on the way to becoming a handsome residential neighborhood. A group of investors called the Mount Vernon Proprietors initiated the development by purchasing the property adjoining the capitol owned by John Singleton Copley, the self-exiled American painter. Streets were laid out and about 60 feet sheared off the top of Mount Vernon to create space for mansions and block houses. In 1800 Bulfinch designed a large, elegant house for Harrison Gray Otis on the crest of the hill, and a few years later he built a row of four-story brick houses on Park Street. The beauty of this new area was further enhanced when Bullfinch constructed his Colonnade Row, a series of 19 houses stretching along Tremont Street across from the tree-lined mall and the Common.

During this same period Bulfinch also designed a variety of public buildings. In 1799 he donated to Fr. Cheverus, the first Catholic Bishop of Boston, the plans for the Cathedral of the Holy Cross. Faneuil Hall was enlarged in 1806 by Bulfinch's skilled hand and 10 years later, on the eve of his departure for Washington, D.C., he created the superb granite building of the Massachusetts General Hospital.

In addition to the development of a residential area on Beacon Hill, a number of large, opulent houses were built in the South End during this same building boom. Several were bought by a new,

Left: "Beacon Hill" was symbolic and actual. The Puritans wanted their community to be a beacon to others, symbolizing their special relationship with God. At the same time, they built a beacon as a lookout on Boston's highest point of land. When winds blew the beacon down in 1789, Charles Bulfinch designed this brick monument in memory of those killed at the Battle of Bunker Hill. The monument still stands in a parking lot behind the State House. (TBS)

Below: This unusual house was built in 1796 by Charles Bulfinch as the summer home of the James Swan family. (TBS)

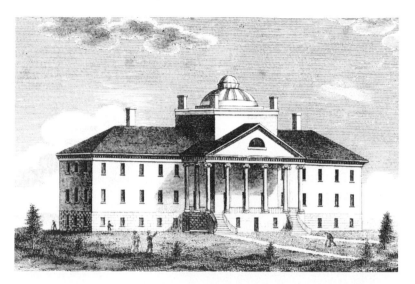

This was the original Massachusetts General Hospital designed by Charles Bulfinch. Construction began in 1816 and the hospital was the site of the first operation performed under ether in 1846. The domed operating room is incorporated into the present MGH complex. From History of Boston, *by Caleb Snow, 1825. (SPNEA)*

distinct class of merchant princes, many of whom were emigres from Essex County—the Lowells, the Higginsons, the Jacksons, the Lees, and the Cabots. This group, along with Thomas Russell, James and Thomas Handasyd Perkins, and Josiah Bradlee, formed a kind of extended family, a kinship group second to none in New England. Their wealth was linked to the development of new trade routes. By 1792 these daring, ambitious Boston merchants had established the Boston-Northwest-Canton-Boston route, trading sea otter skins for silks, chinaware, and tea to be sold either in Boston or abroad.

They sailed from Boston in the autumn, aiming to clear Cape Horn during the Antarctic summer. Still "the passage around Cape Horn," wrote one Boston ship captain, "is the most dangerous, most difficult, and attended with more hardships, than that of the same distance in any other part of the world." With luck these courageous Yankee seamen reached the Pacific Northwest by spring. Once there the Boston Nor'westmen moved along the rugged coast from one Indian village to another, bartering a myriad of goods—trinkets, chisels, molasses, tin kettles, old keys, *anything*—for the glossy, jet-black sea otter skins that the Indians had collected.

It was a dangerous business. In 1803, for example, the Indians near Nootka

Sound attacked the Amory's ship *Boston* and massacred all but two crew members. Several years later, the Winship brothers of Brighton were forced by the fierce Chinook Indians to give up their hope of establishing a permanent settlement in Oregon. If there was no major trouble, it generally took about two years to gather enough skins to set sail for Canton, the next leg of the long voyage.

China was the only market for sea otter skins and Canton was the only port in which Boston traders were permitted to do business. Here, too, negotiations had to be carefully conducted. All of the commissions, presents, and bribes had to be freely given and all the intricate diplomatic maneuvers knowledgeably followed. It was a challenge to which Yankee traders such as John Perkins Cushing (J. and T.H. Perkins' man in Canton for 30 years) responded adroitly and incredibly successfully. When the skins were sold, traders bought tea, porcelain, and silk. With hard bargaining and a bit of luck, it was not uncommon for a Boston entrepreneur to net $100,000 on a single China voyage. (By comparison the average wealth of all residents in the North End was $523 per capita.)

Many of the Boston-China merchants spent money lavishly, chasing an opulent lifestyle. At the same time some used the trade to accumulate capital and later invested it in the development of the new textile industry. One way or the other, an enormous amount of money was pumped into the New England economy by the China trade. The siren song of luxury, feared in the abstract three decades earlier by the old republicans, had become by 1820 a very real problem.

For Bostonians the issue of luxury became a hotly disputed public debate when a Tea Assembly was established. Meeting every other week at Concert Hall for dancing and card playing, this Sans Souci ("Free and Easy") Club, as it was called, was founded by a young, well-to-do group of men and women eager for some "innocent amusement." But its critics, whose attacks on the club filled the pages of the Boston *Centinel* and the *Independent Chronicle,* saw nothing funny or innocent about it. For the issue at stake seemed to the old republicans to be nothing less than the kind of society Boston was creating.

One writer, identified as "The Observer," began the debate by stating the old republican maxim: "Luxury is fatal to a free nation." To the end of his life, John Adams adhered to the same sentiment. Despite his desire to surpass Europe in the cultivation of the arts, Adams was convinced "that the more elegance, the less virtue, in all times and countries." Buildings, mansions, music, painting, and dancing, were simply "bagatelles introduced by time and luxury in change for the great qualities and hardy, manly virtues of the human heart," concluded the old patriot.

The Tea Assembly's defenders rejected the old republicans' arguments. First "A Bostonian" and the Sans Souci Club asserted that their young friends possessed "as great heroic manliness and bravery of soul at this moment as could be claimed at any period." Second the youngsters raised the specter of individualism: everyone had the right to spend some part of their earnings for amusement. Finally "One of a Number" reminded the old republicans of Boston's recent, prosperous history and its consequences. "If you wish to separate commerce from luxury," he told them, "you expect an impossibility."

In many ways the tempest over the Tea Assembly was a tepid version of the statewide and national struggles that contorted Boston politics during the period from 1780 to 1822. From the adoption of the new state constitution through the War of 1812, Boston's political leaders were curiously anxious. From most Americans' point of view, the young republic was a glorious success. But Boston's elite—the Otis's, the Lowell's, and the Cabot's—became disillusioned and increasingly despaired of the possibilities of shaping the character of the American people in the way *they* believed necessary.

Thus until the collapse of the Federalist party and the rise of a new generation of reformers in the 1820s, Boston came to symbolize the dark, provincial side of American politics rather than the bright, national side.

The Massachusetts constitution of 1780 was chiefly the work of John Adams, though James Bowdoin and Sam Adams also were named to the drafting committee by the convention. In Adams' famous phrase the constitution sought to create a government of laws, not of men. It struck a balance between the powers of the legislature and those of the governor, and between the interests of property and those of the people. This old-fashioned notion Adams blended with the radical idea that since the people were sovereign, all governmental institutions were merely different kinds of representations of the people. The governor, therefore, was not an elected monarch but, as the convention declared, "emphatically the Representative of the whole People, being chosen not by one town or country, but by the People at large."

The general frame eventually met the approval of the people of Massachusetts who assembled in town meetings in the spring of 1780 to debate and to decide if they would recommend that the convention ratify the constitution. The Boston Town Meeting—887 voters strong at its peak—met for three days. The chief obstacle to quick approval was Article III of the Declaration of Rights that proclaimed the right and duty of the state to support the teaching of "piety, religion and morality" on the grounds that these virtues were necessary for "the happiness of a people and the good order and preservation of civil government." A majority of Bostonians supported the principle forwarded by Article III, but many people wanted to "Secure the Rights of Conscience and to give the fullest Scope to religious Liberty." Someone suggested that if a citizen could not in conscience support "any of the various denominations among us they may then allot their Money to the support of

Dorothy Quincy married John Hancock and shared in the toil and privation of the Revolutionary War. Living near the State House after 1780, the couple entertained often and, when Admiral d'Estaing was invited to breakfast and requested that his 300 officers join him, Dolly Hancock sent servants to milk all the cows on the Common saying that she would personally deal with anyone who complained. No one did. (TBS)

the Poor." But that motion, as well as other proposed compromises, failed.

The key argument for the article was made by "Hieronymus" in the Boston *Gazette*. He maintained that it did not invade the right of conscience because no one was forced to believe anything. And "Hieronymus" concluded by pointing out that Article III would take effect only if a majority approved. When the question finally was put, the town meeting voted "almost unanimously" in favor of Article III.

Eight years later Bostonians were among those who met in convention to consider the new federal constitution. Heavy taxes, an unsure commercial future, and a violent uprising in western Massachusetts convinced a large majority of Bostonians from every social class that hope for prosperity and order lay with the new instrument of national government. John Hancock and Sam Adams initially were hesitant; but when a mass meeting of mechanics, chaired by Paul Revere, overwhelmingly declared themselves in favor, the old patriots joined the ranks of the constitution's supporters.

Even with their support ratification won by only a narrow margin. The divisions, however, were quickly healed. Before the convention broke up Hancock's newly adopted Federalism was being celebrated in song:

The Squire Hancock like a man
Who dearly loves the nation,
By a conciliatory plan,
Prevented much vexation.
   Yankee doodle. . .

The Federalists' euphoria lasted but for 12 years. During those halcyon days Bostonians were prominent and powerful figures in the new government. But changes were taking place over which the old elite had no control. In 1800 Thomas Jefferson and his democratic supporters defeated John Adams and the Federalists. To the Boston oligarchy Jefferson was the "devil incarnate." Although younger Federalists such as Harrison Gray Otis and Josiah Quincy learned the tricks of courting the votes of the people and emphasized to the "happy and respectable classes" their responsibility to preserve order, they were fighting a rear-guard action and they knew it.

The Boston Federalists' most foolish and bitter gesture against the direction of national politics was their opposition to the War of 1812, "Mr. Madison's War." Every effort by Jefferson to prevent a conflict with Great Britain was vigorously denounced. In 1809 the Boston Town Meeting sent a petition to the Massachusetts legislature claiming that the president's policies were nothing but a "War in disguise"; in 1811 a huge meeting at Faneuil Hall decried the law stopping trade with Britain as "unjust, tyrannical and oppressive"; and late in 1814 the Boston *Gazette* declared that "on or before the 4th of July, if James Madison is not out of office, a new form of government will be in operation in the eastern section of the union."

The Republicans, meanwhile, announced their determination to win the war. They saw it as a test of the experiment in free government. Therefore although Americans

The Boston troops are reviewed on the Common on President Adams' birthday in this 1800 print. The new State House and John Hancock's house are visible in the background. The scene was re-engraved by Charles Goodspeed in 1903. (BPL)

gained nothing tangible from the war, it was widely regarded as a great success. The Federalists were completely discredited and the national party passed into obscurity.

Within Boston, however, the Federalists began to campaign to change the system of government from a town to a city so that they might continue to exercise political control in their own back yard. The town meeting was a disorderly forum that was not capable of meeting the demands of a growing urban center, the elite argued. The Federalists proposed, therefore, that Boston be incorporated as a city, to be governed by a mayor and a common council elected at large.

Following an emotional and sometimes bitter series of debates, the vote in favor of incorporation passed on January 7, 1822. Shortly thereafter Governor John Brooks officially approved "an act establishing the City of Boston." The new charter called for a mayor, 8 aldermen, and 48 councillors elected by wards. A motto from the book of Kings was selected for the city's seal: *Sit Deus nobiscus sicut fuit cum patribus nostris*

("May God be with us as he was with our fathers").

When George Robert Twelves Hewes returned to Boston in 1821 after an absence of nearly 50 years, he was aghast. He had been born in the town and had been active as a young man in the stirring events leading to the Revolution. But the town he had known was gone:

The whole scenery about me seemed like the work of enchantment. Beacon Hill was leveled, and a pond on which stood three mills, was filled up with its contents; over which two spacious streets had been laid and many elegant fabrics erected. The whole street, from Boston Neck to the Long Wharf, had been built up. It was to me almost a new town, a strange city; I could hardly realize that I was in the place of my nativity.

Although the physical appearance of the city had changed, Hewes was pleased to observe that its ideals had not. Bostonians still were committed to the struggle to create a free, humane, and disciplined City on a Hill.

IV
Hub of the Universe

"The demon of reform" is loose in the land, Ralph Waldo Emerson excitedly announced in 1841. Bostonians were indeed busy reforming their society. Dozens of volunteer groups sprang up during the first half of the 19th century to reform the city's religious, political, and economic institutions and to perfect the individual. "Matters have come to such a pass," one observer grumbled, "that a peaceable man can hardly venture to eat or drink, or to go to bed or to get up, to correct his children or to kiss his wife, without obtaining the permission and direction of some. . .society."

As they had been in 1630, Boston's reformers were concerned both with building an integrated, harmonious community and with goading individuals to recognize their moral

responsibilities. They sought to influence the public mind in the interest of some large social transformation. "The reformer," argued one of Boston's most outspoken abolitionists, Wendell Phillips, "is careless of numbers, disregards popularity and deals only with ideas, conscience and common sense." Reformers also shared an unconquerable faith in moral progress.

Most of the men and women who wanted to change Boston during this period were optimistic, motivated by an "adoration of goodness" and a belief in the nobility of man. "We are in an age of improvement," gushed Edward Everett, a Boston-born, Harvard-educated reformer whose speeches sped thousands along the road toward a new society. A few reformers, however, insisted that the road to change should be straighter and narrower. They tended to support only those changes that would help to control the "dangerous classes of society."

Josiah Quincy, the second mayor of Boston, seemed an unlikely reformer however defined. His political career, before his election as mayor in 1823, was characterized by fruitless, vitriolic attacks on Jeffersonianism. By his own admission Quincy was thought of as "a raving Federalist," an "embarrassment" to his colleagues in the United States Congress. Yet during his six terms as mayor, Quincy initiated a series of reforms that substantially improved the quality of life in Boston for decades.

Quincy wanted nothing else from life than to be a politician. His family background, education, and wealth seemed to ensure him of a long and distinguished career in public service. But when he resigned his congressional seat in protest to the War of 1812 and returned to Boston, it looked as though his political life was over. He was bitter. Passed over by his own party for positions he wanted, Quincy adamantly and publicly refused to join in the "era of good feelings." He dabbled. At the Brighton Cattle Show of 1819 he sang the praises of farming and at the same time made money speculating

in urban real estate. Most of all Quincy brooded. "Time, now a days," he wrote a friend in 1820, "spins along without noise or apparent motion. . .Nothing to find fault with, and yet nothing to make [me] happy."

Finally at the age of 48, Quincy narrowly won election to the Massachusetts lower House, one of 15 representatives from Boston. The 1820 session of the legislature was the first in Massachusetts history to begin to cope with the problems of urbanization. In particular Governor John Brooks urged the house to address the growing problems of crime, poverty, and overcrowding at the Charlestown Prison and public welfare.

Quincy responded enthusiastically. He conducted an investigation of the pauper laws, and in 1821 he issued a report that clearly demonstrated the scope and consequences of the problem. He called for an end to direct relief to the poor. Of all methods for aiding the needy, Quincy declared, "the most wasteful, the most expensive, and most injurious to their morals, and destructive of their industrious habits, is that of supply in their own families." He advocated instead institutionalizing the poor, removing them from the temptations in their communities, and rehabilitating them by insisting that anyone who received public funds be taught the lesson of hard labor.

Quincy's report broke with the past. He began by asserting that the civic ties that had transcended class lines and bound communities together in the past were no longer as powerful. Therefore another more realistic approach was needed. While the Quincy report flirted with the idea of abolishing all poor laws and either casting individuals on their own, or throwing them to the mercy of private charitable organizations, it finally was decided that such a strategy would be "inconsistent with a humane, liberal and enlightened policy." The poor, in other words, were acknowledged to be a social problem and therefore a proper object of community reform.

Order and regularity, together with hard work within the institution, would bring the "hope of amendment to the vicious and assistance to the poor." Such a regimen, Quincy claimed, would correct rather than confirm habits of idleness. Inmates of a workhouse would learn "constancy and diligence" and "to obey and respect" in a setting that gave the highest priority to "reformation." The lives of the poor would then be "more comfortable and happy," Quincy predicted.

The report established Quincy as the state's leading authority on poverty and welfare. Not surprisingly, therefore, in May 1821 the Boston selectmen asked Quincy to study the feasibility of establishing an almshouse, where the "honest poor" would be put to work. Early in 1822 the city accepted Quincy's recommendation and a House of Industry was built in South Boston. The design reflected the new philosophy toward the poor. Rather than resembling a large house as had its predecessor, Boston's House of Industry had a rigid, massive,

institutional appearance. At its center was an administrative building, where the keeper and his family lived, with two long wings radiating out from each side—one for men, the other for women.

Before construction of Boston's newest poorhouse was completed, Quincy had become a municipal judge. His interest in poverty, it seems, had led him to study crime. It was not a prestigious position, but he had "the most honorable intentions . . .and the ability to be useful," according to one of his friends, William Sullivan. The same flattering assessment was made subsequently by many others during Boston's first mayoral campaign.

Harrison Gray Otis thought he was going to be the city's first mayor. His friends in the Federalist party told him that he had the backing of "Webster, Lowell, Tudor, all the judges and those whom I know you feel a high respect for." To their astonishment, however, Quincy entered the race, the candidate of the so-called "Middling Interest," shopkeepers and artisans. "A man of forty is a fool to wonder at anything," snorted Daniel

This Staffordshire platter by Ralph Stevenson displays the almshouse on Leverett Street. When it was built in 1800, the almshouse was considered to be the most modern method of housing and caring for the poor. Mayor Josiah Quincy later criticized it by saying it did "not comport with the honor and interest of the town." In 1822 the city built a new House of Industry in South Boston and the almshouse was closed. Photograph by Richard Merrill. (TBS)

Scrimshaw is the art of carving on whalebone and whale ivory. It was popular in 19th century Boston as a result of the large whaling industry in Boston and Salem. This six-inch tooth features a familiar household scene. Photograph by Richard Merrill. (TBS)

Webster, "and yet one is in danger of committing this folly when he sees Mr. Quincy the very darling of the Boston Democracy!"

Webster's elitism caused him to exaggerate. Boston's working-class voters refused to embrace Quincy. "His whole political life has rendered him obnoxious," one North End resident explained. The result was that neither Quincy nor Otis won a majority and both men withdrew before the run off. The voters, therefore, settled on John Phillips, described by contemporaries as "disinterested, considerate and candid." His administration was brief. Halfway through the year he fell ill and announced he would not stand for reelection. Quincy won the nomination and easily defeated his Republican opponent.

Quincy's enthusiasm and energy suddenly seemed boundless. One hour after his inauguration on May 1, 1823, he called the city council into session and presented a plan for cleaning the city's streets. A couple of weeks later he appointed Benjamin Pollard, a young lawyer, to the newly created office of "marshal of the city." In addition to his duties as police officer, Pollard also was charged with maintaining public health.

Cleaning up Boston required a herculean effort. There was no effective system for cleaning the streets and "house dirt" and "street dirt" went uncollected for long periods of time; the city's sewage emptied out into Town Dock right behind the market; and the odor of "noxious effluvia," as Quincy delicately termed it, permeated the center of the city. Within a remarkably short time, however, the mayor and his marshal accomplished what the old town Board of Health had failed for generations to do. The streets were cleaned by teams of sweepers, the refuse collected on a regular basis, and the sewers brought under public control. By the end of his first year in office, 6,000 tons of street dirt had been collected. Boston had become, under Quincy's guidance, one of the healthiest and cleanest cities in America.

The crowded, old market district was the next object of Quincy's vigorous urban reformation project. Since its construction in 1742, Faneuil Hall had been used as a meeting place and a public market. Although it was expanded in 1804 by Charles Bullfinch, by 1820 it was again hopelessly inadequate. On market days the streets around the hall were jammed with carts and there were not nearly enough stalls available for vendors. Quincy proposed that a new market be built, along with a docking facility and several new access streets. Although he

This map of Quincy Market shows changes that were made for this early landfill and urban renewal project. Several streets and buildings were removed and the shoreline was changed to create a broad expanse of land for the new complex (indicated by the shaded area). (TBS)

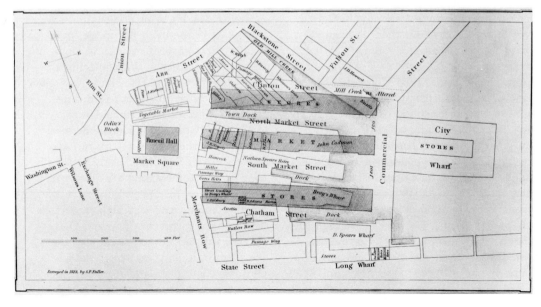

ran into opposition from some members of the council who were alarmed that the city's taxpayers were to assume the cost of his "mammoth project," the mayor won a public referendum approving the expansion.

The cornerstone for Quincy's new market was laid on April 22, 1825, a little over two years after he had become mayor. "Quincy Market," as it immediately came to be called, was a two-story, classically styled granite building, more than 500 feet long with a copper-sheathed dome in the center. In addition to the market building, six new approach streets and a new wharf were constructed. Completed in 1826, the new market complex transformed the city's center. Bostonians swelled with pride. "Boston has long enjoyed the reputation of a neat city," boasted the Boston *News-Letter,* "it bids fair indeed to gain the additional reputation of being a handsome one."

Mayor Quincy was eager to do far more

than change the face of Boston. He wanted to restore the community's organic unity, to make the people of Boston "happy, secure and contented" and aware of "the advantage of a vigorous and faithful administration." One important step toward achieving these goals, according to Quincy, was to reduce crime in the city. His principal concern was protecting society. He had little sympathy for the "vicious poor" or the "hardened criminal," nor was he interested in the debate over how best to rehabilitate criminals. Quincy believed that crime was an inevitable feature of a modern, urban society. The Boston Prison Discipline Society, founded in 1825 by Louis Dwight and Samuel Gridley Howe, tried in vain to convince the mayor that with the proper prison system criminals would be reformed. Howe advocated isolation: "left in total solitude, separated from evil society. . .the progress of corruption is arrested," he argued. The mayor remained unconvinced, but he did agree that the

From the moment Faneuil Hall Market opened in 1826, people called it Quincy Market, in honor of "The Great Mayor," Josiah Quincy, who built the project to serve as Boston's central marketplace. Quincy Market today is the focus of major waterfront restoration efforts, and its specialty shops host thousands of visitors annually. (TBS)

Joy's Building was an early shopping center located on Washington near State Street. Built on the site of Boston's First Church, the building had a circular staircase surrounded by over 40 stores and offices. This lithograph suggests the variety of businesses located in the building and the ways in which they advertised. (BPL)

old Leverett Street jail was grossly inadequate and, therefore, pushed through major improvements.

Howe did succeed in demonstrating to the mayor the need for a separate facility for juvenile offenders. Rather than commit youngsters to the state prisons ("those well-endowed seminaries of crime"), Quincy came to believe that they ought to be segregated from adult criminals and given special attention aimed at making them useful citizens. Completed in 1828, the House of Reformation for Juvenile Offenders in South Boston operated on the basis of a strict regime designed to instill order and method into the boys' lives. For example the youngsters were forbidden to talk to one another as they went about their assigned work; periodically all of the boys were brought together in the gymnasium, where, standing at rigid attention, they were required to shout in unison answers to questions from the superintendent; and they were required to attend chapel each day to listen to a sermon about the benefits of "habits of submission, self-denial and benevolence."

The quasi-military doctrine of the House of Reformation did not guarantee success in the long run. By the 1850s the

city's well-intentioned attempt to rehabilitate delinquent children had lost its special purpose. Moral reform gave way to custodial care, the work ethic to enforced idleness, and young immigrants—Irish Catholics for the most part—accounted for a disproportionate share of the residents compared to their numbers in the general population of Boston.

Mayor Quincy's conservative approach to reform, manifested by his skepticism about the possibilities of rehabilitating criminals, also was demonstrated by his handling of the controversy over education for girls. Compared with other American cities in the 1820s, Boston had an outstanding public school system. More than 7,000 students were enrolled in the city's 72 schools, including a high school for girls. Quincy's commitment to public education in general was not very deep, and by 1826 he was on record as opposing the girls' high school. Although the school was popular and, according to an investigation carried out by the school committee, successful, Quincy charged that the school was "undemocratic" because it admitted girls only by exam (as did the boys' high schools) and was too costly. Resistance by some school committeemen collapsed and in June 1828 the Girls' High School closed its doors. It would be 33 years before the city reconsidered Quincy's judgment that Boston could not "provide fit wives for well-educated men" at public expense.

Well before that time, however, Quincy had been turned out of office. The headmaster of the girls' school publicly attacked Quincy charging him with bias and dishonesty. Others objected to the mayor's autocratic manner and his elitism. On the eve of the election in December 1828 the Jacksonians issued a circular quoting the mayor as stating that if the Girls' High School were allowed to continue "the education of our servant girls will be equal to that of our daughters, and perhaps enable them to force connections with our sons!" Quincy said nothing in his defense and Harrison

Gray Otis became Boston's third mayor.

The democratic upsurge among Boston voters that helped defeat Quincy was part of a national Jacksonian movement. But there were local roots as well. The old Puritan view of the depravity of man and the struggle for salvation that had dominated the Boston mind for nearly two centuries gave way in the early 19th century to a new, optimistic spirit. Without questioning either the existence of God or the authority of the Bible, Unitarians emphasized the goodness of God and the perfectibility of man. They argued that reason was able to clarify Christianity. Unitarianism easily captured the middle and upper classes of Boston. Nearly all the important Congregational pulpits were taken over by Unitarian preachers: Nathaniel Frothingham was at the First Church; Henry Ware Hollis, Professor of Divinity at Harvard, was called to the Second Church; Francis Parkman led the congregation at the New North; and William Ellery Channing, the founder of Unitarianism, spread his gospel of the "adoration of goodness" at the Federal Street Church.

Unitarianism relied on character—defined as the process of understanding, accepting, and acting on moral truths—to bring about social harmony. Creating a moral society was as important to Unitarians as achieving personal salvation. Therefore although Unitarians did not zealously seek converts they did actively engage in various reform programs. Joseph Tuckerman, for example, left his comfortable church in Chelsea in 1826 to become the first Unitarian minister at large to the poor of Boston. He used books, sermons, home visits, and voluntary associations to adapt religion to a society in which life no longer centered on the church. The primary objective of Tuckerman's efforts was the moral improvement of the working class by personal contact with exemplary Christians. Training sessions for middle-class volunteers were held each week at Channing's Federal Street Church. Self-improvement, an "awakening

of a deeper concern" for the poor, also was crucial to Unitarianism's campaign for social justice.

Orestes Brownson, a member of Boston's Transcendental Club, rejected Channing's easy solution to the problem of class conflict. In 1836 Brownson organized a free church for workers called the Society for Christian Union and Progress and preached a doctrine that made Christianity a weapon of class struggle. Most of the men and women who participated in the small circle of Transcendentalism, were neither as Christian nor as radical as Brownson.

Ralph Waldo Emerson, the son of a Boston minister and the descendant of five generations of New England clergymen, began his career as a Unitarian but left the church a few years after he graduated from Harvard Divinity School. He rejected both rationalism and ritualism. In a series of brilliant essays, Emerson articulated the basis for Transcendentalism by emphasizing the virtues of individualism, self-reliance, and self-improvement. "Who so would be a man," he told his audience, "must be a non-conformist." To the youth of America he delivered the reassuring thought: "Trust thyself; every heart vibrates to that iron string." He castigated Bostonians for their single-minded pursuit of wealth and fame, for their obsession with material things. He called upon American scholars to look for ideas and inspiration in the familiar and natural sources of beauty right around them. "We walked this afternoon to...Walden Pond," Emerson recorded in his journal on April 9, 1842. "The world is so beautiful," he wrote half in pain, "that I can hardly believe it exists." Emerson and the Transcendentalists made the unity of nature and man their god.

As Emerson saw it the great peril that threatened the American people was not injustice but a fragmentation of the soul. "The reason why the world lacks unity and lies broken and in heaps," he told a Boston audience in 1837, "is because man is disunited with himself." We must

Brook Farm was a Transcendentalist community, established in 1841 in West Roxbury, near the present West Roxbury High School. Residents and supporters established an innovative school and participated in cooperative work ventures. Financial problems and a major fire in 1846 led to the closing of the farm. (SPNEA)

recover a sense of the whole. Still Emerson welcomed social heterogeneity, Boston as a melting pot. "The energy of Irish, Germans, Swedes, Poles, and Cossaks, and all the European tribes—and of the Africans, and of the Polynesians—will construct a new race, a new religion, a new state, a new literature, which will be as vigorous as the new Europe which came out of the smelting-pot of the Dark Ages," he predicted. It was this robust optimism born of a faith in the common person that made Emerson America's most popular philosopher in the 19th century. He offered something for everyone and thus nourished the ideal of an integrated, harmonious community to which Boston still aspired.

Emerson's critique of materialism and his call to idealistic unity awakened other reformers in the City on a Hill. Women entered a variety of reform movements, to pursue their self-interest as well as to improve their society. Mothers formed groups to discuss how best to raise children. Other women focused on

reforming formal education outside of the home. Moral reformers attacked the double standard of sexual morality and the victimization of prostitutes, exposed the state's dreadful treatment of the mentally ill, and joined in the abolition movement.

Women were entrusted with the morals and faith of the next generation. Local maternal associations and the child-rearing literature of the time were responses to the contemporary cultural and religious elevation of the mother's role. Ministers declared repeatedly that women's pious influence was not only appropriate to them but also important for society. "We look to you ladies," the Reverend Joseph Buckminister told a group of Boston women, "to raise the standard of character in our own sex; we look to you to guard and fortify those barriers, which still exist in society, against the encroachments of impudence and licentiousness."

The women who formed the Dorchester Maternal Association did so because they were "aware of our highly responsible

BOSTON.

situation as Mothers and as professing Christians." The women considered it each member's duty to pray with her children and to read the appropriate, helpful books on child-rearing. One of the most widely read of the advice-to-parents books was Lydia Maria Child's *The Mother's Book*. Born in nearby Medford, Child settled in Boston in the 1820s, where her novels and advice books quickly established her in the city's intellectual and literary circles. She told mothers to train their children to respect authority. A combination of firmness and gentleness, she wrote, would cause children to obey without argument. Should a mother fail in this task, the most dire consequences would result. Another author of an advice book told the Mount Vernon Maternal Association of Boston that the mother of George Washington had said: "A good boy generally makes a good man. George was always a good boy."

Women who joined maternal associations were anxious to shape their children's lives while they were at home. Other Boston women and men joined together during the 1830s to see to it that children were educated properly while in school. But what constituted "proper" education was a matter of controversy that divided Boston's educational reformers.

Infant schools, for example, were hailed enthusiastically in 1829 by the Boston *Recorder*. If the children of the poor were placed in infant schools from the age of two years until age five years when the public school system would accept them, the *Recorder* predicted they would learn "at least a hundred times as much, a hundred times as well, and [would be] a hundred times as happy." A year earlier, prompted by William Russell, an educational reformer who came to Boston from Scotland, 90 women founded the Boston Infant School Society. They were committed to the idea that urban problems—crime, vice, and poverty—could be ameliorated by taking the children of the poor from their families and

inculcating them with the values of discipline and morality.

The Boston school establishment came out in opposition to the society's infant schools and its philosophy. Public school teachers reported that they found children from infant schools "intractable and troublesome." And school administrators publicly doubted the efficacy of the infant school's social mission. "Such is the power of a bad example—especially that of parents," one headmaster declared, "that it will probably do much to counteract the good influence of the infant school."

The final blow to the infant school movement in Boston was struck by Amariah Brigham. In 1833 he published a book called *Remarks on the Influence of Mental Cultivation and Mental Excitement upon Health* that was aimed directly at the theory underlying the infant school movement. Brigham's thesis was explicit: "Too early cultivating the mind and exciting the feelings of children" was one of the most important causes of insanity. The danger of the "hothouse effect" was publicized widely by the very journals that just three or four years earlier had embraced the social benefits of infant schools. Within months after the appearance of Brigham's book all of the infant schools had closed, reformers recoiling from the thought that their benevolence might be contributing to the

With Beacon Hill a residential district and the shoreline filled in, the Shawmut peninsula was getting crowded in 1837. Wharves covered the waterfront, and the only remaining large open space was the Common. (TBS)

mental instability of future generations.

Bronson Alcott was one of a number of young teachers who had been drawn to Boston by the infant school movement. Although the idea failed Alcott acquired a reputation among Boston's avant-garde as an educational Messiah, and in September 1834 he and Elizabeth Peabody launched the Temple School. Thirty boys and girls from some of Boston's leading families became participants in Alcott's revolutionary "love-oriented" educational experiment. By giving praise and affection as rewards, Alcott believed children would learn to behave conscientiously. He held lengthy conversations with his students, probing "the consciousness of the children" and encouraging them to tell the truth about their own feelings. This practice led him to conclude that children were a source of divine revelation, he explained in the preface of his book, *Conversations with Children on the Gospels.* Published in 1836, the book enraged influential Bostonians and resulted in the closing of the experimental school.

Alcott left Boston as he had come—a penniless idealist. Still, from the safety of Concord, Massachusetts, he rejoiced that he had been "saved" by his association with, and study of, children. Years later Alcott's daughter, Louisa May, used her family's trials and joys as the backdrop

Bronson Alcott, a Transcendentalist and an educator, opened an innovative school in Boston in 1834. Although recitation was the common teaching method of the day, Alcott's students wrote in journals and practiced "conversations" which gave them an opportunity to think about their reading and develop their own ideas. (TBS)

for her stunningly successful novel, *Little Women.* Within the confines of their home the fictional March family conducted a pilgrimage, defining as they went the solid values of Boston's middle class.

Most of Boston's reformers, however, doubted the competence of the city's poor and immigrant families to accomplish the goal of transferring society's all-important values of hard work, discipline, and morality to their children. Horace Mann was the most influential spokesman for a generation of school reformers who believed that the solution lay in the establishment of common schools, where rich and poor were educated side by side. Mann had come to Boston to practice law, but he soon found himself drawn to several reform groups. After a decade of work as an all-purpose reformer, however, Mann came to the uncomfortable conclusion that he had been wasting his time trying to reform men and women too far corrupted to be rehabilitated. Therefore in the mid-1830s he shifted his focus from the already-corrupted parents to their children, because, as he put it, "men are cast-iron; but children are wax."

In 1837 Mann was given the opportunity to put his ideas into effect. He became the first secretary to the Massachusetts Board of Education, a position from which he exercised personal leadership over the public schools for 12 years. And over the next generation scores of reformers emulated Mann, hailing him as the "Father of the American Public School."

Mann's initial success in Massachusetts was due in no small part to his connections with the wealthy and powerful. He appealed directly to their self-interest as businessmen whose profit margin depended on a stable, productive work force. After sending out questionnaires to prominent manufacturers, Mann published their conclusions on the "difference in the productive ability...between the educated and the uneducated." Not surprisingly the employers agreed with Mann that schooled workers were worth more than

QUARTER CARD OF DISCIPLINE AND STUDIES IN MR. ALCOTT'S SCHOOL FOR THE WINTER TERM CURRENT 1837.

unschooled. The advantages, spelled out by Mann in his *Fifth Annual Report,* were manifested in the worker's character and habits. Workers who had been educated in a common school showed "docility and quickness in applying themselves to work"; "personal cleanliness"; "standing and respectability among co-laborers, neighbors and fellow citizens generally"; and "punctuality and fidelity in the performance of duties."

These characteristics also were applauded by Bostonians who professed to find an exact correlation between an increase in immigration and social instability. Samuel Bates, chairman of the Boston public school Visiting Committees, explained that "our Public School System is a branch of Government itself; as much so as are our courts, our police, criminal and charitable regulations for the poor." The chief aim of city government in establishing and maintaining schools, therefore, "is its own preservation."

In 1849 the Boston School Committee, composed almost entirely of supporters of Mann, proposed to make schooling compulsory for all children. The committeemen were alarmed about the number of Irish children who were loose in the streets, a condition the schoolmen took as positive proof that the parents were not exercising proper control. And the reformers claimed that when parents failed to do their job, the city had no choice but to intervene. "The parent is not the absolute owner of the child," the Boston School Committee declared in 1853. "The child is a member of the community [therefore] Government has the same right of control over the child, that it has over the parent...Those children should be brought within the jurisdiction of the Public Schools," the committee concluded, "from whom, through their vagrant habits, our property is most in danger."

Boston's Irish community knew why a mandatory school attendance law had been passed. The law was designed, stated an Irish newspaper, to destroy the "work of the Church, and of the Family," to

cause children to lose respect for their parents, their church, and their traditions as Irish. Although school reformers denied such a motivation, they were forced to admit by the 1850s that the city's overcrowded common schools had not broken the chains of poverty.

One supposed Irish tradition that Boston Protestants in particular attributed as the cause of poverty was drink. Ironically the Irish arrived in Boston at a time when the campaign against the evils of alcohol had achieved some success. Per capita consumption of liquor had climbed during the 1820s when the average adult American consumed about 37 gallons of spirits each year, then suddenly leveled off, and by 1840 began to plummet toward an unprecedented low.

Reformers, such as Dr. John Warren who founded the Massachusetts Society for the Suppression of Intemperance, saw themselves as carrying on the work of the Founding Fathers. Anti-liquor reformers asked Bostonians to sign pledges and celebrate their dry oaths on the 4th of July. The symbolism was explicit, as shown by the frequent references in the temperance literature to the struggle for independence. On one occasion a speaker declared that when future generations assembled to honor the Founding Fathers, they would be able to say, "On this day, also did our fathers, of a later generation,

The Quincy School opened in 1848 as an example of the best of modern schools. Its four stories housed 12 rooms (each seating 56 students) plus a 700-seat hall. There were separate rooms for each class and an individual desk for each scholar. (TBS)

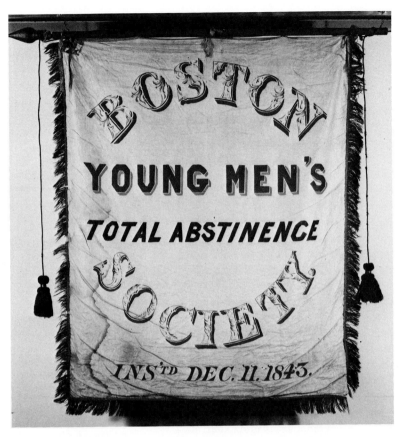

Like other temperance groups, the Young Men's Total Abstinence Society was active in local politics. They educated young men about the dangers of drink in an effort to persuade them to take the pledge of abstinence. Temperance reformers often went on to support other reform groups, many of which optimistically set about improving conditions for Bostonians in the 1840s. (TBS)

declare and maintain a SECOND INDEPENDENCE. . .from Prince Alcohol."

Even though consumption of alcohol was declining, opposition to the temperance movement spurred by the presence of an increasing number of Irish, did not weaken. In order to make liquor less readily available, Massachusetts outlawed the retail sale of distilled spirits in 1838. The law had two unintended effects: first, it clearly demonstrated the Yankee's lack of understanding or sympathy for the cultural alienation and impoverishment that often led the Irish to drink excessively; second, because the new law made mere possession of small quantities of liquor a crime rather than punishing public drunkenness as had the old laws, there were far more clashes between the police and the poor, including the Irish, after 1838.

In addition to a cultural bias, temperance advocates were driven by a belief that alcoholism led to the

destruction of the family or to the degradation of young men and women, especially those who lived in the city. For this reason women's moral reform societies saw an explicit link between alcoholism and male licentiousness and prostitution. Therefore there was a considerable overlap of membership among temperance societies and those groups aimed at eliminating the sin of licentiousness and upholding chastity.

The Boston Female Moral Reform Society had two immediate goals: to reform "fallen" women and to publicize and ostracize men who visited prostitutes. The society's literature expressed the women's rage. "Our mothers, our sisters, our daughters are sacrificed by the thousands every year on the altar of sin," declared the *Advocate of Moral Reform* in 1835, "and who are the agents of this destruction? Why, our fathers, our brothers, and our sons." These Boston women were not accepting the double standard; they urged virtuous men and women to "esteem the licentious man as little as they do the licentious woman." The Moral Reform Society also raised the specter of revenge. Women who had become prostitutes were described as "abandoned girls, who having been ruined themselves by the treachery and depravity of man, have sworn to glut their vengeance by dragging to their own depths in guilt and infamy such young men as might otherwise have been the flower and stamina of our country."

Never a popular position, this assertion of destructive power by women turned out not only to be illusionary but also self-destructive to women's drive for equal treatment. This was demonstrated by a sensational murder trial that took place in Boston in the fall of 1845. In a significant way the question of the guilt or innocence of Albert Terrill, accused of murdering his mistress Maria Bickford, hinged on how women in Boston society were perceived.

Early on the morning of October 27, 1845, a fireman summoned to a house on Charles Street, charged up the stairs through thick smoke to a bedroom that seemed to be the source of the fire and stumbled over the body of a woman. An investigation conducted by the Boston police revealed that the woman's throat had been slashed. There was blood on the mattress, suggesting that the body had been dragged from the bed. The water in the wash basin was thick with blood.

The woman was identified by Joel Lawrence, owner of the house, as Ms. Maria Bickford. Lawrence also told the police that Albert Terrill had been with Ms. Bickford on the evening of October 26th. Several articles of clothing identified as belonging to Terrill were discovered; they were bloodstained and partially burned. In December Terrill was arrested in New Orleans, returned to Boston, and charged with the murder of Maria Bickford. The trial took place in March 1846.

Before the trial even began Bostonians had been treated by the local press to the sordid details of the adulterous relationship between Bickford and Terrill. Readers of the *Daily Mail* and *Daily Times* were told that Terrill was from a solid, successful manufacturing family in Weymouth, Massachusetts. At the time of the trial Terrill was 22 years old; he was married and had two children. Young Terrill deserted his wife and children in the summer of 1844 when he met Ms. Bickford. Like Terrill, she was in her early twenties and had married young. Born and raised in Bangor, Maine, she had married James Bickford, a shoemaker, when she was 16 years old. After three years Marie left Bickford and came to Boston with another man. Once in the city, he abandoned her. Alone, without friends or means of support, Bickford turned to prostitution.

From the time they met in a New Bedford tavern, Bickford and Terrill were together constantly. They traveled together as man and wife, moving from hotel to boardinghouse to house of assignation. At least one landlord, however, refused to tolerate their blatant disregard for the law and morality. The owner of the Hanover House in Boston

brought charges and Terrill was arrested and indicted late in September for adultery. He was bailed out by his brother-in-law and with the help of letters to the court from his wife, mother, father-in-law, and a Weymouth selectman, the judge suspended proceedings for six months on good behavior. On October 21st Terrill was released; he went looking for his lover, Maria Bickford.

While no one witnessed Bickford's murder, all of the circumstantial evidence pointed to Terrill. He had been with her in a room at the Lawrence House on Charles Street on the night of the murder. Between 4:00 a.m. and 5:00 a.m. Terrill had gone to a stable near the Lawrence's and asked to be taken to Weymouth. He talked about a fight with a woman and said something to the carriage driver about a fire. In addition Samuel Parker, the prosecutor, described Terrill as a rogue without moral principles.

Terrill's defense attorney was one of the best in the business. Rufus Choate was a brilliant trial lawyer with years of experience and a flamboyant style. He launched a two-pronged attack that undermined the commonwealth's case. First, Choate attacked the credibility of Lawrence and the other witnesses who had testified against Terrill by pointing out that they worked at a house of ill-repute. Second, Choate worked hard to convince the all-male jury that Ms. Bickford was a depraved woman, a common prostitute without promise or hope of reformation.

Two hypotheses followed from Choate's second argument: Ms. Bickford had committed suicide (somehow managing to throw herself off the bed after she slit her throat from ear to ear). This theory was based on a syllogism: Bickford was a "fallen" woman; women of bad character always commit suicide; therefore Ms. Bickford had committed suicide. Then Choate maintained that even if Ms. Bickford had not killed herself, she was the destructive force. Because she was intent on dragging down Terrill, punishing him, he had to kill to free himself. Terrill was the victim.

The jury acquitted Terrill. Choate's defense, it would seem, played into the prejudices of the nine men who sat in judgment. In fact most New Englanders probably would have reacted similarly, though perhaps they would have shown a bit more sympathy for Maria Bickford. It was a common belief, after all, that young women from rural areas were corrupted by the sin and licentiousness of city life.

Francis Lowell, Nathan Appleton, and Patrick T. Jackson were well aware of this prejudice. For this reason among others, therefore, these wealthy financiers determined to build their new, modern textile factory in the countryside away from the existing urban centers. Lowell, the spot chosen by the Boston Associates, was located 15 miles north of Boston on the Merrimack River. It was a place of great natural beauty with rolling hills on either side of the river. The mill buildings were laid out to take advantage of the setting; there were grassy open spaces between the buildings so that the river could be seen and shrubs and trees separated the factory from the boarding houses. The whole effect was peaceful and inviting.

The rural character of Lowell was not mere aesthetics. The guiding idea was that the moral values of country life could be maintained while simultaneously promoting industrialization. Material advance through technology, in other words, would not sacrifice morality. This was especially important to the Boston Associates because the workers were "the daughters of respectable farmers." Workers in the manufacturing cities of Europe were notoriously men and women of low character and intelligence. But here in America Appleton, Jackson, and Lowell hoped to prove that industrial employment would not inevitably result in physical and moral deterioration. "Ours is a great novel experiment," declared Appleton. "Whatever the result, it is our destiny to make it. It is our mission—our care should be to understand it and make it succeed."

Succeed it did—for a time. Every European visitor sang the praises of the "celestial city." The young women who worked in the mill invariably were described as "clean," "fresh," "moral," and "healthy." Cautious and normally critical, Charles Dickens was surprised to find that the young women workers produced a literary magazine. *The Lowell Offering* "will compare advantageously with a great many English Annuals," Dickens happily concluded. And in the evenings the lecture hall often was crowded.

The Lowell workers themselves did not regard their work and their living arrangement in the same light as the visiting dignitaries. The actual working conditions were not utopian. Women operatives worked a six-day week, averaging 12 hours per day. Bells dictated every activity: beginning at 6:00 a.m. bells awakened the women; they rang again to call the women to and from meals; and bells marked curfew and the end of the day. All the while company officials stipulated that the women "must devote themselves assiduously to their duty during working hours" and "on all occasions, both in their words and in their actions, show they are penetrated by a laudable love of temperance and virtue animated by a sense of their moral and social obligations." If they worked steadily and their behavior was good, the workers earned an average weekly wage of $1.00 to $2.00, exclusive of room and board.

This policy of strict social control was reinforced by the hierarchical arrangement of the Lowell factory system. The directors and officers did not live in Lowell but in Boston. The first chief executive for the corporation was Kirk Boott who lived in an imposing Georgian mansion just below the original factory. Under Boott were the overseers who lived in simple yet substantial houses at the ends of the boardinghouses where the women operatives resided. These quarters were intended to serve as dormitories, six to eight women to each bedroom. Similar arrangements were provided for male mechanics. At the bottom of the hierarchy were the Irish day laborers who built the canals and mill buildings. No housing was planned for this group, and they lived in shacks crowded into an area near a Catholic church called "New Dublin" or the "Acre."

Despite this corporate insensitivity to the needs of immigrant workers and a few brief work stoppages led by women, the Boston Associates' new industrial plan was imitated widely throughout the 19th century. Visitors continued to admire Lowell, praising it as a productive, cohesive, and harmonious community, a reflection of the ideals of republicanism.

Not everyone agreed. A minority of dissident workers and their spokesmen protested their oppressive working conditions and the hierarchical conception of society that sustained them. Among the earliest and most articulate critics of industrialism were Edward Everett and Seth Luther. Everett was a liberal Unitarian who joined with a group of striking East Boston ship carpenters in 1825, taking up their demand for a 10-hour work day. Although the strike failed, Boston workers formed a Workingmen's party committed to electing candidates favorable to the needs of laborers. Everett conceived of more sweeping goals. He told a Charlestown audience that the aim of the party was not simply to "elevate this or that candidate for office, but to promote the prosperity and welfare of working men and. . .to produce *happiness.*"

Everett and the Boston Workingmen's party looked backward to the era when workers necessarily became artisans and independent producers. But by 1832 when the ship carpenters struck again, Seth Luther, a self-educated labor reformer, had no such illusions. Speaking for the striking carpenters, Luther denounced the employers as hypocrites for refusing to allow workers to form unions when the shipyard owners had formed a "detestable combination" in order to drive Boston's workers "into starvation or submission."

During the summer of 1832 Luther

This lithograph depicts the interior of the Glendon Rolling Mill and Forge Works which made sheet metal and machinery parts. Boston didn't have a large factory district but there were numerous small factories and mills, and Boston money financed the large mills in Merrimack Valley communities such as Lawrence and Lowell. (BPL)

published an *Address to the Working Men of New England* in which he attempted to speak to all workers, including those men and women in Lowell. The motives of *all* employers, he argued, sprang from "Avarice," which always "destroyed the happiness of the MANY, that the FEW may roll and riot in splendid luxury." The wretched Irish laborer living in a hovel in Lowell—the so-called industrial utopia—represented, in Luther's view, the vanguard of "hundreds of thousands of the miserable and degraded Population of Europe" who would be enticed to America and thus be degraded by the factory system.

So long as gross inequities existed, he contended, the American Revolution would be unfinished. The imperative of the Declaration of Independence, that "all men are created equal," Luther perceived of as a radical injunction against all social distinctions and he urged workers to unite and demand a fair share for their labor.

In 1834 workers from 16 craft unions heeded Luther's call. They formed the Boston Trades Union (BTU), one of the first organizations of its kind. At its peak, the BTU enrolled nearly 4,000 workers who helped carry the struggle for a shorter work day to the outlying mill towns, including Lowell, where women

This is the banner of The Liberator, *William Lloyd Garrison's weekly newspaper that advocated immediate abolition of slavery. While the slave trade had been outlawed in Massachusetts in 1789, Garrison argued that the textile mill owners and Boston financiers were supporting slavery by profiting from the Southern cotton industry. (BPL)*

operatives struck against wage cuts in 1834 and 1836.

Beginning in the 1830s many Boston reformers shifted their attention from moral reform, education, temperance, and factory legislation to the campaign against slavery in the South. Like the other reforms Bostonians had embraced, abolitionism was motivated by moral frenzy, not economic discontent. "Our enterprise," declared Wendell Phillips, the most socially prominent Bostonian opposed to slavery, "is eminently a religious one, dependent for success entirely on the religious sentiment of the people."

Phillips was an unlikely agitator. He had everything—family, wealth, an education at Boston Latin School and Harvard. In 1835 he opened a law office on Court Street; his success seemed assured. But one afternoon not long after he began his law practice, Phillips came upon a mob that had seized and threatened to lynch William Lloyd Garrison, publisher of the *Liberator* and founder of the Massachusetts Anti-Slavery Society. Such a blatant violation of civil liberty revolted Phillips. He drew closer to the abolition movement. When he married Anne Terry Greene, daughter of a wealthy Boston shipper and a militant abolitionist, he became an outcast in upper-class society. "My wife made me an out and out abolitionist," he declared lovingly years later.

Phillips' assaults on slavery continued to be tolerated by many Bostonians as long as his targets were southern aristocrats. In March 1839, however, he

burned the last of his bridges to polite society when he gave a speech to a massive meeting condemning the Massachusetts legislature for refusing to heed antislavery petitions. Phillips was especially critical of the legislators for rejecting a plea from a group of Lynn women, many of whom were black. According to Anne Weston, a cousin of Phillips, he tore the legislators to bits, "then ground them to atoms, then strewed them on the waters." The result, according to another friend, was that Boston was "convulsed with rage."

Phillips' acceptance of William Lloyd Garrison's leadership was the last straw. Garrison's strategy and style were anathema to everyone outside the movement. His famous declaration, published in the *Liberator* in January 1831, permitted no ambivalence: "I will be as harsh as truth, and as uncompromising as justice. On this subject, I do not wish to think, to speak, or write, with moderation....I am in earnest—I will not equivocate—I will not excuse—I will not retreat a single inch—AND I WILL BE HEARD." For Garrisonians there was no neutral ground regarding slavery: a person was for immediate emancipation or for slavery.

The *Liberator* was not read widely, nor did Garrison's position win many supporters in Boston or anywhere in the North. In its first year the paper had only 50 white subscribers and two years later barely 400. In the black community, however, Garrison and his program was enthusiastically supported. Of course black leaders such as William C. Nell and Benjamin Roberts had been actively opposed to slavery and involved in improving racial relations before Garrison arrived in Boston. In 1826, for example, a group of blacks dedicated to abolition formed the Massachusetts General Colored Association and two years later helped publish and distribute David Walker's incendiary *Appeal* for freedom. Although Walker's approach was rejected by Garrison, he was loved by the black community. He was often a guest in the homes of blacks living on Beacon Hill and in 1833 he was given an inscribed silver cup in appreciation for his commitment to the welfare of black people.

With Garrison's prompting the Boston Female Anti-Slavery Society resolved in 1838 that white abolitionists should make a greater effort to socialize with blacks. The fact that the resolution caused a furor, even among those who were opposed to slavery, made it clear how deep racial prejudice was in the "cradle of liberty." One of the most obvious examples of racial discrimination was Boston's public school system. Barred from attending the white public schools, blacks organized a private school that met in the African Meeting House beginning in 1806. As a result of a legacy from Abiel Smith, a white merchant, the city accepted financial responsibility for the education of black children after 1820.

But separate was not equal. In 1844, therefore, a group of black leaders organized to integrate public education in Boston. They petitioned, investigated,

THOMPSON, THE ABOLITIONIST.

That infamous foreign scoundrel THOMPSON, will hold forth *this afternoon*, at the Liberator Office, No. 48, Washington Street. The present is a fair opportunity for the friends of the Union to *snake Thompson out!* It will be a contest between the Abolitionists and the friends of the Union. A purse of $100 has been raised by a number of patriotic citizens to reward the individual who shall first lay violent hands on Thompson, so that he may be brought to the tar kettle before dark. Friends of the Union, be vigilant!

Boston, Wednesday, 12 o'clock. Oct 21.1835

Left: Boston eventually gained a reputation as the center of abolitionist activity. There was also strong anti-abolitionist sentiment as indicated by this broadside that was circulated before the visit of George Thompson, a British anti-slavery lecturer and organizer. (TBS)

publicized, demonstrated, and finally in 1849 brought suit against the city. Benjamin Roberts, a black printer, asked the School Committee to allow his five-year-old daughter, Sarah, to attend the white school closest to her home. (She passed five white schools on her daily trip to the black school.) Roberts' request was denied. The case was argued before the supreme judicial court by Charles Sumner, an abolitionist and later United States Senator from Massachusetts. Sumner asserted that segregated schools were not only unconstitutional but also damaging socially and emotionally to both black and white children. Segregation of children according to race, he maintained, would create a sense of caste distinction that would make social interaction among blacks and whites difficult or impossible later in life. Such a situation, Sumner concluded, would prevent "those relations of equality which our constitution and laws promised to all."

The court rejected Sumner's plea and ruled in favor of the Boston School Committee's right to set educational policy. Finally in 1855 the Massachusetts legislature passed a law abolishing separate schools. Other racial bars quickly fell; most public theaters were opened to blacks and railroad travel was integrated.

While Boston's optimistic reformers did not achieve their utopian goals, their ideals still burned brightly. Against all odds Bostonians clung to the idea that they could establish a new order, a harmonious community. This ideal would be severely tested, but never forgotten, during Boston's next two centuries of growth and change.

Left: After escaping from slavery in Kentucky, Lewis Hayden moved to Boston and became a leader in the abolitionist movement. Hayden and his wife, Harriet, used their home as a station on the Underground Railroad and assisted numerous fugitive slaves. Hayden was elected to the state legislature in 1873, and served as messenger to the secretary of state from 1859 until his death in 1889. (TBS)

V

The Coming of the Irish

They came to Boston on "coffin ships." Driven
from Ireland by hunger and unbearable
hardship, nearly one hundred thousand Irish
immigrants were spewn upon Boston's shores
between 1846-1849; 15,500 in 1846, 25,250 in
1847, 25,000 in 1848, and 34,000 before the
"Black Forties" ended. Not until 1864 did the
tide abate; by then 2.5 million Irish had
abandoned their homeland.

   The causes of this demographic disaster
were woven into the web of Irish economic life
decades before 1846. A sharp increase in
population at the turn of the 18th century
accompanied by the collapse of agricultural
prices, revealed a serious problem that English
landlords sought to exploit by raising rents
and by converting farmland into grazing land.
By the mid-1840's, therefore, the potato—a

cheap source of food that could be grown easily on the tiny plots of land still held by the Irish peasantry—was the only food of about one-third of the Irish people. In the autumn of 1845 a potato disease destroyed all but a fraction of the crop. After a wet spring and a humid summer, the crop of 1846 was a total failure. The two following years were no better. This crisis was aggravated further by a very poor grain harvest.

Starvation stalked Ireland. The death toll rose sharply. And, as if the horrors of starvation were not tragic enough, the Irish people were forced to endure the most severe winter in memory during 1846-1847. With snow blanketing the fields and roads, with icy winds making outdoor work nearly impossible, thousands died of hunger and from exposure. Malnutrition, poverty, and an inadequate relief program (the British government was reluctant to interfere with the "natural laws of supply and demand"), led to the outbreak of virulent diseases. Typhus, dysentery, scurvy and relapsing fever, reached epidemic levels. Finally, early in 1849 a serious outbreak of cholera added more victims to the grim toll.

Laborers, cottagers and small farmers in the southwestern counties suffered the worst. Corpses were left unburied for days, because people feared the contagion of fever. Dead bodies were discovered lying in the streets of villages and in ditches along country roads. A magistrate from Cork visited Skibbereen in late December 1846 and filed a chilling report:

I entered some of the hovels. . .and the scenes that presented themselves were such as no tongue or pen can convey the slightest idea of. In the first, six famished and ghastly skeletons, to all appearance dead, were huddled in a corner on some filthy straw, their sole covering what seemed a ragged horse-cloth, and their wretched legs hanging about naked above the knees. I approached in horror, and found by a low moaning they were alive; they were in fever—four children, a woman and what had once been a man. . . .

Small wonder that these calamitous years burnt themselves deep into the imagination of the Irish and haunted their descendants for generations. An American relief drive, including a massive effort by Boston's Irish Catholic population as well as a number of the city's prominent Protestants, certainly helped end the terrible crisis. More encouraging, by 1848 the potato blight had run its course. New crops showed no sign of the disease. But for thousands of the survivors there seemed to be no hope for a better future for themselves or their country. The land was ruined; there was no work, only the prospect of eviction.

In desperation they fled from Ireland. Somehow they scraped together the cost of a ticket—about 3 pounds—crossed the Atlantic and for no very good reason many settled in Boston. The city was innundated. In the single year 1847, 35,000 Irish immigrants landed in the city. Most were weak, sick, and half-starved. Few of the "famine Irish" had any occupational skills except for a rudimentary knowledge of farming.

Boston offered little. There were relatively few jobs for unskilled workers. In contrast to other eastern American cities, Boston was not a growing, labor-poor industrial center. This meant Irishmen were forced to take jobs doing back-breaking pick and shovel work for the railroads or the huge Back Bay landfill project of the 1850's and 1860's. To supplement the meager wages men were able to earn at such menial jobs, Irish women sought work as domestic servants. In 1850 nearly two-thirds of the adult Irish work force in Boston consisted of unskilled laborers or domestics.

The sick and destitute were forced to turn to the city's charitable institutions, which were large and newly built but soon overwhelmed. Those men and women who were in need of medical care were sent to a hospital on Deer Island, while the poor and insane were housed in an asylum in South Boston. Despite these modern facilities, there were, according to the *Boston Transcript*, groups of "poor wretches" in every part of the city "resting their weary and emaciated limbs at the corner of the streets and in the doorways of both private and public houses." Between 1845 and 1851 the number of foreign-born paupers supported by public funds increased from 4,000 to 12,000. Alarmed by this threat to the "orderly and peaceful city of the Pilgrims," a Massachusetts Senate Committee asserted that Boston was being turned into another Botany Bay, a dumping ground for Europe's poor and criminal population.

Although the legislators' accusation was widely regarded as nonsense, Boston officials did implement a policy of sending back those people who were discovered to have been "paupers in another country," "lunatics" or "infirm persons." In 1855 more than 600 emigrants were refused admission to Boston and were sent back to Great Britain. The Boston *Daily Advertiser* sympathized with two of those who were evicted, Mary Williams and her infant child, Bridget. "The offense of this poor woman, for which she was thus violently and ignominiously expelled from Massachusetts, was the fact that she was born in Ireland and called a pauper. . . .a crime which Massachusetts punishes as no other crime is punished in America, by banishment. . . ."

Those Irish immigrants who stayed in Boston found living conditions wretched. Because Boston was a city surrounded by water, most of the poor crowded into the already overcrowded sections of the old city. They packed into the North End and around the Fort Hill district so that they could avoid paying tolls to cross over to Cambridge, Charlestown, or South Boston. At mid-century, the average number of people living in a house in the North End was eighteen, as compared to the city's average of ten.

Living conditions were miserable. Old houses, once fashionable, were divided and re-divided to make tenements; deserted warehouses near the docks were filled with immigrant families. Those who were unable to pay the exorbitant rents

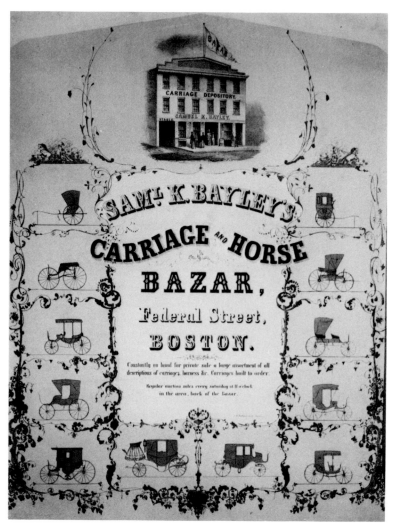

charged by slumlords, were forced into make-shift shanties, or worse, cellars and basements. Without light or fresh air, these underground caverns bred disease and pushed the death rate far above the norm. During the cholera epidemic of 1849, for example, 460 or 60% of the 707 cholera victims in Boston were Irish immigrants.

The deplorable conditions under which the Irish people in Boston were forced to live often led to crime—drunkenness and brawling. Whiskey was cheap (28¢ a gallon) and plentiful. In 1851, City Marshall Francis Tukey, reported that of the fifteen hundred shops selling liquor, nearly nine hundred were owned by Irishmen and almost half were located in the North End and Fort Hill. Tukey and

Boston was known as a walking city, yet horses and carriages were very much a part of the street scene in the mid-1800s. This advertisement for Samuel K. Bayley's Carriage and Horse Bazar suggests the wide variety of carriages available. (BPL)

Mayor John Bigelow pleaded with the Board of Aldermen to drop the "noble experiment" of using "moral suasion" to prevent drunkenness and to substitute strict licensing and tough police enforcement of the law. Within a few years, the Aldermen came around to Tukey's position and the number of arrests for drunkenness soared. In 1856, for example, the Boston police arrested 17,538—14,067 of whom were foreigners, chiefly Irish. Nearly 7,000 of the arrests were for drunkenness and another 3,500 for the related crimes of disorderly conduct and assault and battery.

As well as making more arrests, the police began the practice of raiding notorious areas of the city. In the spring of 1851, Marshall Tukey's men raided Ann Street in the North End. Sixty men and ninety women were swept up in the police net. Thirty-five men were sentenced as "keepers of brothels" and the women as prostitutes. For many Yankee Bostonians, the rowdies on Ann Street were typical of all Irish.

Natural history was a new area of study in the 1800s, as increased travel and literacy brought more people in touch with animal and plant wonders of the world. Entrepreneurs created animal shows with a variety of interesting and little-known creatures. This is an advertisement for one such business. (BPL)

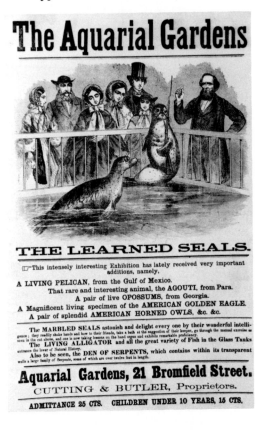

The Pilot, voice of the Boston Catholic community, pointed out that most Irish were good citizens, "quite invisible to the vigilant night police." Others observed that the Irish constituted only about 18% of the state prison population. Critics were quick to add, however, that almost two-thirds of the petty criminals—men and women convicted of drunkenness, assault and other related offenses—were Irish.

Bishop John Fitzpatrick's leadership of the Boston Catholic archdiocese during these hard times was characterized by his sensitivity to the problem of assimilation faced by Irish immigrants and his firm belief in taking a diplomatic approach to the Yankee community. Fitzpatrick was a Bostonian. He was born in Boston in 1812, graduated from the Boston Public Latin School, and after he completed his studies for the priesthood in Montreal and Paris Fitzpatrick returned to Boston in 1830. He was welcomed into an intellectual circle that included Dr. John Warren, Francis Gray, Oliver Wendell Holmes and Abbot Lawrence.

Fitzpatrick shared the chief political and social values of the dominant Yankee community. He regarded as dangerous and subversive any radical or liberal political movements. Indeed he used the pages of The Pilot to urge immigrant voters to elect conservative Whigs rather than Democrats. And, perhaps most important to the hard-working Yankees, Fitzpatrick, as Professor Thomas O'Connor argues in his recent biography, worked hard to impress upon his parishioners the importance of hard work, self-reliance and temperance. Finally, Fitzpatrick firmly believed in assimilation. "We should make ourselves American as much as we can," The Pilot urged. "This is our country now. Ireland is only a recollection."

Of course, Fitzpatrick's social and political beliefs were not necessarily those of his parishioners. Still, it seemed likely, in 1846 when Fitzpatrick was named the third Bishop of Boston that he would enjoy a peaceful, if administratively challenging, tenure. But Fitzpatrick's cordial relations with the Brahmin elite did not prevent the growth of a virulent anti-Catholicism.

Immigrants had not been especially welcome in Boston before 1852 when the American Party, a national political organization, was formed to protect the United States from the "insidious wiles of foreigners." There had been two major outbreaks of anti-Catholicism. Following the publication in 1834 of a sensationalistic novel that purported to reveal in lurid detail what *really* went on inside a Catholic convent, and a series of violent anti-Catholic sermons delivered by the Rev. Lyman Beecher, an enraged mob smashed its way into the Ursuline convent in Charlestown. After allowing the nuns and children to escape, the men set fire to the convent. A crowd of several hundred, including a fire company, watched as the building burned to the ground. Three years later, in June 1837, violence surfaced once again. On a hot afternoon a company of Yankee firemen clashed with a Catholic funeral procession along Broad Street. Mayor Samuel Eliot ended the battle only by calling out the state militia.

The wave of Irish immigrants in the 1840's and 1850's and the birth of the American or Know-Nothing Party, as it commonly was called because its members were pledged to secrecy, escalated and legitimized hatred and bigotry. Many native Bostonians were convinced that the poor, illiterate, hard-drinking, brawling Irish were a threat to their beloved city. As the cost of poor relief soared and the older sections of the city were transformed into slums, native Bostonians grew angry and embraced Know-Nothingism.

Although there are good reasons for doubting the validity of the analysis commonly made about the election of 1853, militant nativists were right when they predicted that the Irish-Catholic vote would be an important factor in all subsequent elections. "For the first time in the history of the state," wrote the *Daily Commonwealth* "the Catholic Church [has] taken the field as a power."

RUINS OF THE URSULINE CONVENT AS THEY APPEARED AFTER THE FIRE IN 1834.

In 1834 the Ursuline Convent was attacked and burned by an anti-Catholic mob, responding, in part, to unproven tales such as Six Months in a Convent, *the story of a young woman forced to remain in a nunnery. The "K.N." refers to the Know-Nothing political party which experienced brief but strong popularity in the 1850s by appealing to anti-Catholic sentiment. (TBS)*

This realization stimulated bitterness among those voters fearful of the power of recent immigrants and led to a Know-Nothing landslide in the state elections of 1854. Know-Nothings captured every one of the senate seats and all but three places in the House. Henry J. Gardner, a former president of the Boston Common Council, was elected governor. Jerome V.C. Smith, a surgeon, an amateur sculptor and a member of the Know-Nothing movement, became Boston's fourteenth mayor.

In his inaugural address Gardner painted a dark picture of the "horde of foreign barbarians" who endangered the republic. The dominant race, he stated, meaning his own, must regulate the incoming class, meaning Irish emigrants. One means of "regulation" was an amendment to the constitution requiring a twenty-one year residence for citizenship. Another was an investigation of Catholic schools, including one in Roxbury.

"Boston and Its Environs," an engraving by J. Poppel, was published in Munich, Bavaria, in 1858. The East Boston Shipyard and the peninsula are featured in the center, bordered by important buildings and scenes of the period. (TBS)

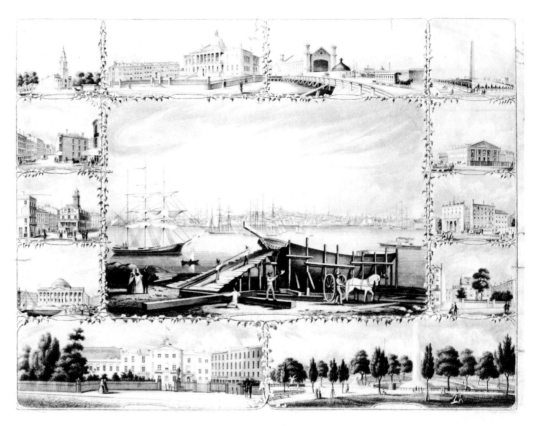

Bishop Fitzpatrick and *The Pilot* did what they could in a quiet way to undercut the nativist movement. Fitzpatrick urged his parishioners to vote as a means of demonstrating their loyalty and commitment as an American citizen. And, he steadfastly refused to develop a separate parochial school system—although many Boston Irish believed that Protestant teachers used "every cunning" to cause Catholic students in the public schools to abandon their faith. Fitzpatrick did write to the Boston School Committee to explain the official teachings of the Roman Catholic church and to emphasize the seriousness with which Catholic students and parents regarded the doctrines of their religion.

Although polite, the school committee was deaf to Fitzpatrick's argument. As they perceived it, the King James version of the Bible, which was required reading every day in Boston public schools, was "nonsectarian" because it was acceptable to all Protestants. Likewise, schoolmasters saw nothing wrong with textbooks which

presented a Protestant world view and mentioned Catholicism only as an example of the corruption and venality against which Protestant reformers rebelled. Boston Catholic parents were so enraged by this situation that many kept their children out of school. In 1854 Barnas Sears, secretary of the Massachusetts Board of Education, stated that the single most important cause for the decline in school population was the opposition of Catholics to the use of the Protestant Bible in the public school system.

While the controversy over education continued until Fitzpatrick's successor, Bishop John Williams began a parochial school system in 1880, the most militant aspects of the nativist movement in Boston collapsed by 1856. Bigotry—especially a prejudice as contrived as the "Catholic Menace"—was simply not enough to hold together a national political organization. Moreover, the issue of slavery had become a consuming passion for men and women in all sections of the nation.

Boston, and the liberal part of the Brahmin community in particular, was the center for the campaign to abolish slavery. William Ellery Channing, Wendell Phillips, Samuel and Julia Ward Howe, and Theodore Parker took the position that slavery was a moral offense that should be purged from the body politic. William Lloyd Garrison, outspoken and uncompromising editor of the *Liberator,* agreed with this analysis, but differed from the polite Brahmins in that he argued for immediate abolition and attacked the United States Constitution for protecting slavery, calling it a "covenant with death."

Most Irish Catholics in Boston reacted negatively to both Garrison and the upper class abolitionists. To begin with, Catholics believed that a number of anti-slavery advocates had been active in the Know Nothing party, that "secret order" of bigots and hypocrites which sought to deny white immigrants their civil rights. The hearts of the abolitionists, charged *The Pilot,* are as "soft as butter" toward the oppressed black laborer in the south, but "hard as flint" toward the white laborer in the north. *The Pilot* also condemned Garrison and his followers because the newspaper was convinced that the kind of militant tactics used by radicals would promote civil disorder and public violence. Fr. John Roddan, editor of *The Pilot,* reminded Boston Catholics that the famed Irish patriot, Daniel O'Connell, had said that "the greatest political advantages are not worth one drop of human blood." Therefore, Fr. Roddan concluded, it would be better if black people remained in "nominal bondage" rather than attempting to win their freedom by force.

The Boston Catholic weekly's conservative views about slavery seemed to be in harmony with the United States Supreme Court's decision in the Dred Scott case. Speaking for the majority, Chief Justice Roger B. Taney, a prominent Catholic from Maryland, argued that Scott had not become a free man as a result of his residing in free territory. Black people, Taney wrote in 1857, were "beings of an inferior order" who possessed "no rights which the white man was bound to respect" and had never been included under the term "citizens" in the Constitution.

Based on these shaky propositions about slavery and black people, *The Pilot* advocated that its readers support Stephen A. Douglas, the presidential candidate of the Democrats in 1860, rather than Abraham Lincoln, candidate of the "Black Republican party" which was supported by the "scattered and broken forces of the know-nothing party." In short, Boston's Irish Catholic community came to almost the same position as did conservative, upper class Bostonians. Both groups feared a black uprising and loathed the social upheaval they believed was caused by abolitionists. Both shared the common prejudices about blacks. Both were opposed to any threat to the textile industry—the "Lords of the Loom" (in Thomas O'Connor's phrase) —because southern secession would endanger profits and the Irish working class because free blacks would compete with poor whites for scarce jobs.

Still, like most northerners, Boston's Irish Catholic community was shocked by the Confederate attack on Fort Sumter in April 1861. Their earlier hostility toward abolitionists and self-interested concern for the economic viability of the cotton textile industry, was forgotten in an outpouring of patriotism, of support for the preservation of the Union. Thomas Cass, an Irishman and former commander of a Massachusetts unit called the Columbian Artillery (disbanded by the Know-Nothings) immediately volunteered to raise a regiment of Irishmen. Governor John A. Andrew enthusiastically accepted Cass' offer and within months the 9th Regiment, Massachusetts Volunteer Infantry, was organized. On June 24, 1861 the 9th marched through the streets of Boston to the State House, where to the cheers of thousands the governor thanked Colonel Cass for having raised "this splendid regiment" and, in a rare gesture of unity and city pride, Mrs. Harrison Gray Otis presented Cass with an American flag and an Irish flag of green silk.

The "Fighting 9th" distinguished itself, fighting courageously in every major campaign waged by the Army of the Potomac. In the bloody battles in the Virginia wilderness the Irish Ninth—led by General Thomas F. Meagher, one of the few prominent Irish Republicans in the commonwealth—never faltered. From this point forward, the patriotism of Boston's Irish Catholics was never again questioned. Indeed, the more favorable climate of toleration even withstood the storminess created by a draft riot in the summer of 1863.

The conscription law that Congress passed in March 1863 was particularly unfair to poor people and immigrants because it permitted wealthy young men either to hire a substitute or to buy exemption for $300. And the quotas established for each Boston ward were weighted in favor of the rich. A Catholic priest confided in his diary a sentiment believed by many working class Bostonians: the government was "drafting poor people, our Irish people."

On July 14, the anger that had been bubbling just beneath the surface exploded. When provost marshalls sought to distribute conscription notices on Prince Street in the North End, a group of women assaulted the marshalls. They soon were joined by hundreds of Irishmen. The police, who had come to the assistance of the marshalls, were forced to retreat to their station house. Mayor Frederick Lincoln called out three militia companies whose first order was to save the armory on Cooper Street. When the crowd tried to break through the doors of the armory, the militiamen opened fire, killing six people. After an unsuccessful foray into Dock Square where there were a couple of gun shops, the crowd melted away into the night.

Although there was considerable anxiety among state and city officials for the next few days, no further rioting occurred. The Catholic Church played an active role in restoring peace in the city. Fr. James Healy, who was acting head of the archdiocese while Bishop Fitzpatrick was in Europe, instructed the Boston clergy to persuade their parishioners to avoid "all fractious assemblies." Following a plan outlined by Fitzpatrick during the tumultuous 1850's, the priests left their churches and patrolled the neighborhood streets, dispersing crowds and calming angry people. As a sign of the new attitude of toleration, Mayor Lincoln distinguished between rioters and Irish Catholics. He publicly thanked those Catholic priests "who labored to preserve quiet among their congregations."

The war greatly increased the degree of understanding between Yankees and Irish. The Irish were no longer treated as unwanted immigrants. Thousands of young men—those in the "Fighting Ninth" and other units—had fought and died to save the Union. While the boys were at war, other changes that signalled a new era were made. In July 1861, Bishop Fitzpatrick was awarded an honorary degree by Harvard University, the first time a Catholic ecclesiastic was so honored. The Boston School Board repealed the law making it compulsory to read the King James version of the Bible in the public schools. And upon the recommendation of Governor Andrew, the legislature repealed the amendment requiring the foreign born to reside in Massachusetts at least two years before they were eligible to vote.

Irish continued to come to Boston after 1865. They were not driven from Ireland as they had been in the "Hungry Forties", but rather they were attracted to the city by relatives and friends, persuaded that Boston was a good place to live. By 1865, too, more than three-quarters of all immigrants came by steamship. The steamers were in every way better—faster, more comfortable, safer—than the "coffin ships" on which the earlier immigrants had come. Those of the "famine Irish" who survived the crossing, had worked hard and begun to

establish themselves in Boston. Each year more of the Irish increased their modest incomes and moved a rung higher on the social ladder.

Still, as late as 1880, over 30% of Boston's Irish remained unskilled workers. More than 10,000 men were common laborers, working irregularly on the docks or a construction project. Over 7,000 Irishwomen were servants for middle and upper class Yankee families. Many of them hated the work. One Irish domestic informed a journalist that she told "every girl I know, 'whatever you do, don't go into service. You'll always be prisoners and always looked down on.'"

A handful of Irish achieved middle class status by the end of the 19th century. In 1880, for example, there were only 18 Irish lawyers out of a total Celtic population of 35,000. Only about 1400 Irish had become businessmen—mostly saloon keepers, morticians, grocers and real estate salesmen. Only 6% of the Irish between 1860 and 1880 made it into the

business and professional classes, as compared to 31% of the native-born Bostonians. According to Geoffrey Blodgett's brilliant study of Massachusetts politics, however, the lowly economic position of the Irish "did not breed automatic resentment among Irish spokesmen toward Yankee domination of

John Boyle O'Reilly began his career as leader of the radical Fenian movement in Ireland. After settling in Boston he became a respected poet and, as owner of the Irish newspaper, the Pilot, *O'Reilly advocated cooperative political relationships among Boston's various ethnic and racial groups. (TBS)*

business and the professions. It remained as much an incentive to greater efforts toward mobility as it did a cause of class hostility." In fact, by the 1870's and 1880's some Irish were able to gain acceptance from Brahmin society without surrendering their ethnic pride.

The foremost example of this phenomena was John Boyle O'Reilly. Born in County Meath, Ireland in 1844, O'Reilly was exiled to Australia for participating in the Irish revolutionary movement. In 1869 he escaped and eventually settled in Boston, where through luck and pluck he landed a job as a reporter for *The Pilot,* then edited by Patrick Donahoe. O'Reilly prospered, becoming owner and editor of the paper in 1876. His advice to a young friend in Ireland, reflected O'Reilly's new status. "Go into business as soon as you can," he told John Devoy, adding, "keep out of these Irish or American political 'rings'."

O'Reilly's drive to succeed in Boston

also included a commitment to his writing. In addition to his editorial work at *The Pilot,* he wrote several romantic novels and dozens of poems and essays. His reputation as a writer won O'Reilly entry into the exclusive Boston literary circle. O'Reilly certainly helped his cause by writing commemorative poems honoring the Yankee heroes of Boston's glorious past and by criticizing his fellow Irishmen's lack of intellectual achievement. "No people," he wrote in July 1877, have been "more neglectful of its poor than the rich and educated Irish in America. What schools and colleges have they endowed?...What reading rooms have they established to keep men from liquor stores and for their mental improvement? None whatever."

O'Reilly's blast overlooked at least one important sign of the Boston Irish Catholic community's commitment to intellectual achievement. In March 1863, Bishop Fitzpatrick's dream of a "college in the city" came to fruition. The Massachusetts legislature approved a charter incorporating Boston College. Although it had taken more than a decade, the hard work and dedication of Fr. John McElroy, S.J., finally resulted in the founding of a college that soon claimed the loyalty of the Boston Irish and whose graduates eventually would break Harvard's grip on the city's financial and legal institutions.

Although he was forced by poverty to leave school at the age of twelve, Hugh O'Brien rose above his humble origins. Born in Ireland, O'Brien worked in publishing before he entered politics in 1875. Ten years later he was elected Mayor of Boston, the first not of native birth. O'Brien proved such a popular and efficient administrator that he was re-elected for four consecutive terms. Despite an occasional gesture to the Irish—the creation of public parks and ordering the Boston Public Library closed on St. Patrick's Day—his commitment to decreasing the tax rate and expanding the powers of the mayor's office—made him appear to be very much the same as his Yankee predecessors.

In 1890, O'Brien and O'Reilly and a few dozen other Boston Irish were celebrated in James Cullen's *History of the Irish in Boston*. Published ten years after Justin Windsor's *Memorial History of Boston*, Cullen's history emphasized that it was "brains not brawn" that distinguished the Irish. Among other signs of accomplishment, Cullen listed all the Irish people who owned homes or businesses in Boston. By contrast, Windsor's four volume *History* all but omitted the Irish and focused on the colonial, revolutionary and early federal periods of Boston's proud—Yankee—history.

Recounting the glories of the Yankee past did not, however, assuage the anxieties of those Brahmins who formed the governing elite. They could now see that their hope of assimilating the Irish into the Boston way of life was hopeless. Some gave up and left the "city on a hill" their ancestors had founded two hundred

READY FOR THE BATTLE!

and fifty years earlier. Others of this elite believed it was their responsibility to maintain the high standards of leadership and the cultural benefits for which Boston was famous. Still others struck back, by working to cut off new immigration, hoping, therefore, to cling to a piece of national political power.

Clearly, Boston's passage from the past to the 20th century was not going to be easy.

John L. Sullivan, an Irish immigrant living in the South End, became one of the best prize-fighters in the country at a time when fights were bare-fisted and lasted as many rounds as the contenders could stand. Sullivan won this bout with Ryan and collected the $5,000 prize. (TBS)

VI
The Athens of America

Boston's old elite had great affection for their town—for its historical and religious traditions, for its town meeting form of government, for its compact size, and especially for its small, homogeneous population. Slow to admit to growth and change, Bostonians had been reluctant to become a city in 1822. As if to deny the break with the past, the new city had not built a city hall. The mayor and city council met first in the Old State House, then for a time in Fanueil Hall, and in the 1850s in the old courthouse on School Street.

Finally, in 1862, Mayor Joseph Wightman pushed through a bill providing funds to build a city hall. Gridley Bryant, Boston's most distinguished architect, was chosen to design the building. Bryant understood the need for a monumental public building that

Previous page: By 1880 most of the Back Bay was filled in and devoted to upper class homes and institutions with a valuation exceeding $100 million. (TBS)

The class picture was serious business for these third-graders at the Winchell School in the West End circa 1890. The class reflects the ethnic composition of the area which was changing from predominantly Irish to Italian and Eastern European. The class size and lack of decoration and visual aids were standard for public schools of the period. (BPL)

would affirm the new Boston. He chose to use the new French Second Empire style which was popular in Europe, but relatively unknown in America. The result was a stately building of white Concord granite, topped with a great dome and flanked by graceful pavilions. To reaffirm the relationship of the city's past and present, a small plaza in front of the new city hall was decorated with the statues of two of Boston's great men, Benjamin Franklin, who had done so much to create a new nation, and Josiah Quincy, who had done so much to modernize an old city.

Although explicitly linked with the past, the new city hall signalled the beginning of a sweeping transformation. From 1862 to 1900 Boston grew more rapidly and expanded further from its original center than it had during its previous 230-year history. The population of the city jumped from 140,000 in 1865, to 341,000 in 1875, to 560,890 in 1900. Before the Civil War Boston had been a town confined to a small tract of 780 acres, but by filling in the marshes and bogs on either side of Roxbury neck and by annexing the

neighboring towns, Boston became, by 1900, a city of nearly 24,000 acres— almost thirty times its original size.

A new cultural tone was present as well, manifested in the rows of elegant brownstone houses, broad tree-lined boulevards and parks, and by the number and quality of the city's newest public institutions. During the last quarter of the 19th century, Boston became the cultural capital of the United States, the "Athens of America."

At the same time, the Brahmin elite that created this new, fashionable, vibrant city feared that its considerable cultural and social accomplishments were endangered by the new immigration from southern and eastern Europe. The 1890 census showed 10,000 Italians and Jews living in the city; by 1910 there were 30,000 Italians jammed into the old North End, and more than 40,000 Jews packed into the West End. The Irish at least spoke English and had a smattering of knowledge about Anglo-Saxon culture. These new people—Italians, Jews, a growing number of Poles, Lithuanians, and Greeks,—spoke a babel of tongues and cultivated their own quite different social customs. The percentage of foreign-born rose to 64% in 1880, to 74% in 1900.

The eastern and southern European Jews and southern Italians who poured into Boston after 1880 settled in the North End. Once solidly Irish, by 1895 there were more Italians and nearly as many Jews as Irish in the North End. By 1920, the Jews had moved into the West End, and the Italians accounted for more than 90% of the population in "Boston's first neighborhood," as historian Paul Tedesco so aptly called the North End.

The Jews were driven from Russia, Poland, and other eastern European countries to Boston to escape the pogroms that threatened their lives, and they came to Boston with the hope of economic success. Jewish immigrants settled primarily in a triangular area roughly bounded by Hanover Street, Endicott Street, and Prince Street. There were some families who lived between the North End and the newer Jewish neighborhood of the West End.

A strong family life was important to members of the Jewish community, but like other immigrant groups, it was often the case that a man came alone in order to earn enough money to bring his family. When the family did arrive, the demands of hard work and long hours sometimes created crises that pulled the family apart. Charitable groups assumed responsibility for the maintenance of families who had been deserted by the husband and father. Although Jews in the North End had a lower rate of desertion than other immigrant groups, desertion was one of the major problems confronting the benevolent associations.

Most of the Jews who came to the North End came from villages or small towns, and many turned to peddling or operating a small store to make a living. An elderly Jewish woman recalled that "everybody who came to Boston would take a basket." The immigrant would fill his basket with merchandise from a store

that extended credit and then set out to sell in a neighborhood which was not yet visited by many peddlers. Those newcomers unable to speak English were taught to say "Look in the basket." Good merchandise, fair prices, credit, and a desire to please bridged the gap between a Jewish peddler and his Yankee or Irish customers.

Jews who owned retail stores formed a financial and social elite in the North End community. Some especially successful businessmen supplied other peddlers, as did Harris Garfinkle and Company and Freedman Brothers. Others sold clothing, such as Michael Slutsky and Richmond, Cohen and Reinherz, who specialized in men's clothing. Yente Rabinowitz owned a small grocery that the family eventually built into Stop & Shop, a food store chain. I.B. Reinherz began as a peddler, then became a steamship ticket agent, and finally a banker.

Not all Jews who lived in the North End were in trade. A majority worked at whatever job they could get. Some used the streetcar to travel to Boston's suburbs where they found work as shoemakers or garment workers. A number of North End Jews drove horse-drawn cabs. Others bounced from one job to another; a man

In 1905 peddlers traveled the streets of Boston and its suburbs bringing a variety of products to residents. Many of the peddlers were recent Jewish immigrants from Eastern Europe, who began business with a horse and cart, and later opened shops throughout the city. (BPL)

who grew up in the North End recalled that "father worked in an iron foundry at Charlestown. Later, he became a street-car conductor and finally he became a *shames* at a Lithuanian synagogue."

Like other immigrant groups, Jews attempted to retain the patterns of European life. Russian Jews were devoutly orthodox and especially determined to maintain religious discipline. There were two main synagogues in the North End: Congregation Beth Abraham, founded in 1873, and Congregation Beth Israel, on Baldwin Place, established in 1890. Synagogue services followed the Eastern European pattern; congregants prayed in Hebrew, although prayerbooks usually had a Yiddish translation. Because they were perceived as more American, reform ideas had a wider appeal among younger Jews in the North End. The children's religious liberalism gradually affected the older generation. For example, the son of one of the pious and learned leaders of the Chevra Shas (Talmudical Society) noted: "While father observed all religious rites in every possible way, he would make certain statements that indicated to me that his ideas were entirely liberal. But living in a community as he was he naturally followed the dictates of the community."

Although there was some tension between younger and older Jews, both groups slowly became more acculturated to American life. As the second generation prospered, they moved out of the North End and were assimilated into the larger Boston community. "By 1910," Paul Tedesco tells us, "the last North End Jews were moving on into the mainstream of society, leaving the North End and its memories of poverty behind them."

The southern Italians who arrived in the North End about the same time as the Jews were not as quick to make the transition to a new American way of life. In part, this was due to the fact that 79 percent of the Italian immigrants who came to Boston did not intend to stay. These "birds of passage," as they were called, came to work, to make money, and then to return to Italy. The number of men who fled the grinding poverty of southern Italy for Boston was staggering: from 1895 to 1920 the number of foreign-born in Boston increased by 76 percent. The Italians of the North End accounted for much of this increase. In 1895, 26.6 percent of the people crowded into the North End were Italian; in 1920, 90 percent. The North End was home to 23,000 people in 1895 and 40,000 by 1920. Only in Calcutta were there more people

The age of these students and the apparent ethnic mix suggests that this was an "Americanization" class. Local settlement houses sponsored such classes in the late 1800s for those seeking American citizenship. The woman in the photograph probably was the teacher. (BPL)

per square mile.

The results of this severe overcrowding were predictable: the infant mortality rate was appalling; sanitation was almost non-existent; and more than a hundred families were living in one room per family. The North End at the turn of the century was Boston's "classic land of poverty." Still, they came. Poor, and illiterate, they depended on *paesani* (Italians from the same village) or a *padrone* (labor contractor) for survival. Because almost two-thirds of the men were unskilled laborers the jobs available to them were limited. They worked on the docks, in the granite and stone quarries, and on the railways, or left the city each day to build a sewer system in Brockton or Beverly or even as far as Northampton. A few sold fruit and vegetables in the market and a tiny number became clerks or professionals. Almost all single women worked and nearly a quarter of all Italian married women worked at least part time in a local garment or confectionery factory. Women's wages were lower than men's.

Because work was scarce, there was fierce competition between the Italians and the Irish, who resented the intrusion of the Italians. Irish gangs controlled the waterfront. During the day anyone could walk through the area unmolested, but after dark the Irish gathered on the street-corners and it became dangerous for an Italian to try to pass through their territory. Often, during the early years, if a Sicilian fishing boat came in after dark the men chose to sleep on board rather than run the gauntlet to their homes.

When the Italians established a numerical majority, the streets and institutions of the North End were more under their control. Although both Irish and Italians were Catholics, the Italians soon formed separate churches. St. Leonard's was founded in 1873, the Sacred Heart Church in 1888. A variety of community benevolent societies, schools, and social clubs sprang from these churches. One of the customary duties of these societies was to honor their patron saint with a yearly festival. The Feast of Our Lady of Grace, sponsored by former villagers from San Sossio Baronia, began in 1903. Sicilian fishermen honored the Madonna each year for her help in protecting the men while they were at sea. A procession during which a statue of the saint was carried around the North End was always a part of the festival.

These children gathered in the North End in 1890 when area residents were predominantly Italian and Jewish. The house with the awning belonged to Paul Revere during the 18th century and was a commercial and residential building until 1908 when it was restored and opened to visitors. The Revere house became a national landmark in 1961. (TBS)

Boston Latin School, the first high school in America, was established in 1635 to prepare young men for Harvard. In the 1890s the growing immigrant population and Irish political advances forced the school to diversify the student body. (TBS)

Societies honoring patron saints were usually carried over from the particular village from which people had come. Although the North End was made up of people from southern Italy, it was divided into separate enclaves of Avilanese, Calibrese, Neopolitians, Sicilians, and a handful of Genoese from northern Italy. Each group had their own dialect, their own *campanelisme,* their own way to maintain "la via veccia," the old way of life and their own section of the North End. People who identified themselves as living on "North Street," "near St. Mary's," "lower Prince Street," or "down on Salem Street" also identified the part of Italy from which their family came, where they went to church, the societies to which they belonged, and often what occupation they pursued.

William DeMarco, a recent historian of the North End who has carefully charted the numerous and distinct enclaves, drives home his analysis with an anecdote about an "impostor,"

I went to Naples from Siracusa, Sicily, in 1905, in search of work. I went to Avellino during the grape harvest season and met my wife. Because I was Sicilian, I was not accepted by her family, so we decided to 'run away, and get married. Of course, we couldn't go back, so we came to Boston, where we found more Avellinese. Since I picked up my wife's dialect quickly, I decided to pass as Avellinese. This worked well. I opened a barber shop which attracted Neopolitians and Avellinese. With a wife who cooked Avellinese-style and my speaking the dialect at my shop, everyone thought I was from Avellino. I passed as Avellinese for almost thirty years, until a paesano from Siracusa told everyone I was Sicilian as part of a bet. By that time I was accepted by the Avellinese, so it did not hurt my business. Twenty-five or thirty years earlier, who knows what would have happened.

These subcultures, or "urban villages," were very much a part of the vitality of Italian immigrant life, but contained two disadvantages. First, Italians in the North End were so divided among themselves they did not participate in city politics. In part, too, this was because of a general distrust of government shared by all southern Italians. The North End was therefore merged with the West and South End wards, and ward boss Martin Lomasney was able to maintain his hold on Boston's political life until the 1930s. Second, the existence of distinct enclaves led Robert Woods and other Yankee urban reformers to despair of ever Americanizing the Italians. They concluded that the Italians lacked two essential Yankee characteristics: a commitment to active citizenship and to the work ethic. Without these qualities, Woods predicted, Boston would remain an urban wilderness.

Although they were anxious about what effect foreigners would have on their city, most Brahmins were still social creatures. As had their Puritan forefathers, they believed in community. While deploring aspects of society, Brahmins never rejected the idea of society. For this reason, they held fast to a belief in stewardship, that it was their special responsibility to see to the well-being of Boston.

The magnitude of that responsibility increased as the city grew. In 1850 the area of dense settlement barely exceeded a two-mile radius from the Old State House. Horse-drawn carriages were a common sight on Boston's downtown streets. Because enormous marshes and tidal basins were the dominant geographical feature, men cramped for space began damming and filling the marshes and flats. Hills were leveled and sea walls built. By the 1850s developers had reclaimed the area around Charles Street and much of the South End, had cut down a big chunk of Beacon Hill, and had completely leveled Fort Hill (the area around Pearl, Milk, and Broad streets) to create a new waterfront area along Atlantic Avenue.

In 1857 a special commission composed of representatives of the commonwealth, the city, and several private developers was formed by the legislature to fill the Back Bay and sell the lands. The project was breathtaking in scope. It called for filling hundreds of acres of tidal flats and a shallow bay to create land west of Arlington Street to Kenmore Square along Commonwealth Avenue and from Beacon Street to the tracks of the Boston and Providence Railroad in the south, and to create a new shore line for the Charles River to the north. Norman Munson and George Gross, two railroad builders, were contracted by the commission in 1858 to carry out this enormous job, in return for four blocks of the newly created land.

The railroad and the steam shovel, two products of new technology, were utilized by Munson and Gross to fill the Back Bay and make the city an integral part of the mainland. The gravel was brought from Needham, about ten miles from Boston, by a specially designed train consisting of 35 cars to which two locomotives were attached. There were three such trains on the road day and night; one arrived at the Back Bay every 45 minutes, dumped its contents and returned to Needham to be re-filled by two giant steam shovels, an operation that took only about 10 minutes. In the first year, 300,000 yards of gravel were taken out of the hills of Needham and 1,400 acres of land were made in the Back Bay.

By 1861 the shore line of the bay was just west of Clarendon Street. Ten years later, Boylston and Newbury streets and the south side of Commonwealth Avenue were filled as far as Exeter Street and the northside reached Gloucester and Hereford streets. The entire area extending to Kenmore Square had been filled by 1882.

Ten years before the Back Bay project was completed, Boston suffered from a devastating fire. The fire burned out of control on November 9 and 10, 1872, causing many deaths and immense property damage. By the time the fire had been brought under control nearly sixty acres of downtown Boston had been reduced to ashes and rubble. This included most of the wholesale and warehouse district in the oldest part of the city, where houses were wedged together and streets were crooked and narrow. Although most of the buildings

were constructed of granite and iron, their owners had in recent years bowed to fashion and the demand for cheap space and had added mansard roofs, wooden frame superstructures covered with tarpaper. The fire easily jumped from one mansard roof to another.

Still, the conflagration could have been controlled but for two circumstances. First, there was an inadequate supply of water. Because Boston had not modernized its water system, commented a reporter, "there were more engines than water; the water pipes were too small to supply the draught of more than two engines." The second handicap was the complete absence of horses. All that year, horses in New England had suffered from a contagion of distemper, known as epizootic, or "horse disease," which incapacitated the animals and sometimes killed them. When the fire began, therefore, fire-fighters from Boston and neighboring towns were forced to pull their engines themselves, often for miles.

When the fire burned itself out, and while the extent of the damage was being assessed, two reforms were called for: the widening of the streets and the

prohibition of mansard roofs. No such ordinances were passed. "Building brokers," indifferent to safety and architectural beauty, jammed a greater number of plainer, taller buildings into the area than had been there before the fire. In this process, small shopkeepers and tradesmen, many of whom periodically came into Boston from the country to sell a wagonload of goods, were forced out, victims of big business's, demand for efficiency. The lasting effect of the Great Fire of 1872 was to speed the transformation of Boston into a collection of distinct sections, each with its own social and economic characteristics.

The attractions of the newly made Back Bay, for example, were obvious: it was detached but not remote from the business section; its neighbors were Beacon Hill and the Public Garden; and it was new and expensive. Boston's wealthiest families were able to create an unusually homogeneous upper class environment. They flocked to the Back Bay, building large five-story houses of brown sandstone inspired by the Second French Empire style of the 1860s, a considerable number of chaste but elegant brick houses, a number of homes whose vigorous Romanesque style was developed by Henry Hobson Richardson in the 1870s, and a rich profusion of homes in other styles, including those homes built during the classical revival in the 1880s.

A few mansions in the Back Bay were designed to look like medieval castles or 16th century chateaux with the lavish sculptural decoration of the Renaissance. The Albert Burrage mansion at 314 Commonwealth Avenue, for example, was built in the same magnificent style as W.K. Vanderbilt's Fifth Avenue mansion in New York. Charles Francis Adams' home at 20 Gloucester Street was not as ostentatious, but its heavy masonry towers and arched entrances affected a medieval style that was quite grand.

The Back Bay quickly became the center of Boston's intellectual and cultural life. The public buildings in and around Copley Square, in particular, symbolized

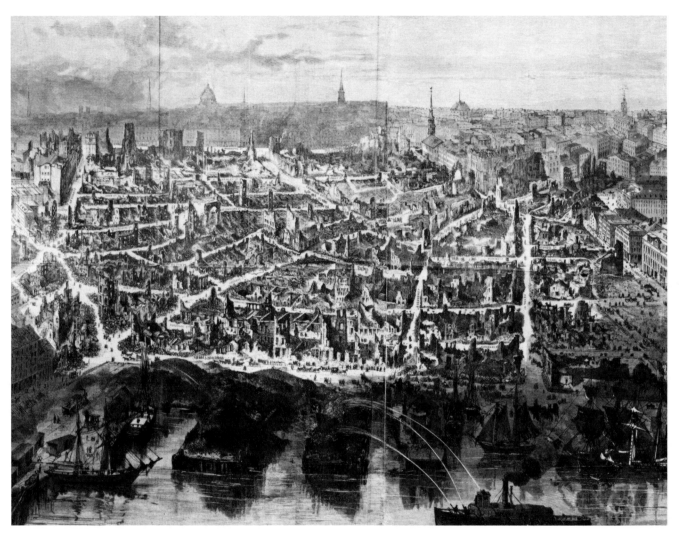

the city's new vitality. Without benefit of a plan—it began as an awkward space caused by the odd angle at which Huntington Avenue started off—a handsome square gradually took shape.

Located on the south side of the square, the first permanent home of the Museum of Fine Arts was completed in 1876. Designed by Sturgis and Brigham, it was a curious-looking striped red brick and terra cotta Victorian Gothic structure that housed the museum's growing collection of paintings and sculpture. The museum featured frequent exhibits from its permanent collection of old masters, as well as shows focusing on modern French paintings that had been purchased for the museum by Boston artists who traveled abroad.

Above: The 50th anniversary of Quincy Market was celebrated with a parade of stallholders representing businesses that had been located in the market since it opened in 1826. (SPNEA)

Facing page, top: This was a women's ward at Boston City Hospital before 1900. The hospital treated the poorer classes and people avoided being admitted to the hospital if they could since the recovery rate was not high. The plain walls and floors and tightly wrapped bedridden patients suggests the unpleasantness of a hospital stay. Courtesy, Boston University Library

Facing page, bottom: The Bigelow Operating Room at Massachusetts General Hospital was used to teach Harvard medical students in 1893. (SPNEA)

On the east side of Copley Square H.H. Richardson designed the masterpiece of his short career. Trinity Church, the Episcopal Church of the South End, led by the most distinguished clergyman of his day, the Reverend Phillips Brooks, was begun in 1873. A massive Romanesque structure with a single tall tower similar to those built in the 12th century, Trinity posed several engineering problems because it was built on "made land." First, Richardson had to figure a way to support the tower weighing more than 9,500 tons. He accomplished this by sinking four huge truncated pyramids of solid granite deep into the ground. Second, Richardson poured a mass of gravel more than thirty feet deep, through which 4,500 piles were driven into the bedrock. Finally, he decided at the last moment to omit the top fifty feet of the central tower and to reduce the height of the walls by several feet.

Trinity Church was consecrated on February 9, 1877. Alexander Rice, the governor of the commonwealth, Frederick O. Prince, the mayor of Boston, more than one hundred clergymen, and the warden and vestrymen of the church walked in procession to their seats, reciting Psalm 24. Reverend Brooks and several of his old friends shared the

service, speaking from small platforms projected over the five full-width steps leading to the spacious apse. The bishop of Massachusetts celebrated Holy Communion, bringing the memorable service to a close.

Several of Boston's major cultural and educational institutions were located near Trinity Church. Just one block east of Copley Square, the Boston Society of Natural History built a three-story brick museum (now Bonwit Teller's), and one block west, at Boylston and Exeter streets, the Harvard Medical School moved into a large facility chosen for its proximity to both Massachusetts General and City Hospital in the South End. Nearby, the Massachusetts Institute of Technology—known commonly as "Boston Tech"—was established in 1872. Presided over by the distinguished scientist William Barton Rogers, MIT pioneered in the effort to link high-quality scientific education and industrial research.

The Boston Public Library, opened in 1895, completed Copley Square. Built on land granted by the commonwealth, across the Square from Trinity Church, the library's splendid Renaissance building not only housed a vast collection of books, but manuscripts and original materials given to it by Brahmins who spent a

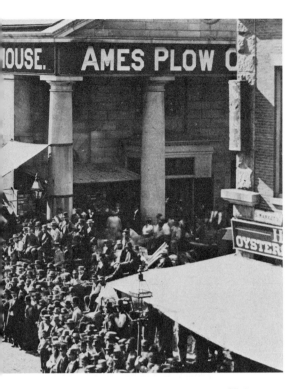

Higginson, by contrast, was committed to using his vast personal fortune to hire an orchestra of "sixty selected musicians and a conductor and paying them all year" so that he had the "right to all their time needed for rehearsals and concerts." Indignant critics of professionalism attacked Higginson's restrictive contractual arrangement with his musicians as "deluded wealth with arrant charlatanism." Most Bostonians, however, supported Higginson, pointing out that the quality of the Boston Symphony Orchestra depended upon the dedication of the players.

After eight months of preparation under

lifetime traveling and collecting. Heir to a fortune derived from textile mills, Thomas Gold Appelton bought a collection of valuable 17th century engravings in Rome which he donated to the library. Many other acts of civic generosity followed.

Founded in 1881 by Col. Henry Lee Higginson, the Boston Symphony Orchestra owed its origins to the city's long and deep interest in music and to Higginson's personal desire "to have a part in some good work which would leave a lasting mark." In the decades prior to Higginson's publicly announced intention to form the Boston Symphony Orchestra, Boston had supported an opera company—though a division over the relative merits of Italian versus German opera created what a critic labeled "the battle of the Operas"—as well as the Handel and Hayden Society (founded in 1815), four magazines devoted to music, and a professional music school. After the Civil War two symphonic groups were added to this early medley: the Harvard Musical Association, which devoted itself to classical programs; and the Boston Philharmonic Orchestra, formed in 1872 in response to the demand for more modern music. Neither group had solid financial backing or permanently employed professional musicians.

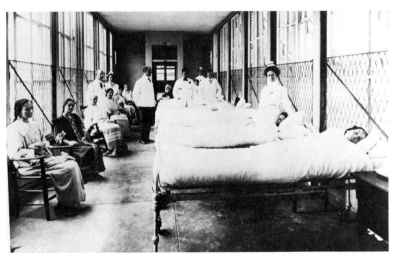

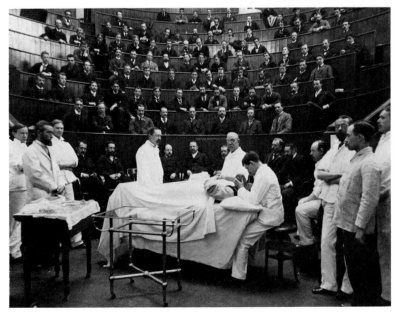

the direction of Georg Henschel, a German-born singer-pianist-composer-conductor, the Boston Symphony Orchestra gave its first concert on October 22, 1881, in the Boston Music Hall. The orchestra gave 20 Saturday evening concerts and an equal number of public rehearsals during its first season. Bostonians were delighted. A total of 83,359 people flocked to hear the orchestra. Indeed, the Boston Symphony Orchestra was so popular ticket speculators did a brisk business, spoiling Higginson's plan to make available inexpensive seats for "impecunious students and lovers of music."

In subsequent years the Boston Symphony Orchestra became a more disciplined and widely known orchestra. There was some grumbling among the musicians about the music director's penchant for long, grueling rehearsals, but Higginson cleverly undercut their complaints by offering those who stayed summer employment playing popular concerts, or "Pops." He also arranged a post-season tour in 1886, to help achieve visibility. Higginson's strategy paid off: critics in the cities on the tour praised the orchestra for the quality and precision of its playing.

Although they were proud of their orchestra, Bostonians were not as quick as outsiders to praise it. They seemed to prefer to indulge in what Philip Hale, long-time music critic for the *Boston Home Journal* and the *Herald,* called "A Boston Habit," the tendency "to be of a critical spirit concerning everything that pertains to art..." Any new piece of art, Hale observed, causes "many of the unemployed an unrest that only finds relief in spoken opinion and in long letters to the newspapers." But for every self-appointed critic, Hale found—and applauded—an equal number of amateur choral singers, "men and women (who) quietly attend the necessary rehearsals and go through the inevitable drudgery attending the preparation for a concert..." such as the performance of the *Messiah* given each year by the Handel and Hayden Society. Such

dedication to music, Hale concluded, "is a surer sign of true musical interest than the buying of seats for Symphony concerts at an exorbitant price."

Mrs. Isabella Stewart Gardner was a wealthy, flamboyant, not-all-together-proper Bostonian who belied Hale's characterization that the rich knew nothing about the arts but were willing to pay a high price to sustain the illusion that they did. Mrs. Gardner was the city's most famous and knowledgeable private collector of art. Born in New York, the daughter of David Steward, a wealthy department store owner, Isabella married a proper Bostonian, John Lowell Gardner in 1860. From that time until her death in 1924 at the age of 85, "Mrs. Jack," as she was popularly known, did "everything that Proper Boston women do not do, and then some." Among other outrageous acts that set Bostonians' tongues wagging, she drank beer rather than tea, walked down Tremont Street with a lion on a leash, became a Buddhist, and spent thousands of dollars on clothes and jewels. Her portrait, painted by John Singer Sargent in 1888, pictured her in a lowneck, tight-fitting black evening dress. After a brief public exhibit caused a rash of risque comments, Mr. Gardner demanded that the portrait never be shown again.

Despite her eccentric behavior, Mrs. Jack was an intelligent, careful collector of fine paintings by Titian, Vermeer, Rembrandt, Raphael, Whistler, and Degas. To house her collection she bought a Florentine palace and had it shipped piece by piece to Boston where it was rebuilt in the Fenway. On New Year's night 1903, Mrs. Gardner staged a grand opening of her palace for Boston society. While the Boston Symphony Orchestra played, Mrs. Jack allowed her guests to pay homage to her, to recognize—however grudgingly—that she was the queen of Boston society. When the concert concluded, she signaled for a large mirror to be moved so that the magnificent palace courtyard, filled with flowers, was visible to all the guests. There was at first, one man wrote, "an intense silence broken only by the water trickling in the fountains; then came a growing murmur of delight and one by one the guests pressed forward to make sure it was not all a dream."

Proper Boston society was even more impressed when it was learned that according to Mrs. Gardner's will, the palace and its magnificent art collection were to become the property of the people of Boston. It was an act of civic responsibility worthy of the most proper Bostonian. Henry Lee Higginson recognized Mrs. Jack as a Brahmin: "You and I have held the same view of life and its duties," the benefactor of the Boston Symphony Orchestra told her.

Other outsiders who made a contribution to the city's development also eventually won accolades from Boston's elite. Three businessmen, Isaac Rich, Lee Claflin, and Jacob Sleeper, active Methodists, founded Boston University, which was chartered officially in 1869. The University began with a school of theology, later linked to a college of liberal arts and ultimately to professional schools of law, medicine, and music. At his death, Rich, son of a Wellfleet fisherman, left Boston University a gift of several million dollars. The bequest turned to ashes, however, when the Great Fire of 1872 consumed all of the downtown property Rich had left to the university. His vision was intact, and although Boston University was forced to struggle in cramped quarters on Beacon Hill for several decades, it established itself as a great university long before it moved in 1939 to its present Commonwealth Avenue campus.

John Simmons was another Boston businessman who dreamed of founding a college to serve his adopted city. He was a farm boy from Rhode Island who made a fortune in the clothing business and real estate during the last half of the 19th century. In his time the clothing business was organized as a "putting-out system," a method which used the labor of poor, immigrant women working in their homes. Simmons made money, but he was

haunted by the vision of those working women who were degraded because they had not been able to develop their intellect. When he made his will, Simmons endowed a college whose primary purpose would be to offer professional education for women. Simmons College opened the doors of its Fenway campus in 1901.

Just a few years later, Boston College left its original home in the South End and moved to Chestnut Hill. According to Rev. Charles Donovan, the historian of Boston College, the move was probably precipitated by an article that appeared in a Jesuit magazine in 1898, critical of the mingling of high school and college students, as was the case at Boston College. The author argued that American Jesuit colleges had lost a good bit of their prestige because good college students were "ashamed to be seen in the company of so many 'kids.'" Father Thomas Gasson apparently agreed. When he became president of Boston College in 1907, he moved the college to the spacious rural location in Chestnut Hill.

The new, open site implied nothing; the curriculum at Boston College remained a fixed classical course of study. Students were required to master Greek and Latin, "as they are languages with a structure and idiom remote from the language of the student, the study of them lays bare before him the laws of thought and logic." This rationale, which first appeared in the academic catalogue in 1894, was articulated by Fr. Timothy Brosnahan, president of Boston College from 1894 to 1898.

Fr. Brosnahan's statement emerged from a controversy with Charles Eliot, then president of Harvard. In his inaugural address in 1869, Eliot had vowed to turn Harvard into a great world university. He subsequently opened up the curriculum, introducing more scientific courses, and giving students a wide choice among subjects. This so-called elective system was necessary, Eliot maintained, in order to equip Harvard men with the ability to solve complex modern problems.

During his campaign to encourage

secondary schools to adopt the elective system, Eliot chose as a whipping boy the fixed Jesuit curriculum, which he said had "remained unchanged for 400 years." Fr. Brosnahan took up the defense of the classical curriculum, pointing out first that many Protestant college administrators were opposed to the open system. Finally, Brosnahan attacked Eliot as "pathetically naive" for denying that some graduates of Boston College were as well, or better, educated than some graduates of Harvard. Eliot was unmoved.

While the quality of university education was the chief concern of the Protestant and Catholic elite, most Bostonians were enmeshed in the process of creating a new life for themselves and their children. From among the city's earliest immigrant groups a middle class was emerging. Second, and third-generation Irish and Germans were eager to leave their original ethnic centers and take their place in the general life of the American middle class.

In the 1870s and 1880s thousands of Bostonians, ranging from those in the upper middle class—lawyers, brokers, large storeowners, manufacturers—to those in the central middle class—teachers, salesmen, contractors—to the artisans, office workers, and sales personnel who constituted the lower middle class, moved to the suburbs. Specifically, these groups left the crowded inner city for the spaciousness of the three formerly independent towns of Roxbury, West Roxbury, and Dorchester. Before 1870 these towns were mere villages; in 1870, when the suburbanization process was well underway, the towns had a population of 60,000; by 1900 they had boomed to 227,000.

Both real estate speculators and individual families wanted the modern services—schools, libraries, water, gas and sewer—offered by the city of Boston. The main water and sewer lines, therefore, were run as rapidly as possible out to the principal suburban streets, connecting the fast-growing towns with the central city system. Roxbury residents voted to give up their independent identity and become part of Boston in 1868; Dorchester made a similar decision in 1870, and West Roxbury in 1874.

Although there was a tendency for

In 1868 Boston annexed the predominantly Yankee, Protestant town of Roxbury. The streetcar, coming along such streets as Humbolt Avenue, helped bring new people to Roxbury as upwardly mobile Irish and then Jewish families moved into Roxbury Highlands. (BPL)

particular ethnic groups to settle in distinct areas, the general economic mobility of second- and third-generation immigrants meant that the ethnic composition of Boston's new suburbs reflected the city's population proportions of about 30 years earlier. In 1880, for example, the foreign-born and their children made up about 46 percent of Dorchester's population; by 1905, the percentage had risen to 57%. Not surprisingly, the dominant ethnic group in 1880 was Irish, but by the turn of the century, Canadians, Russians, Germans, and Jews left the working class districts of the inner city and moved to Dorchester in significant numbers. This steady flow of ethnic groups to the suburbs demonstrated the continued openness of metropolitan society in general and of Boston's ability in particular to provide a middle class environment for the children of its immigrants.

Boston's suburban growth was made possible by the development of the street railway. Not coincidentally, Sam Bass Warner tells us in his book *Streetcar Suburbs,* "many of the founders and investors in street railways were real estate speculators who wanted to attract new customers for their land." Henry Whitney, for example, established the West End line to Brookline in 1887, where he owned a large tract of land. A short time later, Whitney bought enough stock in several competing companies to effect a merger and create the first urban transit system in the nation. In 1888, Whitney began replacing the horse-drawn cars with electric streetcars and expanded further into the suburbs. He defended his monopoly by arguing that street railways had a positive "moral influence" on city development; street railways made it possible for workingmen to own homes and to escape the debilitating effects of living in crowded tenements.

Indeed, according to their promotors, street railways added significantly to the quality of all Bostonians' lives. By offering cheap transportation to parks and cemeteries outside the city, family togetherness was bolstered. On Sundays, thousands of Bostonians traveled out from town to spend the day at Castle Garden Amusement Park, or Norumbega Park in nearby Newton, or Forest Hills Cemetery, or Arnold Arboretum.

Within the city, the elevated railway and the subway—the nation's first, in

Center Street, in Jamaica Plain, was a typical business area in a streetcar suburb with its variety of stores and services, a thriving real estate company, and a new apartment building. There were similar scenes in Dorchester, West Roxbury, and Brighton. (SPNEA)

Frederick Law Olmsted designed Boston's park system in the 1880s. Olmsted also created Central Park in New York City, Mount Royal in Montreal, Golden Gate Park in San Francisco, and hundreds of smaller parks and residential gardens and estates. Courtesy, National Park Service, Frederick Law Olmsted National Historic Site

1893—made travel easier for both workers and shoppers. After 1901 people were able to speed across town from Sullivan Square in Charlestown to Dudley Station in Roxbury in just twenty minutes on the el. And, according to a brochure distributed by the Boston Elevated Railway, such a trip would be not only fast, but an aesthetic experience as well. The stations used building materials "with finesse and ingenuity, from large sheets of copper molded into classical details to heavy steel beams forming complex compositions, some of delicacy, others of power." And the elevated platforms, the company boasted, "provide travellers with unusual panoramas of Boston as well as views of the tracks which seem to float inplausibly between houses, commercial buildings, and distant tree tops."

For some Bostonians, fast, efficient transportation, however aesthetically pleasing, was a sign of the "devouring eagerness and intellectual strife" of city life. In an attempt to do something about curbing the excesses of city life, Charles Eliot Norton of Harvard invited his friend Frederick Law Olmstead to Boston. Olmstead was the most famous landscape architect in the nation. Among scores of other projects he had designed Central Park in New York City and the park

system linking Buffalo and Niagara Falls, and played a major role in the planning of the capitol grounds in Washington, D.C. In Boston for a conference sponsored by the Lowell Institute, Olmstead read a paper, "Public Parks and the Enlargement of Towns," that was a detailed explanation of his views on the planning of cities.

He believed that cities symbolized mankind's historic social progress. At the same time, he acknowledged the rising rate of social problems caused by the closer proximity of people. Therefore, Olmstead concluded, one of his principal goals was to create an environment that would make possible calm recreation and be conducive to a healthy state of mind. In other words, he believed parks were civilizing forces. They were also great democratizing experiences, bringing people of all classes together.

The Boston City Council had a much more mundane goal in mind: to do something about the danger and stench from the polluted, stagnant Muddy River, a tidal swamp and creek left over from the time when all the Back Bay was a shallow body of salt water. Olmstead offered to remedy the problem, but only if the Muddy River were made a part of a whole new park system for Boston. In 1877 his elaborate plan to form a green belt of pleasure drives, parks, and ponds around the city was accepted. His proposed Arborway and Fenway would give access to the western suburbs and link Franklin Park and the Arnold Arboretum to the Charles River and to tree-lined Commonwealth Avenue which ran downtown to the Public Garden and the Common.

Muddy River was the first segment of Olmstead's "Emerald Necklace." Although it appears to be the fortunate preservation of a piece of natural wilderness, the Fens was created entirely by Olmstead from rotting tidal flats on a barren river edge. He made a charming fen-like wooded area around the Muddy River while separating the sewage from the stream by way of a hidden conduit. The Fens was linked with

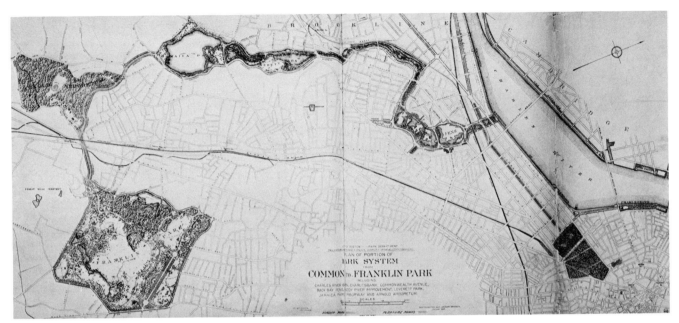

Commonwealth Avenue in Back Bay, then on to the Riverway to Jamaica Pond and the Arnold Arboretum, an experimental horticultural area managed by Harvard College. In what was called the West Roxbury Highlands, he created Franklin Park, then carried the concept through Columbia Road in Dorchester to the South Boston beaches and Castle Island.

The work of almost two decades, it was a magnificent accomplishment. Olmstead took great pride in having completed the first metropolitan system of parks in the United States. In 1893, he urged his colleagues to concentrate their best efforts on other projects in Boston. In their historical and educational impact they were, he declared, "the most important work of our profession now in hand anywhere in the world."

Not all landscape architecture conformed to Olmstead's ideals. His parks were designed to encourage contact between Boston's rich and well-born and the city's immigrants. However, many of the wealthy abandoned the dream of cultural integration, opting instead for protection and isolation. For example, in 1882 the nation's first exclusive, private country club was established in Brookline by J. Murray Forbes, a member of one of Boston's oldest families. Proudly

consuming immense acreage for the benefit of a few golfers, The Country Club was touted as "a rendezvous for a colony of congenial spirits." Or, in more blunt language, no immigrant need apply.

The establishment of private preserves for the wealthy and public parks for the poor epitomized the ambiguous character of Boston society at the end of the 19th century. For Samuel Eliot Morison, a young Boston Brahmin who later became a Harvard professor, the new century "was a high moment of hope and glory — (with) vistas of progress looming ahead...This opening year of the new century for me, marked the transition from childhood to youth....Those last years of the nineteenth century were a great time for a boy to grow up in Boston." Morison's youthful observation was correct; Boston did have much of which to be proud. But what young Morison didn't notice amidst the self-congratulatory celebration was the tendency of members of his class to look anxiously for islands of security in a Boston society that had become so diverse that culture, education, and government seemed to be threatened. The "proof" that their fears were real came in 1905 when John F. Fitzgerald, an Irish Catholic ward boss, became mayor of Boston.

Boston's park system is called the "Emerald Necklace" because it is a string of green jewels, beginning with the Charles River Basin and ending at Franklin Park. Current work on a bike path and park land from Forest Hills to South Station will make the string a complete circle. Courtesy, National Park Service, Frederick Law Olmsted National Historic Site

VII
Ward Bossism and James Michael Curley

Barney McGinneskin wanted to be a cop, one of Boston's finest. But he was Irish. And, in 1850, that was enough to disqualify him. Although more than one-third of Boston's population at this time was Irish, they had almost no political influence, no access to jobs on the city's payroll.

Power was in the hands of a wealthy, Yankee elite. Nearly two-thirds of the city's Aldermen between 1838-1850 were either merchants or lawyers; more than 90% of the men who were elected mayor during that same period were well-to-do attorneys or businessmen. All were Protestants. Nearly all were descended from one of New England's founding families. Like the priestly Brahmin class of ancient Hindus who performed the sacred rites and set moral standards, Boston's

Above: A common sight in the West End, the hurdy-gurdy man attracted the attention of children of all ages. (TBS)

Previous page: Mayor Curley threw the first ball of the season at Fenway Park in 1924. (BPL)

leaders perched on top of a modern caste system in which they were recognized as the superior group. The Lorings, Grays, Lowells, Everetts, Cabots, Shaws, Forbes, Winthrops, Peabodys, Cushings and Saltonstalls proudly and naturally assumed responsibility for the city's political life.

A shakeup in state politics in 1850 led the Boston wing of the Whig party to which the Brahmin's belonged to look—however reluctantly—to conservative Irish Democrats in order to counter an ascendant liberal coalition. One part of the deal was a promise by the Whigs that an Irishman would be added to the Boston police force. Barney McGinneskin was that Irishman. He was 42 years old, a cabby, and had been a taxpayer for 22 years when he was interviewed by the police board. McGinneskin wanted the job for very practical reasons: a policeman earned $2.00 a day—nearly twice what a common laborer was paid—and it was guaranteed work all year.

Following a careful investigation and a lengthy interview, the police board recommended McGinneskin to the Board of Aldermen. Initially only John Bigelow publicly objected, stating "that it is a

dangerous precedent to appoint a foreigner to stations of such trust." Other critics, including the City Marshall Francis Tukey soon joined Bigelow. Opposition grew until the entire night shift of the Boston police department marched to the polls to elect Benjamin Seaver mayor in the hope that he would bar McGinneskin from joining the force.

The policemen miscalculated badly. Mayor Seaver was unwilling to acknowledge publicly his anti-Irish bias. Rather, he re-instated McGinneskin and fired the entire night shift. By this point, however, McGinneskin was exhausted and embarrassed and he resigned.

While Irishmen joked—"there goes the force"—McGinneskin's struggle, together with the development of Irish political power in the last quarter of the 19th century, eventually opened the police force to Irishmen. By 1871 there were 45 Irish policemen; in 1900 an even 100. This dramatic change was brought about by a handful of shrewd, ambitious and energetic Irishmen who seized control of their neighborhood by providing help to their own people when they were unable to get what they needed from any other source. "The earliest leaders," William Shannon writes, "organized the Irish voters as a battering ram to break the power of a hostile majority."

The political machines built by Irish ward bosses in Boston developed out of family and neighborhood loyalties, from old country ties; and, most importantly, from the idea that politics was a struggle for power among competing groups. Yankee political leaders, to the contrary, took the position that a good citizen was called to "service", motivated by the ideal of civic responsibility, and committed to the goal of a stable, moral community. Because of their working class backgrounds, Irish politicians were far more practical minded. They entered politics as a career because, if successful, politics made possible rapid upward mobility for the ward boss and his Irish neighbors.

Beginning in the late 1880s, Boston's

political life began to be transformed by the new Irish ward bosses. John F. Ftizgerald—"Honey Fitz"—controlled the densely populated North End, "Smiling Jim" Donovan's sartorial elegance and flashing spending habits endeared him to Irishmen in the South End, Joe O'Connell used his power to dominate Ward Twenty in Dorchester, and Pat Kennedy directed East Boston. The most powerful and successful ward boss was Martin Lomasney. Known as the "Mahatma," Lomasney ran Ward Eight in the West End for more than fifty years. He knew what politicians wanted—votes—and he knew what the people needed—"food, clothing and shelter." There has to be someone in every ward to turn to for help, he once told a friend. "Help, you understand, none of your Yankee law and justice, but help." In exchange for the votes "his people" delivered to an office-seeker, Lomasney demanded and got access to jobs which he distributed to his loyal supporters. It was simple: power and patronage went hand in hand in the Irish neighborhoods.

In 1895, in the midst of a severe economic depression, a number of Irish ward bosses united to elect Josiah Quincy IV, the last of the Yankee Democrats, mayor of Boston. Quincy responded to the demands of working people by ordering

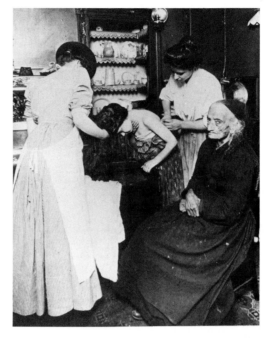

The "visiting nurse" served people who could not get to a doctor. Here a nurse, in striped dress, is visiting these women and teaching them about haircare. Courtesy, Visiting Nurse Association, Boston University

city departments to hire organized labor for specific projects and by establishing a city owned printing plant staffed by workers whose benefits included paid holidays and the 8-hour day, still regarded as a rare and bold innovation. Indeed, Quincy's experiment in municipal socialism caused him to lose the support of at least one Irish ward boss, Patrick "Peajacket" Maguire. He told his followers that they would "forfeit public confidence and come to grief" if they

Sleigh rides were popular in Boston around the turn of the century. This view of Beacon Street was taken following a 1901 snowstorm. (BPL)

The Boston subway, which began operation in 1897, was the first underground railroad in the country. This group of dignitaries and conductors made one of the first official trips under Park Street. (BPL)

listened to the siren song of radicalism.

Elected mayor in 1902 and again in 1905, Patrick Collins was more to the liking of those ward bosses who wanted city government to be less socialistic and more Irish. Collins came to Boston at age four, fleeing famine-stricken Ireland. Forced to leave school before he was twelve, as well as an apprenticeship as a machinist a few years later, because of militant anti-Catholic bias, Collins flirted with radicalism. He joined the Fenian Brotherhood—the political culture developed by Irish nationalists battling British imperialism—and helped form an upholsters union. Still, he threw himself into his work, winning promotions and achieving prosperity. In 1867 Collins was elected to the Massachusetts House and three years later he became the first Irish Catholic elected to the state senate. He studied law, served three terms in the United States Congress, and became a wealthy man, director of the International Trust Company.

By the time Collins became mayor (the second Irish Catholic) his youthful flirtation with radicalism was long forgotten. His conservative fiscal policies earned him the support of a great many Republicans, and his conservative demeanor, the admiration of the Brahmin elite in general. Collins was hailed as an

example of how an illiterate Irish immigrant could be transformed by residence in Boston into a sober, responsible citizen.

Mayor Collins' sudden death in 1905 cleared the way for Fitzgerald, the North End ward boss, to run for the city's highest office. "Honey Fitz" won easily, becoming the first American-born son of Irish parentage ever to be elected mayor of Boston. Municipal reformers despaired. Fitzgerald was not only regarded as a brash opportunist, but a representative of the corrupt ward system of patronage politics that spelled doom to the old Brahmin ideal of disinterested political service.

To counter the frightening prospect of a complete Irish-Democratic takeover, Yankee "progressives" formed the Good Government Association. Calling for reform, the institutionalization of professional and efficient processes to improve city government, and commited to supporting candidates who were qualified by education, breeding, and experience, the GGA threw its weight behind James Jackson Storrow in 1910.

The GGA firmly believed that Storrow, an able, civic-minded banker, could beat Fitzgerald. In part the Yankees' optimism stemmed from a series of changes that had been made in the city's charter between 1907 and 1909. First, in an obvious move to cripple the Democratic ward bosses, city elections were to be non-partisan. Second, a special Finance Commission, composed of prominent, independent citizens, was formed to oversee "all matters pertaining to the finances of the city." Third, the mayor's term of office was extended from two to four years, but his patronage powers were reduced considerably.

These reforms, together with the candidacy of Storrow, led the Brahmins to believe they had found a short cut through the Yankee-Irish conflict. But the reformers had ignored a democratic imperative—majority rule.

"Honey Fitz" launched a vigorous campaign that exploited the economic and social differences between Celtic and Yankee. Specifically, Fitzgerald charged that Storrow was trying to buy the election. The aggressive Irishman called upon Storrow to make public his total assets as well as the amount of money he was spending on the campaign. Storrow refused. He angrily maintained that he was doing nothing wrong; and he insisted, in typical Yankee fashion, that his word was his bond.

Fitzgerald seized upon Storrow's wealth and arrogance and made it the key issue in the campaign. "Honey Fitz" criss-crossed the city's wards, on some evenings visiting as many as eight clubs, meeting halls, and taverns, enjoying food and drink with the crowds, giving a rousing speech and then singing a chorus or two of his theme song "Sweet Adeline" before moving on. Stiff, awkward and shy, Storrow was no match for Fitzgerald.

Although the business community regarded Fitzgerald with loathing, "Honey Fitz" did not attack basic Yankee values. His campaign slogan was "A Bigger, Better and Busier Boston," and he was an untiring promoter of the port of Boston. In short, Fitzgerald was colorful, but respectable enough for the Catholic clergy and the emerging "lace curtain" Irish. He defeated Storrow by 1,402 votes.

Fitzgerald's narrow victory marked a

turning point in Boston political history. It signaled the end of Yankee control and the emergence of a new Irish-style of politics. Using the personal networks created by ward bosses to stage rallies and meetings of all sorts, an Irish candidate for city office made scores of appearances in order to convince voters that he was one of them.

Fitzgerald's energetic campaign style was matched by his drive once in the mayor's office. He built schools and playgrounds, founded a hospital, and extended the subway to Cambridge. He also increased the pay of city laborers and gave all city employees a half-day off on Saturdays. His solid record and charismatic personality seemed to insure Fitzgerald of a second four-year term.

It came as a complete surprise, therefore, when a young, aggressive Congressman named James Michael Curley announced that he was going to oppose Mayor Fitzgerald. After a good deal of hesitation, "Honey Fitz" withdrew. In his place the panicky Democratic City Committee chose a scholarly lawyer from South Boston, Thomas Kenny. The Good Government Association quickly endorsed him, and both Fitzgerald and Storrow backed him against Curley. Not a single ward boss sided with Curley. Not one newspaper endorsed him.

The latest addition to Boston Consolidated Gas Company's fleet of vehicles for transporting workers to the job is seen in this circa 1905 photograph. Courtesy, Boston Gas

North End ward boss, John F. Fitzgerald, was a popular and tireless mayor who served in 1906/07 and again from 1910 to 1913. (BPL)

This fit perfectly with Curley's two-fisted style. He loudly and crudely assaulted everyone who opposed him and appealed directly to the people by tapping into the deep-seated anger and envy of the Irish working class. Curley ridiculed the Democratic City Committee as "a collection of chowderheads"; branded the GGA as simple-minded "goo goos"; and denounced Yankee business leaders as "the State Street wrecking crew." At the same time, Curley assured the voters that he would be independent and accessible to everyone. He would be the people's mayor, fighting the people's enemies.

Curley wound up his 1914 campaign in his opponent's home district. "I'll be elected mayor of Boston, and you don't like it," he boasted to a hostile audience. And then he threw out a challenge: "Here I am. Does any one of you bums want to step up here and make anything of it?" Curley won by more than 6,000 votes, carrying sixteen of the twenty-six wards, including all the working class sections of the city.

The style and substance of Curley's politics came from his experiences as an Irish "slum brat" in Roxbury. Growing up in the "waterfront slum of ward seventeen," he wrote in his autobiography

I'd Do It Again, the mansions in the Back Bay "seemed like castles." His father's death in 1884, when James Michael was ten, meant that he and his brother and his mother all had to work to maintain the family. Sarah Curley sometimes found work as a maid in one of the wealthy homes on Beacon Hill, or as a scrubwoman in an office building along State Street. James Michael sold newspapers after school until he graduated from grammar school. After that he took a job delivering groceries in a horse-drawn cart and then, briefly, as a machine operator at the New England Piano Company. Hard work and long hours taught young Curley that "barons...exploited Irish labor." He learned that he "belonged to an Irish Catholic minority...despised socially and discriminated against politically." It was this sense of rage and the possibility of rapid upward mobility that brought Curley into politics. "Curley," the Boston *Transcript* observed sarcastically in 1933, "was born not with a silver spoon, but with a wooden ladder in his mouth, which he proceeded forthwith to climb."

Curley began his audacious climb as soon as he reached voting age in 1895. As always his approach was a frontal assault. He challenged "Pea Jacket" Maguire, long time boss of Ward 17: first Curley won Maguire's seat on the Common Council; next young Curley seized control of the ward's Democratic Committee. Now he was boss.

But Curley's ambition, his flamboyant style, and his egotism made him unsuited for the stale game of petty politics played by the old-style ward boss. He was not the least bit interested in being a cog in someone else's machine. He sought to be the most powerful figure in Boston politics, the one person to whom thousands would look for jobs, of course, but also for inspiration and revenge. His poor Irish followers were thrilled to learn, for example, that Curley had told the Harvard Board of Overseers: "The Massachusetts of the Puritans is as dead as Caesar, but there is no need to mourn the fact. Their successors—the Irish—had letters and learning, culture and civilization when the ancestors of the Puritans were savages running half-naked through the forests of Britain. It took the Irish to make Massachusetts a fit place to live in."

Curley's aggressive—and to the Irish, funny—attacks on wealthy Yankees, were matched by his showy appearance, oratory, and life-style to create an image that delighted his constituents. Strikingly handsome, Curley usually wore a black coat, white vest, gray-striped trousers, a gray soft hat, and a velvet-collared Chesterfield coat. He affected a Harvard accent and developed a mellifluous speaking voice that was his greatest political asset. Shortly after he was elected mayor in 1915, Curley left Ward 17 for a magnificent house he had built in Jamaica Plain. A huge dining room, mahogany paneling and a winding staircase were only a few of the house's expensive features. Although his detractors gossiped and an inconclusive public investigation was launched, Curley's working-class supporters didn't begrudge his life-style, nor did they doubt that he was still "one of us."

Curley's political strength also had a practical basis. During his first term on the Common Council in 1900 he sponsored a bill that ended the practice of laying off city laborers without pay during inclement weather while clerks and foremen remained on the job and drew a full salary. Likewise, in his first term as Mayor of Boston, Curley helped working people by firing nearly 600 city employees who had been appointed by Fitzgerald or had worked for Thomas Kenny's election. "Mr. Fitzgerald has left in office a number of people who are hostile to me," Curley announced, "and as I have no desire to be ambushed in my own camp, I am removing them."

Soon the corridors of city hall were crowded with voters who came looking for jobs and favors of every description. Curley saw every one of them, rewarding those who had been his loyal supporters

and friends. More than personal demagoguery or mere showmanship, this process—the beginning of Curleyism—realigned political power in Boston. Curley's move to take into his own hands the distribution of all city jobs, cut the political legs out from under the ward bosses. From now on, Curley alone would dispense patronage.

In a city plagued with chronic unemployment, jobs were the chief means of patronage. Therefore, Curley began a series of building projects. (He "rivaled Caesar Augustus as a monumental builder," a recent historian has quipped.) He greatly enlarged Boston City Hospital, created a number of smaller health units in the neighborhoods, and developed the mudflats along the South Boston ocean front into a recreational mecca that included miles of beaches, several bathhouses, and a solarium. Elsewhere in the city Curley built playgrounds, stadiums, and parks. He expanded the subway system, extended the tunnel to East Boston, and undertook to widen and pave thousands of miles of streets. In short, Curley set in motion an energetic government that provided tangible and enduring benefits for Boston voters.

Curley's construction projects were expensive and soon conservative businessmen and bankers were howling. They contended that "Curleyism" was irresponsible, that his reckless spending would bankrupt the city or at least send the tax rate soaring. Curley brushed aside these criticisms; tax money was meant to be used to help the people. Besides, he pointed out, the tax rate had inched up slowly—from $1.15 to $1.80—during his tenure in office, while it had skyrocketed during the terms of his immediate predecessors.

Curley did admit—with his political tongue in cheek—that he may have been too compassionate toward those in desperate need. "I have known what it is to be hungry," he wrote in 1929, "and I have known what it is to be cold, and if I have sometimes erred in response to the dictates of the heart rather than the head, perhaps I am not altogether to blame....My sympathies and purse have been ever freely given to those who stood shivering in the shadow of adversity." His critics called this kind of rhetoric pure demogoguery, but thousands of Bostonians believed he was sincere.

His actor's skill for personalizing issues and his commitment to using government to resolve those issues, made it possible for Curley to dominate Boston politics for more than thirty years. His triumph wasn't easy; he made enemies as well as friends. First, the ward bosses fought him. They wanted their patronage powers restored. To accomplish that, the bosses entered three Democratic candidates in the race for the mayor's office in 1917, two of whom had Irish names. The winner was Andrew Peters, a conservative Yankee.

The bosses victory over Curley was short-lived, however. He waged a spectacular campaign in 1921, defeating John R. Murphy, a respected veteran Boston politician. Curley derided Murphy's experience: he was "an old mustard plaster that has been stuck on the back of the people for fifty years."

Curley won by fewer than 2,500 votes. Once again he began knocking down old buildings to make way for new construction projects. Within two months after he was sworn in, Curley had reduced unemployment from 75,000 to 45,000. While his enemies charged that he produced an "administrative wilderness," even they had to concede that he did get things done.

Because a provision of the city charter prohibited a mayor from serving successive terms, Curley made a bid to become governor of Massachusetts in 1924 but he was defeated by Alvan T. Fuller, a Republican. Curley's constant appeals to emotionalism and to the prejudices of the Irish working class made it difficult for his candidacy to transcend Boston's city limits.

Curley's formal announcement that he intended to run for mayor again in 1929, therefore, surprised no one. The GGA

backed Frederick Mansfield, a conservative Irish Democrat who had previously served as state treasurer and president of the Massachusetts Bar Association. Mansfield made Curley the issue; Curley wisely made "work and wages" the focus of his campaign. He proposed a fifty year program for public work in Boston. With new construction at a standstill and unemployment increasing daily, Curley easily won the endorsement of the Boston Central Labor Union and of his old foes, the ward bosses. Curley's margin of victory was smaller than he (and other experts) had predicted, but as a floral tribute, placed in front of city hall on the day after the election proclaimed — Curley was *still* "Champion of Them All."

But Curley's old formula of personal patronage was hopelessly inadequate as the recession of 1928-1929 became the Great Depression. As the lines of unemployed men and women grew, the search for a quick remedy caused the rift between Curley and the Council to grow.

Of course the mayor loved it. He encouraged confrontation. Labeling his old Yankee enemies "tools of Wall Street," Curley chastized them for not using their "vast wealth" to help "those in need."

Curley's tough rhetoric and his early alliance with President Franklin Roosevelt propelled him into the governor's office in 1934, his only state-wide victory. His two years on Beacon Hill were at once tumultuous and disappointing. Curleyism was wearing thin, especially among the "lace curtain" Irish who lived in Boston's suburbs, and even among the younger generation who remained in the city but whose emotional attachment to an ethnic neighborhood was much less intense than their parents.

In 1936 Curley suffered a major defeat. He was beaten in a race for the United States Senate by the young, inexperienced Yankee, Henry Cabot Lodge, Jr. The following year Curley lost on his home turf. Maurice Tobin defeated Curley by more than 25,000 votes. Although Curley became mayor of Boston once more when

he won a fourth term in 1945, the days of "Curley's Boston"—of Yankee baiting and personal power—were gone. All that remained was the legend.

Curley's notoriety began in 1903 when he took a civil service exam for one of his constituents. His ruse was discovered, however, and Curley was sentenced to sixty days in the Charles Street jail. Showing not the smallest hint of embarrassment, let alone repentance, Curley boldly explained, "I did it for a friend." To his supporters, Curley's action was not a crime but a heroic gesture.

Thousands of Bostonians claimed to have been the recipient of James Michael's personal generosity and concern. "He really cared about us and took care of his own," an Irishman from Brighton recalled. Another added, "If you were in trouble or needed help, you could always count on Curley."

Because he used power to help the poor, Curley was characterized as a Robin Hood by those who felt oppressed by Yankee Boston. When he was convicted of misappropriating city funds and sentenced to prison (after serving five months, his sentence was commuted by President Harry Truman) the man-on-the-street asked, "How can you call it stealing, if you take the money and give it away to people who need it?" Or, as one South Boston Irishwoman put it: "He never kept a cent of it for himself. He was always giving money away to people who needed it."

Curley's final, hapless bids to be mayor (1951 and 1955) did nothing to tarnish his legend. When he died in November 1958, Boston wept. Countless stories of his largesse and his larceny were retold. He was loved for his sentimentality and cursed for his divisive use of power.

Both characterizations are correct. Why else would there need to be two statues of James Michael Curley—one seated on a park bench seemingly listening attentively to someone in need of help, the other stuck in a speaking pose, pausing perhaps to enjoy one of his slashing rhetorical attacks on an opponent.

Facing page and left: When Bostonians erected a statue of longtime mayor, James Michael Curley, they decided to build two to represent both the public and private qualities of Curley's tenure—the official leader of the city and the friend of hundreds of individual citizens. Courtesy, Boston Art Commission

VIII
Turmoil and Triumph

For many Bostonians the first half of the 20th century is memorable only for two thrilling victories by the Red Sox: in 1918, behind the pitching and hitting of Babe Ruth, the Sox won the World Series; and in 1946, when "The Kid," Ted Williams, batted the Bosox to their second American League pennant. The years between these two triumphs were one long string of inexplicable, heartbreaking failures for Red Sox fans. ("Some Bostonians criticize art, some music, some Harvard," noted a local pundit, "but most just criticize the Red Sox.") Bostonians' unconquerable faith in mankind was tested in more serious ways as well. These were tumultuous years, characterized by a wave of protest by blacks and women demanding equal rights, a devastating epidemic, a rash of bitter strikes often

Above: In the late 1800s, when blacks began moving from the West End to the South End and Roxbury, the African Meeting House was sold to a Jewish congregation. The Museum of Afro-American History purchased the structure in 1970 and is renovating it in collaboration with the National Park Service. (SPNEA)

Previous page: Mayor Curley adjusts the microphone for Franklin D. Roosevelt during the 1932 presidential campaign. Curley supported Roosevelt despite pressure from the state Democratic leadership to back Al Smith. (BPL)

aggravated by a fear of Bolshevism, the trials and execution of radicals Sacco and Vanzetti, the Great Depression, and the rapid and disruptive effects of the transformation of Boston's economy.

Because it had been the intellectual center of the abolitionist movement, Boston was popularly known as "Freedom's Birthplace," a label that paid homage to the myth of racial equality. The central conception of the myth was the notion that Boston was the ideal place for black people to live during the early decades of the 20th century. Like all powerful myths, that of Boston's special commitment to racial equality did influence Bostonian's perception of reality and also therefore, their behavior. But it also masked reality, the ugly marks of social and economic injustice and discrimination. Before he left North Carolina in 1928, Edward Cooper was told, "When you get to Boston the only way you'll know you're colored is to look in the mirror." "I had been here just three weeks," Cooper recalled, "and I was called a nigger for the first time in my life."

Soon after 1890, Boston's black population increased rapidly, though it remained small in proportion to the city's growing white population—never more than 2 percent before 1940. In 1890 there were 8,590 black people living in Boston, nearly 12,000 in 1900, and 16,350 by 1920. As a result blacks burst out of the West End, where they had been congregated, on the northwestern slope of Beacon Hill, and began moving into the South End, and by the 1920s into lower Roxbury. They moved into the old brownstone apartments that dotted the area between Washington Street and Columbus Avenue; then, in the early 1900s, along Columbus Avenue and Tremont Street into the upper portion of the South End. When, by the 1930s, the black community numbered more than 20,000, it extended into Roxbury by way of Dudley Street and Massachusetts Avenue.

Within the South End-Roxbury ghetto Boston's black people built a viable and proud community, although they were subjected to a virulent racism. Job discrimination, for example, systematically deprived black artisans of their trades. This meant that many men were forced to seek low-paying, unskilled jobs in the railroad yards and station of the South End. Job discrimination also accounts for the fact that married black women worked in much greater proportions than their counterparts in other immigrant groups. While only 5 percent of all white married women worked, nearly 30 percent of all black married women worked outside the home. It was also quite common for black families to take boarders into their homes so that they might cut living expenses and boost their income, which was the lowest in the city. By utilizing these various survival strategies, the black family held together.

The black churches of Boston helped provide stability for the family. They were agencies of social control, centers for adult education and an arena for political action. Indeed, Robert Hayden claims in his study of *The Black Church in Boston* that churches "represent pillars of strength, the foundations on which black life in Boston have been built and survived." It is not surprising, therefore, that the church was often the first institution established when the black community expanded into the South End and Roxbury. By 1915 the Fourth Methodist, Twelfth Baptist, the People's Baptist and the Columbus Avenue A.M.E. Zion church all had moved from the West End into the South End of Roxbury. The Charles Street A.M.E. church remained in the West End until 1939, when it too moved to Roxbury.

The Reverend Reverdy Ransom was pastor of the Charles Street church while the population shift from Beacon Hill to Roxbury was occurring. Because he had such a towering reputation as a speaker, however, many black people chose to attend Charles Street rather than a more conveniently located church. In 1905 the Reverend Ransom spoke in Faneuil Hall commemorating the one hundredth birthday of Wendell Phillips and William Lloyd Garrison. The *Boston Transcript* reported that Ransom's speech "stirred a crowded audience of Negro men and women. . .as no white speaker has been able to stir them throughout the whole series of Garrison addresses at previous meetings. . . . They cheered, they shouted. . .they threw their handkerchiefs and hats in the air."

Like other black clergymen, Reverend Ransom also was an important political leader within the black community. He spoke out forcefully against racial prejudice. Although he conceded that discrimination in Boston was not as brutal as it was in the South, he argued that "where it appears it is nonetheless deadly and humiliating. The aloofness of manner, a politeness of speech and the kid glove handling of social and economic contacts," Ransom told his audience, "are under the surface, just as hard and unyielding as one finds in the solid South." In fact, he added, "one feels it more on the soil that was dedicated to freedom than on the Southern soil that fell on deaf ears. To outsiders, Boston

continued to be perceived as a marvelous example of racial harmony. And because white Bostonians rarely had contact with black people living in the South End-Roxbury ghetto, that myth was perpetuated. In fact, as we have seen, blacks in Boston were victims of racial injustice. But they continued to struggle for complete equality.

Black protest in Boston was led by William Monroe Trotter, editor of the *Guardian* and a militant activist in the campaign for civil rights. Trotter devoted his life to protesting anything that drew a color line. He demanded full and immediate equality. Therefore, he adamantly rejected the conciliatory, gradual strategy espoused by Booker T. Washington, who had laid claim to national leadership in a speech he made at the Atlanta Exposition in 1895.

Washington assured his audience that "the wisest among my race understand that agitation of questions of social equality is the extremest folly." Progress and prosperity for black people, Washington argued, will come "in

Residents gathered at the Swift River Hotel in 1916 for the centennial celebration of Enfield's incorporation. By 1940 the town had been dismantled, the hotel removed, and the river valley flooded to create the Quabbin Reservoir. (SPNEA)

proportion as we learn to dignify and glorify common labor. . . ." If blacks had economic opportunity, Washington believed, whites would eventually "blot out" race prejudice and establish absolute justice. To Washington it seemed that he was not giving up much in such a compromise.

Trotter believed otherwise. Angrily, he pointed to the disfranchisement of blacks, to lynch mobs, and to the doctrine of "separate but equal" as proof that white America was building a caste system which relegated black people to a status of inferiority. He filled the pages of the *Guardian* with invective, lashing out at Washington as a traitor to his race.

The criticism of Trotter and his group mounted to such an extent that Washington decided to come to Boston to challenge his opponents on their home ground. More than two thousand black people packed into the Columbus Avenue A.M.E. Zion Church on a hot July night in 1902 to hear Washington. Trotter had organized a group of hecklers who began to hiss Washington when he came onto the platform. Refusing to let him begin his prepared speech, they shouted questions about his attitude on civil and political rights. Trotter jumped onto a chair and demanded the right to speak. People pushed and shoved, shouted, fights

broke out. The police rushed into the church, ousted the hecklers and hauled Trotter and his sister off to jail.

Trotter's tactics were condemned and he was branded an extremist by newspapers across the nation. But he had a disregard for popularity. As he saw it, his function was not to maintain polite debate, but to stimulate people to action. To be sure, sometimes his passion caused him to be unwise and unfair in his attacks. But his cause was just and he staid the course.

On Patriot's Day, April 19, 1915, Trotter led nearly two thousand singing, chanting, black Bostonians up Beacon Street toward the State House. They marched to protest the showing of a new film, *The Birth of a Nation,* by D.W. Griffith. Trotter charged that the film provoked racial antipathies and hatred and was damaging to the image of black people. The film was not art at all, but propaganda designed to appeal to the idea of white supremacy.

The Birth of a Nation cost nearly $60,000 to produce, ran for two and one-half hours, and cost patrons a minimum of $2.00 per ticket. The focus of the film was the Cameron family of South Carolina, a tragic victim of black rapine. After losing two sons in the war, the Cameron's home is looted by vicious black soldiers and their daughter Flora leaps to her death rather than succumb to the advances of a black man. Still other travails follow until the Klan, a band of hooded, armed riders, came to the rescue. White audiences cheered.

Before the film opened in Boston, Trotter and several activist clergymen met with Mayor James Michael Curley and Police Commissioner Stephen O'Meara. They demanded that the film not be shown, or, if shown, that two especially objectionable scenes be cut. Curley's answer was evasive, causing Trotter to organize a protest at the Tremont Theatre where *Birth of a Nation* was playing to packed houses.

A large crowd of blacks gathered outside the theatre on the night of April

17. They first tried to buy tickets, but were refused. A melee occurred during which several blacks forced their way into the theatre. Once inside they shouted epithets and hurled rotten eggs and tomatoes at the screen before they were arrested. Outside, angry blacks and whites scuffled until the police intervened shortly before midnight.

Trotter's protest march, designed to pressure Governor David Walsh into banning the film in the interest of public safety, temporarily united the black community. Supporters of Washington's cautious approach to change joined with members of the recently formed Boston branch of the National Association for the Advancement of Colored People and with Trotter's militant group. Still nothing happened.

Because he believed that the civil rights of black Americans were being ignored, Trotter was not very enthusiastic about President Woodrow Wilson's call "to make the world safe for democracy." He was a loyal American, but he refused to participate in a meeting called by the Secretary of War to undercut "unrest among the colored people." Rather, in June 1918, Trotter brought together in Washington, D.C., under the banner of the National Liberty Congress, a group of militant blacks who petitioned the Congress to make Wilsonian idealism a reality at home while black soldiers fought and died in Europe. Essentially, the NLC demanded an end to racial segregation and the integration of the armed forces.

Nothing happened. Trotter called for black representatives at the approaching peace conference so that the American racial crisis would be brought to the attention of the world. The State Department refused to issue passports to Trotter or the other delegates. Crushed, he returned home to Boston in the summer of 1918 and sat by helplessly as his wife died.

By the late summer of 1918, Bostonians began to believe that the rumors of a German collapse and of an impending armistice were true. Perhaps now the sickening parade of black-bordered newspaper stories about death—"Gassed Dorchester Soldier's Funeral Today," "Boston Flyer Downed"—would stop. But rumor was not yet reality and at Fort Devens, thirty miles west of Boston, and at other camps thousands of soldiers still were being trained for combat in France.

Recruiters for World War I urged men to enlist, assuring them it would help to protect American womanhood. Photograph by Leslie Jones/Boston Herald. (BPL)

Boston residents converted the open space of the Common into a "victory garden" during World War I. The service buildings were temporary. (TBS)

Major General Henry McCain, who commanded the new Twelfth Infantry Division at Camp Devens, announced on August 20, 1918, his firm intention to have the division ready for embarkation to France in fourteen weeks. Less than three weeks later, thousands of General McCain's soldiers were hospitalized, stricken with influenza or pneumonia. Both were killers.

The Camp Devens hospital normally accommodated two thousand; by mid-September there were 8,000 men who needed treatment. The death rate was accelerating at an alarming pace. During a single 24-hour period the *Boston Globe* reported 66 men had died.

A navy ship tied up at Commonwealth Pier in Boston reported eight cases of influenza on August 28, 58 the following day, and 119 on the third of September. On September 11—the day the Red Sox won the World Championship—the navy announced that 26 sailors stationed in Boston had died from influenza or pneumonia.

Boston's public health officials initially were skeptical and poorly informed about the dangers of the epidemic. Although army and navy doctors had concluded by

early September that "air and sunshine and an avoidance of crowds" were the best preventative measures that could be taken, Bostonians insisted upon holding mass rallies for the Liberty Loan campaign and jamming into Fenway Park.

Influenza raced through the city. The hospitals were inundated. Doctors and nurses worked nonstop. From September 1918 to March 1919 the Massachusetts Department of Health recorded more than 85,000 cases of influenza. Each day the death toll mounted. On September 14, 21 Boston residents died; on September 24, the *Globe* reported 109 deaths; and on October 1, the grim number reached 202. By spring more than 6,000 had died, about 1.5 percent of the population of Boston.

Everyone knew death. There was no end to the tragic stories told by the survivors. Visiting nurses often walked into scenes of horror, like those of the Black Death in the 14th century. They drew crowds of supplicants, or people ran from them fearing that their white dresses and gauze masks carried the disease. One nurse found an eight year old in his pajamas lying on the sidewalk. She took him into his home and found his father

In the months following the end of World War I, hundreds of residents died during a worldwide influenza epidemic. Tents were set up on the grounds of City Hospital to accommodate the numbers of ill Bostonians. Courtesy, Boston University Library

sick and exhausted. Three other children and their mother seemed on the edge of death. When a Catholic sister was asked by a reporter for the *Boston Evening Transcript* to describe her most recent case, she replied, "Well, the mother just had died, and there were four sick children in two rooms, and the man was fighting with his mother-in-law and throwing a pitcher at her head."

Although the epidemic continued through the fall of 1918 and the summer of 1919, the ban on public gatherings was lifted on October 21, 1918. "Boston is wide open once more," trumpeted the *Globe.* "Everything will be done today to make folks forget the epidemic and its awful price," added the newspaper.

But bright lights, a movie, and a soda were not enough to dispel completely thoughts of the dark days through which people had just passed. Many were forever changed by the influenza epidemic. Francis Russell was seven years old in 1918 and lived on top of Dorchester Hill from where he could see Boston and the ships moving silently in and out of the harbor. He bought thrift stamps at 25¢ each as his part in the Liberty Bond drive, and had a birthday cake without

frosting so that the Belgians wouldn't starve, and ate peaches and saved the stones and baked them dry so that they could be used in gas masks. He watched the funeral processions pass by on Walk Hill Street and saw the coffins pile up and noticed that "Pig-eye" Mulvey set up a circus tent that billowed in the wind to hold the coffins that came faster than the grave diggers could dig. One day he and his friend sneaked into the cemetery and watched a funeral. A man with white hair chased them away.

When Francis walked home that

Newsboys from the Boston Globe pause for a group photograph before fanning out across the city to sell their newspapers. Photograph by Lewis Hines. (BPL)

On January 15, 1919, a truck carrying a reported 2,300,000 gallons of molasses exploded and sent a huge wave of syrup down the streets of the North End. Twenty-one people were killed and 150 were injured. Photograph by Leslie Jones/Boston Herald. (BPL)

evening he became conscious for the first time of the irreversible rush of time. "And I knew then," he recalled years later, "that life was not a perpetual present, and that even tomorrow would be part of the past, and that for all my days and years to come I too must one day die."

Clearly World War I and the influenza epidemic were traumatic experiences for Bostonians. The postwar period was not much better. Protest, strikes, and paranoia often characterized the period from 1919 to 1929.

A number of Boston women were deeply involved in the struggle for and against the right to vote and to earn a decent living. Maud Wood Park, for example, was an activist who was born in Boston in 1871. Park's brilliance won her a scholarship to Radcliffe College from which she graduated in 1898. Her commitment to reform was already evident: she was one of two members of a class of seventy-two to favor votes for women, a decision which led her to join the Massachusetts Women Suffrage Association. During the next few years she helped two other Boston women, Vida Scudder and Emily Balch, found a settlement house in the South End, organized the College Equal Suffrage

League, and established the Boston Parent-Teachers Association.

In 1915 Park threw herself into the effort to pass a referendum favoring votes for women in Massachusetts. The MWSA sought to dramatize its cause with street meetings and a variety of publicity stunts. The strategy failed, however, due in large part to the opposition by the Catholic Church and a group called the Massachusetts Association Opposed to the Further Extension of Suffrage to Women. Many women who belonged to this group were themselves active in the reform movement; they held positions on the State Board of Charity, the Massachusetts Prison Commission, and the Boston Overseers of the Poor among others. They argued that voting would not help advance those reform interests which women held in common. Mary M'Intire echoed the sentiments of the Boston archdiocese. Women's participation in politics, M'Intire wrote in the *Boston Sunday Herald,* would necessarily take them outside the home and, therefore, endanger the family.

Although the referendum lost decisively, Park gained a great deal of valuable experience, especially in dealing with politicians. In 1917 she became head of the National American Womens Suffrage Association's lobby in Washington, D.C. Here, at last, her persistence was rewarded: the House and Senate approved the 19th Amendment in 1919 and the necessary ratification by the states was completed on August 26, 1920.

That same year Park became the first president of the League of Women Voters, an organization that sought to use the lobbying skills honed during the suffrage campaign to win approval for various other reform measures. Most working class women in Boston tended to be more concerned with immediate problems—a living wage and decent working conditions.

In April 1919, for example, Julia O'Connor led the Boston Telephone Operators out on strike. The International Brotherhood of Electrical Workers supported the women's union, nearly six thousand strong. Telephone service was tied up throughout New England, which so alarmed the business community that the women's demands for an increase in wages (from $16.00 per week to $19.00), better hours, and cafeterias in some of the exchanges, were agreed to after only a week of negotiations.

Although their grievances were just, the women who belonged to the International Ladies Garment Workers Union did not have as much success as the telephone operators. Florence Luscomb, an organizer for the ILG and an activist in the women's suffrage movement, denounced the conditions under which women had to work in Boston garment shops. "Safety and sanitary conditions required by Massachusetts laws were not enforced," Luscomb charged in 1921. The lighting was poor, there was trash on the floors, the toilets were filthy, but neither the owners, who had organized the Boston Clothing Manufacturers' Association to fight the ILG, nor the Commonwealth would take any action. A long, bitter strike resolved nothing: the garment union was weakened and the Boston clothing industry began to move to the South where there were no unions and an abundance of cheap labor.

Breaking the garment workers union did not end labor strife in Boston. On July 4, 1918, five thousand New England fishermen began a strike that lasted thirty-eight days; the maritime workers followed. Nine days later the elevated railroad workers stopped working. For four days during a summer heat wave, Bostonians were forced to walk. An editorial in the Boston *Herald* expressed the anger shared by many: "Every self-respecting person must have a feeling of disgust over the thought that an army of public service employees can get their wages raised by so despicable a performance as quitting their jobs while an adjustment is pending. . . ."

Still, the workers won their demands and other workers who also were suffering from the effects of low wages and postwar inflation began to consider a similar course of action. In February 1919 more than a thousand policemen, meeting in the Intercolonial Hall in Roxbury, voted by a large majority to empower their executive committee to open negotiations with the American Federation of Labor for a union charter. On August 1, 940 policemen voted to join the AFL. Not one man voted no.

While the petitions favoring affiliation with the AFL had been circulating in each of the 19 police districts, a new Boston police commissioner was appointed by Governor Samuel McCall. Edwin Upton Curtis was a 57-year old Republican who had no previous police experience and was an uncompromising martinet. William Allen White characterized Curtis in *A Puritan in Babylon* as a man who "embodied the spirit of traditional wealth, traditional inherited Republicanism, traditional inherited skepticism about the capacity of democracy for self-government and a profound faith in the propertied classes' ultimate right to rule."

The policemen were predominantly Irish Catholics. They worked seven days a week, with one day off in fifteen. Day patrolmen, in addition, had to spend one night a week in the station house on reserve. Even during their free time the patrolmen could not leave the city without express permission. James Long of the LaGrange Street station grumbled: "We had no freedom, no home life at all. We couldn't even go to Revere Beach without the captain's permission." The police also complained about the condition of the station houses. Most of the stations were old, bug-infested and overcrowded. In the Court Street station, just behind City Hall, there were four toilets and one bathtub for 135 men.

When Commissioner Curtis learned that the Boston police had been chartered by the AFL, he issued an official addition to the rules of the department. "No member of the force," he stated, "shall belong to any organization, club or body composed of present and past members of the force which is affiliated with. . .any organization, club or body outside of the department. . . ." Veterans' groups were exempted. Moreover, Curtis added that policemen were not employees, but state officers.

The patrolmen were angry and determined for a showdown, which they were confident of winning. On August 19 the men elected John F. McInnes, a veteran officer with a distinguished war record, president of their local. His first public statement was polite and mild. "I decry strike talk," he said, but added that the men firmly believed they had a right to organize a union.

Commissioner Curtis bolted into action. He ordered Superintendent Crowley to call in all policemen's night sticks, cancelled all vacations for "division commanders, lieutenants and sergeants" and set in motion a plan to recruit a volunteer police force. And following a brief, perfunctory hearing, Curtis dismissed 19 men, including McInnes, whom he held responsible for organizing the union. "WAR ON POLICE UNION IS ON," the *Herald's* headline shouted!

Monday, September 8, 1919, was a sweltering, humid day when the policemen jammed into Fay Hall to take a strike vote. First they were encouraged by a shouting, red-faced, James Moriarity from the Boston Central Labor Union which represented 100,000 workers. He told the men that the BCLU had resolved "to bring victory to the police or quit." Individual locals—the plumbers, mechanics, and typographers—also vowed to support the police. Second, the 19 suspended patrolmen pushed their way into the hall and were greeted by loud, long cheers and prolonged applause. The excitement was so intense that President McInnes actually held the men back from taking a strike vote then and there. McInnes wanted to be sure Commissioner Curtis would carry through his verdict.

At the afternoon roll call in station houses across the city, Curtis' order formally suspending the 19 men was read. The men were told to clear out their lockers and turn in their badges,

revolvers, and signal box keys. Outside several stations crowds had gathered. When the suspended men emerged carrying their uniforms, the crowds applauded.

Now that Curtis' action was official, McInnes proceeded to a vote. The strike sentiment was overwhelming: 1,134 men voted to strike; only two were opposed. In South Boston a huge crowd assembled outside the station house waiting for those patrolmen who did not strike. When they appeared, first youngsters and then others pelted them with ripe tomatoes, mud, and rocks.

Governor Calvin Coolidge, tight-lipped as usual, called together in his office Commissioner Curtis, who arrived with a revolver strapped to his waist, and Mayor Andrew Peters, who was extremely nervous. Peters wanted the state guard mobilized, but Curtis insisted, "I am ready for anything." Coolidge knew that if he called out the guard prematurely it would be political suicide. He sided with Curtis.

Meanwhile, Jordan Marsh and other large, downtown businesses, fearful of vandalism, organized their male employees into a security force, arming some of them. Curtis approved the swearing in of 100 volunteer police. Scores of young Harvard men, middle-aged lawyers and

Co. A. 1st Motor Corps. Police Strike Duty, Boston, Mass. September. 1919.

bankers, and a retired admiral were issued badges and a night stick and instructed in the rudiments of police work by those few patrolmen who had stayed on the job.

There was some trouble that first night. Crapshooters gathered in boisterous knots on Boston Common, an angry crowd set out toward one of the station houses intent upon teaching the "scabs" a lesson, and teenagers snake-danced their way through city streets in complete disregard for people hurrying home from work. On Washington Street someone lobbed a brick through the window of a shop and within minutes it had been looted, stripped bare. Again the sound of glass shattering; again the crowd surged through a store.

"A night of disgrace," the *Herald* called it. "Somebody blundered. Boston should not have been left defenseless last night." In fact, while there were scattered incidents, most Bostonians had been able to go on with their life as usual. But Coolidge had seen enough. He called out the state guard. His terse statement, "There is no right to strike against the public safety anywhere, anytime," swung public opinion against the strikers and vaulted Coolidge into national prominence.

At the same time both the AFL and the BCLU weakened and back-pedaled away from their earlier support for the striking policemen. Curtis cleverly

recruited an entire new police force largely from among unemployed war veterans. The strike was over. The men scattered, defeated, alone now.

The police strike erupted in the midst of the worst red scare in the nation's history. Some hysterical newspaper accounts even claimed that Boston's striking policemen were Bolsheviks. People were on edge. Everyone feared a violent outbreak. In 1919 a May Day parade composed of a lusty band of radicals was set upon by an angry mob, and later the headquarters of the Socialist Party in Boston were destroyed.

Cardinal O'Connell, Archbishop of Boston from 1908 to 1944, abhorred violence. In an address celebrating the centenary of the Archdiocese in 1908, O'Connell briefly reviewed the history of Puritan-Catholic antagonism. At the same time he saluted those Bostonians who had worked to create a good, moral community. Those "good men whose ashes have mingled with New England soil...did their duty well," he said. Now, O'Connell continued, it is time for Catholics to shoulder the responsibility for fraternal charity and civic duty. And, like those "good men" who built the "city on a hill," O'Connell reminded his listeners that the cement that held together a republic was education, public morality

The National Guard Motor Corps was mobilized during the Boston police strike in September 1919. Governor Calvin Coolidge was catapulted to national prominence by his harsh treatment of strikers. Over two-thirds of the striking policemen lost their jobs. (TBS)

and the protection of the rights of property.

These themes characterized O'Connell's tenure. He revitalized the Boston parochial school system, established three Catholic women's colleges—Emmanuel in 1915, the College of the Sacred Heart in 1924, and Regis in 1927—and encouraged and aided his alma mater, Boston College. He was an outspoken opponent of "modernism," whether it manifested itself in women's fashions or pseudoscientific theories of human behavior. O'Connell also believed that the basic political institutions of American life were under attack in the 1920s. He recognized the inequities of industrial society, but he was quick to denounce those whom he suspected of being socialists or communists. As O'Connell perceived it, there was good cause to be on guard against reds.

Many Bostonians—Catholic and Protestant alike—shared O'Connell's political perspective. The city's anxious, belligerent mood was a result, in part, of a national campaign against radicalism launched by the Attorney General of the United States, A. Mitchell Palmer. On January 2, 1920 Palmer and local police launched a series of sweeping raids. More than four thousand "radicals" were arrested nationwide, about eight hundred in greater Boston. Half of those arrested—nearly all of whom were recent immigrants—were chained and marched through the streets of Boston to be transported to Deer Island.

Two Italians who were members of an East Boston anarchist group who were not swept up in Palmer's raid, but feared they soon would be, hid their literature and armed themselves. On May 5, 1920, Nicola Sacco and Bartolomeo Vanzetti were arrested in Bridgewater, charged with armed robbery and the killing of a paymaster and his guard.

Believing they were being arrested for anarchist activities, Sacco and Vanzetti lied about their politics and friends when they were interrogated. Because witnesses at the South Braintree holdup gave conflicting testimony about whether either Sacco or Vanzetti had been present, they were found guilty largely on the basis of their behavior when arrested. According to Judge Webster Thayer—who had boasted he would get those "anarchist bastards"—Sacco and Vanzetti's conduct before and after their arrest showed a "consciousness of guilt."

After a few hours of deliberation, the jury found the two men guilty. "They kill an innocent man!" Sacco shouted in a shaken voice as the judge and jury were leaving the courtroom. Years of appeals proved fruitless. The death sentence set by Judge Thayer in 1921 was carried out on August 22, 1927. Shortly after midnight, in the Charlestown jail, Sacco and Vanzetti were electrocuted.

As in life, so in death, various political groups squabbled over who should assume responsibility for the bodies of the two men. Finally a committee decided to use Joseph Langone's funeral parlor in the North End. For three days, from August 25 through Saturday, August 27, the bodies lay in state. 100,000 people filed by the two coffins.

In 1937 Harvard University presented an honorary degree to William Cardinal O'Connell. Here the archbishop stands with retired Harvard president, A. Lawrence Lowell. Courtesy, Archives of the Archdiocese of Boston

Left: The Boston archdiocese received a large financial gift from the Keith family, whose fortune was made in the RKO theater chain, early in the 20th century. Cardinal O'Connell endowed Keith Academy and Keith Hall in Lowell; here students from these schools meet their benefactor before his residence in Brighton. Courtesy, Archives of the Archdiocese of Boston

On Sunday morning crowds lined Hanover Street silently awaiting the funeral procession. At 1:30 in the afternoon, a column of mounted police forced their way along the narrow street forming a barrier between the people and the path the hearse would take. Behind the two hearses came open cars heaped with flowers and two limousines carrying family members. 5,000 marchers followed in close-packed ranks. It was a gray day. A heavy drizzle soaked those marchers who made it all the way to Forest Hills cemetery. Inside the small chapel Mary Donovan, who had volunteered to help the Defense Committee six years before, spoke a few, bitter last words: "You, Sacco and Vanzetti are the victims. . . .Massachusetts and America have killed you."

While Sacco and Vanzetti still were struggling to prove their innocence, Congress, in 1924, passed the National Origins Quota Act which limited immigration from Europe to 150,000 a year and allocated most of the places to Great Britain, Ireland, Germany and Scandinavia. Members of the Immigration Restriction League of Boston were delighted. Founded by three young Brahmins in 1894, the League enrolled dozens of Boston's oldest families, including the Lees, the Paines, the Saltonstalls and the Warrens. Congressman Henry Cabot Lodge also

added his voice to the cause of immigration restriction. He argued that those races "most alien to the body of the American people" should be excluded.

Immigration restriction cut the flow of unskilled labor to Boston, but by the 1920s the demand for blue-collar workers was less than it had been. Boston's economy was diversified, characterized by light industry and periodic building

Sacco and Vanzetti were convicted of murder and executed in 1927, despite protests by thousands who felt that the men did not receive a fair trial. Courtesy, Boston Globe

These women were demonstrating machines that by 1932 revolutionized commercial communications and record-keeping and opened thousands of clerical jobs for women in Boston. (BPL)

booms. The impact of the Great Depression was, therefore, somewhat less severe in Boston than in cities dominated by large industries. More than half of the labor force in Boston never lost a day's pay. Still, between 1933 and 1940 about 100,000 workers (25 per cent of the labor force) were unemployed. Everyone knew of someone engaged in a desperate struggle.

A barely literate Charlestown woman who was receiving relief wrote to President Franklin Roosevelt that it was "terriably huiating to Mother and Father to feed three children, say nothing about keeping a roof over there head and trying to give them nurishment to strengthen them for school." However difficult some people's lives became, pride still was important. A black worker wrote to the WPA in 1936: "I do not want to be taken care of. I want to work and support my family."

Generally those Bostonians who suffered the most were men and women who lived in areas of the city which had

been the most depressed at the time of the crash. The bulk of the unemployed came from "the Boston where acres of ugly wood tenement houses line the drab streets; where ten dollars a month rented a three-room flat in a wooden fire trap without heat, lighting, running water, or indoor toilet." Specifically, the groups that were most likely to be unemployed or dependent on some relief program were the Italians of East Boston and the North End, the Irish of Charlestown and South Boston, blacks from the South End-Roxbury ghetto, and the most recent immigrants from Eastern Europe. Unemployment in the Italian North End was 50 percent higher than the city as a whole, and three times as high as the Back Bay. More than one-third of all employable workers in the oldest neighborhoods of the city still held no jobs in the private sector as late as 1939.

Elected to his third term as mayor in 1929, James Michael Curley used every trick in his patronage grab bag to help the jobless. As a stopgap, he immediately hired workers to clean up the city for its tercentenary celebration. And in February 1930 he hired 1,000 men to shovel snow at $5.00 a day. More drastic measures were needed. Unemployment worsened.

Unable to get an increase in state and federal funds and faced with skyrocketing municipal relief rolls (from 1929 to 1932 the number of families aided by the city increased six times), Curley reluctantly endorsed a private philanthropic campaign. Hoopla became the order of the day. A wrestling match at the Boston Garden raised $5,000; football teams from Boston College and Holy Cross played a benefit game on Thanksgiving day; and a "carnival for the unemployed" was held at Braves Field featuring, among others, the current world heavy-weight champion, Boston-born Jack Sharkey, the Red Sox, the Braves and aviator Amelia Earhart. These events created some excitement but failed miserably to stir the public into aiding the unemployed.

Likewise, Boston's jobless workers did

As the Depression deepened, this sound truck made the rounds to various Boston banks, urging people not to withdraw their money. (BPL)

not benefit as much from the various New Deal programs as they had hoped. A feud between Mayor Curley and President Roosevelt and a lack of cooperation between New Deal administrators and Boston's ward bosses badly undermined the effectiveness of federal relief programs. According to Martha Gelhorn, an employee of the Federal Relief Agency in 1934, Boston's management of federal emergency relief was so "blatantly bad" that the government's efforts had become "an object of disapproval (if not disgust) for the unemployed classes."

By the late 1930s the New Deal had gained a better reputation among Boston's workers. Legislation such as social security, unemployment insurance, workmen's compensation, and housing loans, together with more federal jobs, made it possible for Bostonians to regain some measure of prosperity and stability.

The Great Depression had a dampening effect on many aspects of Boston's life, but not its enthusiasm for sports. As far back as the turn of the century, Yankee

reformers had argued that physical activity would help overcome the debilitating impact of city life. Social workers like Robert Woods, who were concerned about "inferior amusements degrading the people," advocated the physical and moral benefits of organized sports, especially for the immigrant working class.

Proper Bostonians were less keen, however, about the behavior of the city's sports fans (short for fanatics). In 1914 when the Boston Braves swept four straight games from Connie Mack's powerful Philadelphia Athletics, 25,000 baseball fans unable to get tickets swarmed onto the Common opposite the *Herald* building so that they could see the score posted on a giant billboard. When the Red Sox won the World Series four years later the celebration was much more subdued—Boston boys were dying in France and the deadly influenza had begun to take its toll—but when the following year the Knights of Columbus and the City Council designated

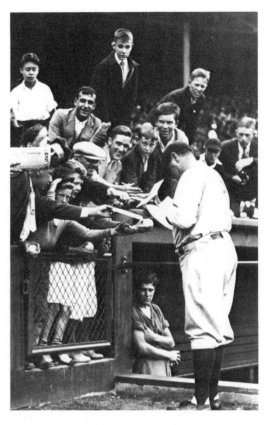

Above: Here Ted Williams hits one of his two world record-breaking homeruns in the 1946 All Star game at Fenway Park. Williams played for the Red Sox from 1939 until 1960 and set many records. He was fifth in all-time homerun percentage, second in walks. (BPL)

Above, right: Babe Ruth began his career with the Red Sox in 1914, and was traded to New York after six years. There he amassed one of the best records in baseball: first in homerun percentage and walks, and second in homeruns, runs, and runs batted in. Babe Ruth returned to Boston to play with the Braves his final year in the game. (BPL)

September 20 "Babe Ruth Day," Fenway Park rattled and shook as it never had before. Fans shouted, clapped, whistled, roared, and jumped up and down when Ruth broke a ninth inning tie by driving a home run over the left field fence.

After 1920, when Ruth was sold to the New York Yankees, the glory days of Boston baseball were mere memory for twenty-eight long years. In the interim college football eased the pain for some sports fans. For Brahmins the Harvard-Yale game—THE GAME—was the highlight of each fall season. For the city's Catholic ethnic groups, the Boston College Eagles were the team to cheer. Its roster in 1939 read like an ode to the melting pot—Charley O'Rourke, Chet Gladchuck, Henry Toczylowski, Gene Goodreault, and the first black player at Boston College, Lou Montgomery. The team was coached by 30-year-old Frank Leahy, whose arrogance belied the fact that he was beginning his first season as a head coach.

Leahy was immediately popular with Boston's fans and sports writers. Following a reverent reference to his old coach, Knute Rockne, the *Boston Globe* raved, "Rockne lives again in Frank Leahy." Leahy's Eagles began with an

easy romp, rolled to victories over Temple, Auburn, and Detroit, and then, in a game played in a raging snowstorm before 41,000 people at Fenway Park, Boston College beat Holy Cross 14-0.

In December 1939 Boston College accepted a bid to play Clemson in the Cotton Bowl. Thousands of alumni, students, and Boston fans cheered lustily when the team's special train pulled out of South Station for Dallas. Star running back Lou Montgomery was not on board. Black players were not allowed to play in the segregated South. "Sure I hate not being there," Montgomery said, "but I know there isn't a man on the team that doesn't hate the fact that I can't be there." After losing 6-3, Leahy told Montgomery, "Lou, if they had let us bring you along we wouldn't have lost." "I'm always going to believe that, coach," Montgomery replied.

The Eagles were an even better team in 1940. Along with most of the starters from the previous year, Leahy had recruited a hard-running Polish kid named

Mike Holovak. Once again, Boston College ended its regular season by beating Holy Cross (a last minute, heart-stopping 7-0 victory) and accepted an invitation to play in a post-season bowl game. This time the Eagles would meet the Tennessee Volunteers in the Sugar Bowl. Tennessee was a slight favorite, but with less than three minutes left to play, O'Rourke sprinted twenty-four yards for the winning touchdown.

Boston was delirious. A crowd estimated to be 100,000 stood in the snow at South Station to welcome its heroes home. Later, at a testimonial to the team, Leahy spoke emotionally about his attachment to Boston College. "I told these lads at halftime they were upholding the honor of dear, old New England," Leahy said. "I told them. . .I would always be with them. I love Boston College and will never leave it." A month later he became the head coach at Notre Dame.

Boston College had some good years after Leahy's departure, but as Jack Falla, historian of Boston College sports, puts it, "the flood tide of success slowly, almost imperceptibly, began to recede." The Sugar Bowl victory in 1941 climaxed one of the last "normal" sports seasons. By the end of the year the United States was at war and strapping young men from colleges and professional teams were playing more serious games.

Ted Williams, who enlisted in the Marine Air Corps shortly after hitting .406 in 1941, returned to the Red Sox after the war along with Dave (Boo) Ferris, Dom DiMaggio, Bobby Doerr and Johnny Pesky. With good pitching and plenty of power, the Red Sox were the pre-season favorite to win the American League pennant. But manager Joe Cronin had come close too many times to be overconfident.

Williams, on the other hand, boasted publicly that he was betting all takers $100 that he would be the American League batting champion in 1946. His arrogance sprang from the phenomenal physical skills that everyone agreed he

Eleanor Roosevelt visited Simmons College in 1944 to talk with students about the problems faced by returning servicemen. Photograph by Leslie Jones/Boston Herald. (BPL)

possessed. His insistence on perfection, however, often caused Williams to be angry, usually with himself, but sometimes with fans and always with sports writers. His moody behavior earned him the label "baseball's foremost problem child." He refused to chase an obvious foul ball, stood with arms folded over his chest while playing left field, and announced, "They'll never get me out of the game running into a wall after a fly ball." Still, at mid-season Williams had fifteen homeruns and was hitting .351. Boston fans either loved him or hated him with a passion.

The Red Sox won forty-one of their first fifty games in 1946, largely on the strength of Williams' and DiMaggio's hitting and Pesky's and Doerr's brilliant play in the infield. The team easily raced to the American League championship. When the Sox clinched the pennant after winning the first game of a double-header, Boston fans could wait no longer. They poured onto the field with gifts for every player. Later they danced and laughed and cheered their way through the streets of Boston until well into the night. How sweet it was!

Now, at last, Boston was ready for a new beginning.

IX
New Boston

One hundred years had passed since Boston's first city hall had been built. The glory of old Boston represented by the city hall on School Street had receded well into the past by 1962. "Boston was a hopeless backwater, a tumbled down has-been among cities," the *Globe* sadly concluded. It was a huddle of old, low-rise buildings—the tallest of which was the Customs House Tower built in 1914—clustered around a somnolent waterfront. When the Rev. Seavey Joyce flew into the city in 1946 to join the faculty at Boston College, he wondered as he looked out of the airplane to the city below, "where is Boston?"

When the plan to build a new civic center was launched in 1962, therefore, it was perceived as one part of a strategy to recapture Boston's glory days, to rekindle civic

pride. Much more than bricks and mortar were needed. Not even a decade of sports thrills provided by the Celtics and the Bruins could lift the spirits of old Boston. Post-war Boston was divided still between Protestant and Catholic, confused and angry about the impact of a growing, militant, black population, anxious about its economic future and in need of new political leadership.

In 1945, James Michael Curley was re-elected mayor for the fourth time. Curley was 71 years old. His career had begun at the beginning of the century and by design had always symbolized polarization and stasis. Curley's re-election half a century after he began his career served to emphasize the hold that the past had on Boston. To make the links even clearer, Curley spent part of his term in the federal penitentiary in Danbury, Connecticut, for mail fraud, an odd parallel to his jail sentence in 1903 for civil service fraud.

During the five months that Curley spent in jail, his place in city hall (the old city hall) was taken by city clerk John B. Hynes. The son of Irish immigrants, Hynes was born in Boston in

1897. Forced to leave school at an early age to help support his family, he worked first for the telephone company then, after service in World War I, he was able to get a job with the city while studying law evenings at Suffolk University. He passed the bar in 1928, but remained a civil servant. Moving from department to department, Hynes earned a reputation as a serious worker and a good bureaucrat. After 23 years in city service, he reached the pinnacle of the bureaucracy when he was named city clerk in 1945.

As was his style, he worked quietly and efficiently during his acting mayoralty, winning him the nickname "Whispering Johnny." Pardoned by President Truman after five months in jail, Mayor Curley triumphantly returned to the city and dismissed Hynes' efforts with the words "I accomplished more in one day than Johnny Hynes did in five months." Underestimating the appeal of Hynes' style, Curley had set the stage for his own defeat.

No one gave Hynes a chance when he announced that he was going to run for mayor in 1949. Quiet, a career bureaucrat who had never held an elective office, and

Previous page: Copley Place, which occupies 3.5 million square feet between Copley Square and the South End, features two major hotels, four office buildings, a shopping center with restaurants, a 15-cinema complex, 100 units of housing, and parking for 1,400 cars. Courtesy, The Architects Collaborative, Inc.

Right: The 1956/57 World Champion Boston Celtics. Standing left to right, Walter Brown, Dick Hemric, Jack Nichols, Bill Russell, Arnie Risen, Tom Heinsohn, Harvey Conn, Lou Pieri. Sitting, left to right, Lou Tsioropoulos, Andy Phillip, Frank Ramsey, Red Auerbach, Bob Cousy, Bill Sharman, Jim Loscutoff. Courtesy, Boston Celtics

without a political base in the neighborhoods, Hynes seemed destined to fall back into obscurity. But he ran an effective, hard-hitting campaign that appealed to the growing number of middle class Irish-Americans who were tired of the old ethnic rivalries and the old-fashioned style of the ward bosses. "Curley's day has passed," announced Hynes. "And I respectfully remind this tired and battle-scarred political war-horse that the majority of his votes are now in the cemeteries of an era long past."

In fact, a new political coalition composed of younger, more affluent Irish, Italians, Yankees, and Jews was formed to support Hynes. In striking contrast to Curley's bombast, Hynes conducted an impersonal, dignified campaign, and shockingly upset Curley, beating him by 11,000 votes. Curley had had his last hurrah.

The desire for a more conciliatory "new Boston" that manifested itself in Hynes' election, was stimulated in other ways as well. The long and fruitful relationship between town and gown that had served Boston so well in the past once more played an important role in the development of the post-war city. Specifically, many of the scientists who had been brought to MIT during the war to develop military projects stayed in the Boston area after the war in order to put what they had learned to commercial use. Over 100 new "high tech" companies were begun by scientists from MIT in the immediate post-war years. Both private and public institutions helped launch this new industry. Boston banks provided venture capital and the federal government appropriated funds to build a highway around Boston that opened up easily accessible space.

From Gloucester in the north to Braintree in the south, Route 128 had been planned to relieve urban traffic congestion, not to be a focal point for scientific enterprise. But just at the time of its opening in 1951 the new high tech companies were beginning to outgrow their early, informal, start-up quarters and

Boston is a city of neighborhoods that once were separate towns. Annexation increased the city's size and resources, and expanded city services including gas, electricity, and public transportation. Brookline alone remained independent. Courtesy, Boston Redevelopment Authority

were looking for space. The land adjacent to Route 128 was ideal for the new style of industrial park required by this industry, and it was within easy distance of the intellectual community in Cambridge and the financial community in Boston. And, according to an urban development expert interviewed in the 1950s, the high tech companies were enormously distrustful of the city. Still, the development of high tech along Route 128 offered the city a growth industry and the prospect of economic revitalization, because the bankers, lawyers, accountants, and other service companies connected to high tech suddenly needed more downtown office space.

Another hopeful sign for Boston in the early 1950s was the beginning of a consensus between Yankee businessmen and Irish politicians. These groups had distrusted one another for decades, and that hostility had done much to cause the city's stagnation. Ephron Catlin, who was a senior official of the First National Bank of Boston, recalled that in the minds of those in the business community "there was a feeling that Boston was in

Political notables joined Archbishop Richard J. Cushing on the reviewing stand of the Holy Name Society parade in 1947. From left are Senator Leverett Saltonstall, Senator Henry Cabot Lodge, Governor Robert F. Bradford, the Archbishop, and Mayor John B. Hynes at far right. Courtesy, Archives of the Archdiocese of Boston

the hands of supercrooks. Nobody had ever seen an honest Irishman." The leadership to break this impasse came from Rev. Seavey Joyce, then dean of the School of Management at Boston College. Bringing together leaders from banking, the utilities, industry, and politics to discuss the common problems of the city sounds obvious in retrospect, but it was a precedent-shattering move in 1954. The Boston Citizens Seminars, as Joyce called the meetings, began in a mood of nervous uncertainty, but soon moved to a spirit of accommodation that surprised and pleased the participants. These seminars provided the format for several decades of shared efforts to develop a civic consensus.

That a Roman Catholic priest took the lead in this civic effort reflected the new religious rapprochement that was beginning to emerge. Catholics had been a majority of the city for over half a century but still maintained a posture of defensiveness that had roots in their earlier status as an unwanted, maligned immigrant minority. Under the leadership of the austere William Cardinal O'Connell the Catholic Church had concentrated on its own affairs while maintaining a position of detachment from the city's affairs. O'Connell's long episcopate came

to an end in 1945, and his successor, Archbishop Richard J. Cushing, was animated by a fresh new spirit. Cushing, a native of South Boston was an earthy, charismatic figure, as approachable as O'Connell had been remote. Cushing was fully as ambitious for his church as O'Connell had been, and set in motion an ambitious building program of parishes, schools, and hospitals. But he also had a concern for Boston that was quite different from that of his predecessor. "I'm for everything that will promote Boston's welfare," he announced at his installation as sixth bishop of Boston. He began to reach out to establish better relations with Protestants and Jews. Delighted at his openness, these other Bostonians responded, and for this reason the national ecumenical movement had a special meaning for Boston.

The third hopeful sign that contributed to the development of a "new Boston" came from the federal government in the form of an urban renewal program. Realizing the stagnant conditions in many cities in the aftermath of the long Depression and World War II, Congress had instituted a program to revitalize the downtown sections of cities such as Boston. The late 1950s and the early

1960s were the golden age of federal largess. But it was a new and complex program that required sensitive handling. Many problems stemmed from the failure of planners to understand that often the so-called "blighted areas" that appeared to need massive change and/or demolition were also neighborhoods of people who could not be disregarded. The conflict in interests between downtown revitalization and neighborhood preservation was not easy to reconcile, and it is not surprising that Boston officials were not always able to determine how federal funds should be used to the city's best advantage during these years.

One of the first large urban renewal projects, begun during the Hynes Administration, was the Prudential Center complex in Back Bay. It was initiated by an out-of-state corporation because no Boston firms were yet willing to build on so large a scale. A pioneering project, built on abandoned railroad yards in the Back Bay, the "Pru" did not conflict with a neighborhood, but nonetheless was inordinately difficult to start. The project involved a tangle of decisions including legal rulings about blighted land, legislative permission for air rights, city guarantees on financing, and design problems. Building the Pru gave a tremendous psychological boost to the city. A *Globe* columnist optimistically wrote in 1958, "All the daring and imagination in this country today is not being spent on launching space missiles. Boston and Prudential are shooting for their own moon."

The West End project was launched in the same year as the Pru. Under the control of the Boston Redevelopment Authority, it was asserted that the West End—the area between the back side of Beacon Hill and the Charles River—was "so clearly substandard that sweeping clearance of buildings is the only way the area can be restored." Once home to 23,000 people mostly Italians and Jews, the West End's population had declined to about 7,000 in 1957. Poor, old, and inward-looking, they were dubbed "urban villagers" by Herbert Gans, a sociologist who made a critical study of the process of urban renewal.

Although the Boston Redevelopment Authority began planning the redevelopment of the West End in 1953, public hearings were not held until 1957. There were a few protesters, but the inhabitants were too disorganized and too powerless to stop the juggernaut of renewal. In January 1958, the federal government and the city signed the final agreement, and a month later the demolition began, and went on inexorably for the next 18 months.

The stupidity of this approach was soon appreciated. There was widespread national recognition that it was ridiculous to destroy a neighborhood to save it. This negative reaction did not prevent another of Boston's early urban renewal projects from getting underway. The "New York Streets" neighborhood in the South End was also marked for destruction without regard for the people who lived there. This was also justified by the rationale of "slum clearance." Black political leader Mel King later reminisced about that justification. "There was a series of articles (about the demolition) that called the area Boston's 'Skid Row.' I was surprised," King wrote, "because I had always called it home." The city cleared the area to attract light industry, but 30 years later there are still large amounts of vacant land in this part of the South End, another testimony to the fallibility of the planning process as well as its insensitivity to neighborhoods.

Yet another neighborhood fell victim, although only partially, to government improvement projects. To alleviate traffic congestion in the center of the city, the Central Artery was built. A massive "green monster" of elevated highway snaking through the middle of the city, from South Station across the Mystic River to Charlestown, the Central Artery caused the demolition of part of the North End.

The bitterness aroused by the wrecking ball approach to redevelopment paralyzed urban renewal in Boston. Poor people in other parts of the city, who were organized politically, were fearful that their neighborhood was next. "TO HELL WITH URBAN RENEWAL," angrily proclaimed a huge sign posted in Allston. South End activist Kay Gibbs complained that the process was manipulative. People didn't know—or weren't told—recalls Gibbs, "that they could hold out for relocation to the place of their choice." She and others now were determined not to allow bureaucrats and bankers to push them around.

By the time Mayor Hynes' term ended in 1959, it was clear that any new plans for urban renewal would have to be much more sensitive to the needs of the people in the neighborhoods. It was also apparent that Hynes's initiatives had not yet restored confidence among potential investors or revitalized the city's sagging economy. John Hynes had been a conciliatory mayor in a hopeful time, but the old Boston still seemed the same. The mayor's race in 1959 seemed to offer Bostonians more old politics. It was generally believed that John E. Powers of South Boston would succeed Hynes. Powers was deeply involved in city politics; he was undisputed boss of Ward Six and he had run a close second to Hynes in 1955. Then president of the Massachusetts Senate, Powers also had solid labor backing and endorsements for the mayorality from local newspapers. His close identity with the political world, his links to all the traditional bases of power, and his high visibility as a politician made Powers the solid favorite.

Powers' opponent in the run-off election was John Collins, former city councilor and then registrar of probate for Suffolk County. Collins was less well-known than Powers, but shared the same background: he was a native-born Bostonian of Irish heritage who grew up in Roxbury, attended local schools, and graduated from Suffolk University Law School in 1941. Immediately after graduation, Collins enlisted in the army and rose to the rank of captain before he was

discharged in 1945. Collins also had considerable local political experience. However, Powers had much more the image of the "pol," the old-style political operator. Collins, appearing to be more the disinterested public servant, sought to distance himself from Powers by linking him to old-style politics and to underworld figures with the slogan, "Stop Power Politics."

Collins had other advantages. His courageous comeback from a crippling bout with polio in 1955, which left him confined to a wheelchair and crutches, conjured up an image in the voters' minds of Franklin Roosevelt. A handsome, clean-cut man, Collins was able also to enhance his wholesome political image by appearing on television and contrasting himself with Powers, a short, tough, arrogant "little Napoleon."

Collins' campaign touched a nerve in the electorate that the experts had not identified. Boston voters rejected the old-style politics represented by Powers and embraced the politics of civic improvement, what Collins called the campaign for a "new Boston." Collins was swept into office by 24,000 votes. He saw his victory as a mandate to change the face and spirit of Boston, a formidable job. "After I took office in 1960," he recalled years later, "I remember going into (old) city hall. The place smelled, the toilets were overflowing, the front of the building was covered with pigeon droppings. The linoleum floor was so dirty that you couldn't tell what color it was. There was a kind of malaise of the spirit—we were all kind of ashamed. People had given up on Boston."

Not Collins. He immediately reactivated the coalition of bankers, politicians, and academics put together by Hynes and began a search for a strong administrator from outside Boston to lead the Boston Redevelopment Authority. In 1960 he persuaded Edward J. Logue, an experienced city planner from New Haven and an Irish Catholic, to become development administrator in order to give urban renewal a more professional

and more forceful direction. At once, Logue made it clear to Bostonians that he too rejected the wholesale demolition that had characterized earlier urban renewal programs. "It is the function of distinguished architecture and imaginative city design," he said, "to see that beauty is the hallmark of the renewed city. Beauty once flourished in Boston. It must again."

Collins next involved the two most powerful segments of the private sector, the financial establishment and the Catholic Church, neither of which had been enthusiastic about his election. He appointed Msgr. Francis Lally, a public spirited priest who was editor of *The Pilot* as chairman of the Boston Redevelopment Authority. He coordinated all planning initiatives with the sensitive neighborhoods and the financial community. "The Vault" as the financiers' planning committee was popularly known, was headed by Ralph Lowell, president of the Boston Safe Deposit and Trust Company and director of the Lowell Institute.

Under Collins, Logue, and Lally, urban renewal went full speed ahead—carefully.

Collins announced a "90 Million Dollar Development Program for Boston" which included renewal of both the downtown and the neighborhoods. Indeed, 25 percent of the land area of the city came under this plan. The Government Center projects alone, in the view of Walter Muir Whitehill, were "almost as dramatic in their effect upon the topography of Boston as the filling of the Back Bay."

The new city hall, set in a broad open space covering some 60 acres previously occupied by Scollay Square, Haymarket Square, and Bowdoin Square, was the focal point of downtown development. The design characteristics of the entire Government Center area had been established by I.M. Pei, an internationally known architect who had studied Boston since his student days at MIT. The city hall itself was designed by Kallman, McKinnel and Knowles, a New York firm chosen from a national competition. Their design, richly modern and iconoclastic, was hailed by Whitehill "as fine a building for its time and place as Boston has ever produced." Surrounded by the refurbished Sears Crescent building and the John F. Kennedy Federal Building,

Above: The curved street in the foreground is Cornhill, a crescent of attached buildings that was the bookselling center of the city circa 1900. The corner building in the foreground is the Sears Block and in the distance is Faneuil Hall with a flag flying from its cupola. Quincy Market is visible behind Faneuil Hall. (TBS)

Right: The Old Howard was the most popular vaudeville theater in Boston. Its closing in 1953 marked the end of Scollay Square's heyday. The area was totally redesigned during the urban renewal of the 1960s. Photograph by Leslie Jones/Boston Herald. (BPL)

the completion of Government Center demonstrated a spirit of cooperation and innovation rare among government agencies. Almost two-thirds of the money for this development came from the federal government which was motivated, in part, by a desire to stimulate private investment in new office skyscrapers.

But it took awhile for Logue to convince local bankers to take the risk. For example, in 1961, the only bidder to develop a downtown site near Government Center was a British firm. "Every bank advised them not to build," recalled one Boston banker. The success of their venture was assured, however, when the State Street Bank agreed to move into the $22 million office tower. From that hesitant beginning, private development came gradually, then with a rush that remains unabated. The "Boston Boom" was on.

By contrast, the neighborhoods continued to feel threatened by urban renewal. Because Collins and Logue were committed to upgrading existing housing whenever possible rather than wholesale demolition, their plan gained some community support. Middle-class blacks in Roxbury welcomed the Washington Park project; the new gentry in the South End

were delighted to be provided with parks, streets, and loans for refurbishing their town houses; and Charlestown residents were generally pleased with Boston Redevelopment Authority plans. But for many poor people the results of urban renewal seemed to be the same as they were in the West End: disregard, destruction, and dispersal.

Before he left office in 1967, at the expiration of his second term, Mayor Collins moved into the unfinished new city hall, to dramatize his special relationship to the new Boston. Certainly, no one challenged his claim. He had set in motion far-reaching plans that drastically changed the appearance of Boston. At the same time, other changes became visible during Collins' administration over which he had no control. Boston underwent a demographic revolution.

The population of Boston changed in two significant ways in the years after 1960. First, the number of people declined from the 1950 high of 800,000 to 575,000 in 1980. The Boston metropolitan area remained one of the 10 largest in the nation, but the city itself dropped to 20th.

Second, the composition of Boston's population was very different after 1960. The old white ethnic balance in the city that had come about in the wake of European immigration half a century earlier was destroyed by the influx of blacks and other minorities. Boston became a racially diverse city. As with the great ethnic immigration of the 1840s, Boston experienced significant racial immigration later than most large cities. Again in parallel with the 1840s, the changes that came with this influx were sharply resisted. The spirit of religious and ethnic accommodation that had come to mark the new Boston of the 1950s was supplanted by the bitterness of racial strife.

There was movement within greater Boston that stimulated profound changes, as well. Many of the children of immigrants, newly prosperous after World War II, moved to the suburbs. At the same time a small but significant number of students and professionals were attracted by the city's vibrant economy. These new "gentry" tended to be more liberal than whites in Boston traditionally had been and were less concerned with the old issues of the city. Taken together, this new gentry and the older traditional ethnic white population totaled 390,000 in 1980 and accounted for 70 percent of the city's population. The differences in their politics, however, meant that they did not form a cohesive bloc.

The influx of the gentry gave a fillip to the old elite residential areas of the inner city that had been neglected for decades. Back Bay and Beacon Hill had their Federalist and Victorian facades burnished and became prestigious addresses again. Other inner city neighborhoods experienced gentrification for the first time. In the South End, for example, long-time residents were amazed when brownstone homes that their immigrant owners could not sell for $5,000 in 1950 were being sold for more than 10 times that amount a decade later. Gentrification was a process that for better or worse inexorably spilled over

into other parts of the city, including the North End, the waterfront, and Charlestown, delighting some residents while angering many others.

The older ethnic neighborhoods were threatened by population shifts among non-gentry too. Some of the shifts came from a loss of their own population as neighborhood people moved to the suburbs. South Boston, for example, lost more than half of its 1950 population of 50,000 in the three decades that followed. Other demographic shifts came from expansion of new neighborhoods which caused destabilization of traditional ethnic "turf" in a way reminiscent of the 19th century. Newer Bostonians—blacks, Hispanics, Orientals,—were pressing on older established neighborhoods of Jews in Mattapan and North Dorchester, of Irish in Roxbury and Jamaica Plain, and what had seemed permanent homes became bitterly contested turf.

The shifts that threatened old white neighborhoods reflected the expansion of racial neighborhoods. The established black neighborhoods in Roxbury had been created about 1900 by black Bostonians displaced from the West End by Eastern European immigrants, as well as by newcomers from the South. Together they

This modern view shows the City Hall Plaza created during the 1960s. Cornhill Street no longer exists, although the Sears buildings were restored. City Hall faces the plaza, and behind it are Faneuil Hall and Quincy Market. Photograph by Peter Vanderwarker.

The Robert Gould Shaw Memorial, erected in 1897, honors the first black regiment from Massachusetts to fight in the Civil War. The sculpture, located across from the State House, was restored recently and the names of the soldiers in the regiment were carved into the granite. Photograph by James Higgins. Courtesy, Ann Beha Associates

created a community of more than 25,000 people in the area around Massachusetts and Columbus avenues in the South End. In the post-war years black migration to Boston increased steadily. Although blacks accounted for only 2 percent of the total population in 1950, that percentage jumped to 9 percent in 1960, 16 percent in 1970 and to 22 percent in 1980. After 1960, therefore, the South End-lower Roxbury ghetto became too small to house all the newcomers, and blacks began to expand into the remainder of Roxbury, past Dudley Station and to Mission Hill and Fort Hill, along Blue Hill Avenue through Dorchester beyond the G & G Deli, past Franklin Field and by 1968 were approaching Mattapan, and Jamaica Plain near the Bromley Heath public housing project. Suddenly there was a new neighborhood configuration and a large black community in the city.

As a result of this increase, the black community became more dynamic, more complex, and more assertive. Before 1960 Shag and Balcolm Taylor ran black politics in the South End-Roxbury area. From their Tremont Street pharmacy, the

Taylors organized meetings and rallied black voters to support white politicians such as Curley, in return for which they were given a few city and state jobs to distribute, were chosen delegates to the Democratic National Convention, and were allowed to run an after-hours social club. They were ward bosses. But as Mel King points out in his book *Chain of Change,* the Taylors' power "was more illusory than real;" it was dependent upon the "white power structure's handouts rather than organizing the community to demand satisfaction of Black needs."

Royal Bolling, Sr., was the first black politician to ignore the Taylors and to organize people in the Franklin Park area around specific community issues. Something of a black political renaissance followed Bolling's successful campaign for state representative in 1960. In 1962 Edward Brooke was elected attorney general, the first black to hold a state office in Massachusetts; four years later he became the first black United States senator since Reconstruction. In 1967, Tom Atkins, executive director of the Boston branch of the NAACP, was elected to the City Council.

During these same years Melnea Cass, long-time activist and president of the Boston NAACP from 1960-1962, and Otto and Muriel Snowden began Freedom House, and Elma Lewis created the cultural center that bore her name. Other black activists, including Mel King, created organizations that challenged the Boston Redevelopment Authority and the School Committee, sponsored rehabilitated housing and agitated successfully for jobs through the United Community Construction Workers, the New Urban League, and the Boston Job Coalition.

With new leaders and specific goals, the black community was ready by the mid-1960s to tackle school desegregation in Boston. Specifically, Citizens for Boston Public Schools decided to run a slate of candidates for School Committee in 1965. Although the Citizens group had some success—all five Citizens' candidates made the final election and for the first time in the city's history a greater percentage of black voters than whites cast ballots in a primary election—the campaign also made heroes of John Kerrigan and Louise Day Hicks, two incumbents. Hicks won almost 90 percent of the votes cast for School Committee by appealing to the alienation of white voters.

In the summer of 1967, Hicks announced she intended to run for mayor. "You know where I stand," she said simply and frequently. It was a code for anger, alienation, and racism. She was against busing and for law and order. At least one of her supporters had no trouble reading between the lines: "I'd like to see the next mayor take a gun and shoot every goddamn nigger in the city," a man from Jamaica Plain told Alan Lupo, a reporter for the Boston *Phoenix*.

There were other candidates who wanted to succeed Collins. Ed Logue, who had resigned from the Boston Redevelopment Authority in order to run, told Boston voters he was a progressive. He promised "planning with people" would save the city. John Sears, a Beacon Hill Republican, likewise spoke politely about remedying the troubles in the neighborhoods. He too was a progressive.

The final candidate was Kevin Hagan White. Once dismissed as "Joe White's boy" or as a "lightweight," by 1967 Kevin White had served three terms as secretary of state, the youngest person in the history of Massachusetts to hold that office, and won a reputation as an articulate reformer who was a tireless campaigner. White inherited political ambition and the connections to realize his passion for public office from his father Joseph, the most prominent "pol" in Boston before 1950, and from his father-in-law, William "Mother" Galvin. Born in Boston in 1929, White was educated at Tabor Academy, Williams College, Boston College Law School, and, most importantly, in the parlor of his West Roxbury home.

White's strategy in the race for the mayor's office in 1967 was to set himself

Martin Luther King led hundreds of Bostonians in a march against racism and discrimination in 1965. King is seen in front of the first poster as the march moves along Columbus Avenue, near Massachusetts Avenue. (BPL)

apart from his opponents. By championing neighborhood reforms, White easily distinguished himself from Ed Logue, who could not shake the charge that he was interested only in downtown development. White out-maneuvered Hicks by stressing his reasonableness and his grace under pressure. "The thing most voters don't consider," White said to a reporter casually, "but which is vitally important, is emotional stability. You've got to remember that's power you're giving a man." It was a thinly disguised, brilliant attack on Hicks' inability to cope with the emotional uproar that her anti-busing rhetoric stimulated.

The second part of White's strategy was to put together a new coalition that included liberals, the new gentry, a variety of older ethnic groups, especially Italians who had felt left out of city government because it was dominated by Irish, and the newly invigorated black voters. At the same time, though, White was careful to retain his connections with the traditional Irish bloc with whom he shared his roots.

On election day, White's coalition

delivered. Blacks voted more heavily than they had previously, and the Italian community gave him a majority of its votes. Even in those Irish wards Hicks carried, White did well. When it was over, Hicks had won half of the city's wards and nearly 90,000 votes. She had lost. White won by about 12,000 votes. In 1971, he won a second term, trouncing Hicks by more than 60,000 votes. Using a similar strategy, White won two more terms, beating City Councilor Joseph Timilty in 1975 and again in 1979.

White's 16 years in city hall may be divided instructively into two parts: the early liberal years during which he focused on the city's neighborhoods, and the second two terms during which he relied more heavily on a political machine and focused most of his attention on developing the downtown. During the early years White also had aspirations for state and national office, and so sought to cultivate an image as a neighborhood-oriented urban activist. He vigorously moved about the city authorizing Little City Halls, community

schools, and new fire and police facilities throughout the neighborhoods. He served as champion of local neighborhood activists in East Boston and Roxbury, creating the image of a dynamic chief executive who was concerned with the ordinary lives of the people.

In all this White was advised by an attractive group of professionals, most of whom came from outside the city. He recruited such people as Robert diGrazia, who modernized and cleaned up the police department; Hale Champion who succeeded Logue at the Boston Redevelopment Authority; personal aides Barney Frank, later a U.S. Congressman; Robert Kiley, subsequently director of New York City's public transit; and Robert Weinberg who became a director of Mass Port. At the same time, White paid close heed to the ethnic and racial aspects of his coalition by appointing significant numbers of blacks and Italians to city hall; he did not neglect the still significant Irish population either. White's style was that of the polished, urbane liberal, so that he was able to court the

After years of neglect and a major fire, most people expected this church to be razed. Instead, architect Graham Gund designed an award-winning residential complex, keeping the tower and street facade of the church and creating an interior courtyard where the sanctuary once stood. Photograph by Peter Vanderwarker.

national press even as he served as champion of the local neighborhood interests.

The development of the downtown area begun during the Collins years became a glittery showplace during White's last two terms. The building boom—one of the most dynamic in the nation—resulted in more than forty new buildings, many of them great towers. With its first "Manhattan-style" skyline and a dizzying array of modern architecture, observers like Fr. Joyce would no longer ask themselves "where is Boston?" A galaxy of new buildings have appeared, including the silvery H-shaped Federal Reserve Bank Building on Atlantic Avenue, the "pregnant" Bank of Boston Building on Federal Street, the stark red towers of 60 State Street, the sheer glass Hancock Tower, and the glistening Copley Place in Back Bay. Still the demand for new office space continues unabated. Nine new office buildings will be available by 1985.

The building boom was a manifestation of a major change in the city's economy. In the decades since 1960, Boston has become a world center of financial and business services. Belden Daniels, a lecturer at MIT, stated recently that "Boston is the most integrated financial service center in the United States outside New York. There are $300 billion of capital held in downtown Boston." It is estimated that one-third of the assets of the mutual fund industry and half of the American securities held by foreign banks are in Boston banks. The number of lawyers, accountants, and engineers with offices downtown has tripled since 1960.

The downtown retail district, too, has thrived. Although some major stores have failed since 1970, Filene's and Jordan Marsh have made major investments in their downtown stores. The astonishing success of Fanueil Hall Marketplace—visited by 15 million people a year—has proved that there is a bright future for the downtown retail trade.

The old was protected as well. The spectacular if unanticipated success of the Quincy Market restoration provided a

Mayor for a record 16 consecutive years, Kevin H. White's liberal early years were marked by the establishment of Little City Halls and various youth activities. White's last years were controversial, however, when he was criticized for putting downtown business interests ahead of the needs of neighborhood residents. (BPL)

national model for such projects and gave encouragement to the historic preservation movement. From Winthrop Square and Church Green in the Old South End to Lewis Wharf on the waterfront, restoration of the past became a nationally known Boston characteristic.

Showy public events were also an integral part of Mayor White's efforts to transform and enhance the image of Boston. Large, impressive, city-wide events—Summerthing, the Tall Ships, Queen Elizabeth's visit, the Bicentennial, the Pope's visit, and First Night—brought hundreds of thousands of people together to celebrate Boston. Kevin White's career seemed as promising and glamorous as the city.

Still, White could not ascend beyond the orbit of the city. He ran unsuccessfully for governor of Massachusetts in 1970, and his hopes for the vice presidency in 1972 went unfulfilled. Then, in 1972, Federal District Court Judge W. Arthur Garrity heard a suit brought by a group of black parents

Bill Rodgers greets the crowd after running the 1978 Boston Marathon in the record time of 2:09:27. Immediately behind Rodgers is Mayor Kevin White, and to his right, Will Cloney, director of the Boston Athletic Association, and Governor Michael Dukakis. Photograph by Matt Delaney.

who charged that the Boston schools were deliberately segregated. In June 1974, Garrity ordered the School Department to implement a massive, system-wide busing plan to end racial segregation. The School Committee is relatively autonomous in Boston, and White had not been involved in school policy beyond the building of schools. Similarly, he had little input into Garrity's decision, but he supported it and worked publicly and strenuously for its implementation. Inevitably he was caught in the turmoil that surrounded busing in the city, and like the city itself he was tarred.

Education and educational policy in Boston had been a focal point for protest for a decade before the order to achieve desegregation was issued by Judge Garrity. White liberals had attacked the

system in books such as *Death At An Early Age* a volatile polemic by Jonathan Kozol, and *Village School Downtown* a more tempered but no less devastating analysis of Boston schools by Peter Schragg, and had tried to reform the schools through the "Citizens for Boston Public Schools." Blacks had more personal complaints about the quality of the education offered to their children, and about the segregation of blacks within the system, whether as a result of housing patterns or deliberately drawn district lines. There were mounting protests by blacks, including student boycott of classes, busing by parents to white schools in the city in "Operation Exodus," and busing of black students to suburban cities under the Metco Program. The protests were given recognition by the passage of the Racial Imbalance Act, initially sponsored by Rep. Royal Bolling in 1965, and by the establishment of a "magnet school." Named for a black activist of an earlier day, the William Monroe Trotter School was built in Roxbury; yet there was little or no change in School Committee policy.

The School Committee did not inspire confidence. Its members had a spotty record for competence and honesty. Worse, the committee had proved impervious to change through electoral reform, and its chairman, Louise Day Hicks (and her slogan, "you know where I stand") had become the symbol of intransigent white Bostonians who would resist integrated education at all cost. For others the School Committee became the symbol of all that was wrong with old, divided Boston. A deep hostility that focused on the committee badly divided Bostonians. Its obstinance in the face of black appeals for equal education and its apparent invulnerability to change created a bitterness among liberals. Likewise, the insistent calls for change increased the bitterness of those who resisted that change and sought to control their children's lives within their neighborhoods. All this brought about a brutal, sometimes violent confrontation between blacks and whites.

In its first phase, Garrity's plan called for busing between South Boston and Roxbury, pitting working class Irish against poor blacks. "We cannot permit our city to be polarized by race or paralyzed by fear," Mayor White told Bostonians during a special evening telecast on September 9, 1974, three days before the busing plan was to be implemented. He looked and sounded confident, but he was not. Despite hundreds of meetings with parents, students, the police, and politicians, during which he promised to enforce the law and to protect every single student, White knew that the anti-busing people were determined to cause trouble, perhaps determined enough to turn Boston into another Belfast. South Boston was the center of resistance. "Southie is having a nervous breakdown, a collective nervous breakdown," White told Bob Kiley, his closest aide.

The battle began on September 12. Police, buses, monitors, and students were assembled at an abandoned shopping mall near South Boston High. A helicopter circled overhead. Additional police encircled South Boston High. Periodically, they sallied out, pushing the demonstrators back, breaking up gangs armed with rocks and bottles. Day after day, week after week, for two years the violent struggle went on. "They were invading our territory," a South Boston youngster replied when asked about racial prejudice, "Southie is my home town, not theirs. Yeah, it was war all right."

In the end, peace was won. In April 1976, tens of thousands of Bostonians staged a march against violence. Speaking to the huge crowd, White did not claim that Boston's problems were ended; he hailed the beginning of the end. "Liberty was born in Boston," he reminded the crowd, "and it will flourish here so long as courageous people of high moral principle are willing to speak what is in their hearts."

Certainly, the busing crisis had shown that there were many courageous people in the city. Still, the halcyon days of the New Boston were over. Boston was seen as a racist city. Eventually, the passions died down and busing became a way of life. In the process the school system changed from 70 percent white and 30 percent minority to the reverse, 70 percent minority and 30 percent white. The system itself shrank in size from 90,000 students to 55,000. The educational results are mixed.

Although he and the city he loved were battered by the school crisis, neither White nor Boston gave up. White's final years were marred by controversy and scandal. Still, his bond with the city was so strong that no one could be certain whether he would run for a fifth term. He chose not to, and retired undefeated. He and the people had created a New Boston.

X
Promise

The campaign to become mayor of Boston in 1983 was historic. It began as usual with a large field, but it was soon evident that only three were realistic possibilities for the run-off: David T. Finnegan, an establishment-backed moderate, who was sometimes talked about as Kevin White's protege; Melvin H. King, a long-time black activist and former state representative from the South End; and Raymond L. Flynn, a populist, and a former state senator from South Boston. Finnegan was the early frontrunner, spending five or six times more money than either Flynn or King. Despite his carefully crafted, lavish campaign, Finnegan was eliminated and King and Flynn finished in a virtual tie (47,432 votes each). For the first time in the history of Boston a black man was in the run-off election for mayor.

Up to this point, King had not been taken seriously by many voters or by the media. By late September, however, King had not only shown that he could get votes, but he had abandoned his dashiki for a suit and tie and put together a new constituency, a "Rainbow Coalition" consisting of blacks, hispanics, Asians, and a sprinkling of liberal whites along with women, gays, and the elderly. He campaigned in the neighborhoods amongst the have-nots. Black voters were especially excited because the victory of Harold Washington in Chicago made King's campaign to be mayor of Boston seem like the beginning of a new era. Eager volunteers registered nearly 53,000 new voters during the months preceding the election, almost half of whom were blacks and other minorities.

Ray Flynn also portrayed himself as a candidate of the people. An All-American basketball player at Providence College, a graduate of Harvard University Graduate School of Education, a city councilor and a state representative who had opposed busing in 1974, Flynn gradually changed his ideas and his behavior in the nine intervening years. Running on a nearly identical platform as King, Flynn differed in that he insisted that Boston's problems were a result of class, not race. Flynn argued, for example, that *all* poor people in the city's neighborhoods were victims of White's mania for downtown development.

The final campaign was hard fought, but without racial hostility. Both King and Flynn spoke in every neighborhood and usually came away with the respect of those who listened, if not the votes. Outgoing Mayor White summed up the feeling of most Bostonians when he said, "How times have changed. A man or woman being black is not a prohibition on being mayor. . .I did not believe that 10 years ago."

Still, Flynn easily defeated King by a whopping 66 percent to 44 percent, a split largely along racial lines. Flynn won by huge margins in the white ethnic enclaves of South Boston, Charlestown, East Boston, and West Roxbury. King ran well in the South End, Dorchester, Roxbury, and Mattapan, but his Rainbow Coalition attracted only 20 percent of the city's white votes. Political analysts are quick to point out, however, that the city's white population is declining while its minorities are on the rise.

Ray Flynn spent New Year's Day putting the final touches on his painstakingly prepared inaugural speech. Outside of city hall that same day, Flynn, carrying under his arm a hardbound copy of *Kennedy: A Time Remembered,* bumped into Kevin White and White's press secretary, George Ryan. Like Flynn, Ryan walked book in hand, his an inscribed gift from the outgoing mayor titled *10,000 Jokes, Toasts and Stories.*

Without doubt, Ray Flynn cut a radically different figure from that of his suave, witty, and urbane predecessor. His attitude about his new position, as had been his entire mayoral campaign, was

Above: Dramatic urban construction is documented in this scene. The older, red-brick Boston nestled along the Charles River and the two highest buildings before 1960, the golden-domed State House and the Customs House, are seen peeking around the large tower on the right. The earlier scene is dwarfed by the scale of the office towers that now dominate the skyline. Courtesy, Boston Redevelopment Authority

Left: Fort Hill, a standpipe built on the highest point in Roxbury, served as a defense during the Revolutionary War by providing a clear view of any travelers on the roads approaching Boston. The structure has recently been renovated and is seen from many points in Boston. Courtesy, Boston Redevelopment Authority

Above: This house is typical of those built in and around Boston in the late 1600s. This is the Reverend John Hale House in Beverly, a community north of Boston. No houses dating from this period remain within Boston proper except for the Paul Revere House. Courtesy, Jeffrey Howe

Top left: The first newspaper in America was issued in Boston in 1704. The Boston News-Letter was a record of local affairs and ship movements. Later in the 18th century newspapers played a significant role in keeping colonists informed about activities and ideas which culminated in the Revolution. First National Bank Blotter Series. (BPL)

Top right: America's first chocolate mill was built in Dorchester in 1765, through the collaboration of Irish immigrant chocolate-maker John Hannon, and Milton physician, Dr. James Baker. The mill grew into the Baker Chocolate Factory which produced chocolate until 1963. Then, as a division of General Foods Corporation, the company moved to Delaware. First National Bank Blotter Series. (BPL)

Bottom left: The Committee of Public Safety was responsible for stockpiling supplies and preparing for conflict. Members included Dr. Joseph Warren and Paul Revere. First National Bank Blotter Series. (BPL)

Bottom right: In June 1775 Congress established the Continental Army, uniting the militias of each colony under federal control. George Washington took command of the troops July 3, 1775. First National Bank Blotter Series. (BPL)

Top left: The new state government of Massachusetts adopted the codfish as its emblem. The codfish replica hung in the Old State House until 1798, when, with great ceremony, it was moved to the New State House. First National Bank Blotter Series. (BPL)

Top right: The Massachusetts Charitable Fire Society attempted to minimize the effects of fire in Boston. The society provided monetary relief for fire victims and stimulated research into better fire-fighting techniques. First National Bank Blotter Series. (BPL)

Bottom left: Eighteenth-century medical care was primitive. The Boston Dispensary, provided a central clinic for medical advice and treatment. The Good Samaritan became the dispensary symbol. First National Bank Blotter Series. (BPL)

Bottom right: The first public high school for girls in Boston was established in 1826 through the support of Mayor Josiah Quincy. Quincy lost political support when he opposed a second girls high school on the unusual grounds that the experiment was so successful it would cost too much money to expand. When the first school closed a short time later, public education beyond elementary school was not available to Boston girls, First National Bank Blotter Series. (BPL)

Right: The Bijou Theater opened in 1882. A broad horseshoe balcony and Moorish architecture and decoration created an exquisite setting for an audience of 1,000 people. The theater, with ingenious scenery-moving devices and electric lights, was described as the "dainty parlor of the Boston places of amusement." (TBS)

Far right: As ready-made clothing became popular and profitable, many tailors changed from making individual items to buying and selling new factory-made clothes. George Brine's family was in the tailoring business as early as 1840, and the clothing store across from Old South, advertised in this poster, operated until after 1890. (BPL)

Bottom: Boston was a center for writers and literary culture in the 1840s, partly due to effective, low-cost printing and publishing techniques. Long after the American literary center had moved to New York, printing businesses from that early period, such as J.E. Farwell and Company, were still operating. (BPL)

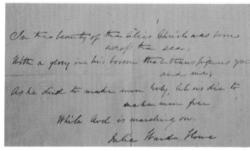

*Above: The Ritz
maintains the traditional
scale and materials of
the original design.
Courtesy, Boston
Redevelopment
Authority*

*Top left: Fashionable
women adorn the menu
from the Ritz-Carlton's
New Year's Eve cele-
bration of 1921. (BPL)*

*Far left: This advertis-
ing card was distribu-
ted by Avery Lactate
Co. in the late 1800s.*

*Left: This baby has
been tempted into good
behavior with a plate of
Hecker's Buckwheat
cakes. Boston distrib-
utors of Hecker's Buck-
wheat were George Nazio
and Howard Knight.*

Above: Ruggles House was built in 1764 on Brattle Street in Cambridge. Courtesy, Jeffrey Howe

Above right: Harrison Gray Otis built three Bulfinch-designed homes. This is the third house where Otis and his family resided from 1806 until his death in 1848. Courtesy, Boston Redevelopment Authority

Right: Near the waterfront is a small block where the crooked alleys and original buildings of 18th-century Boston have been preserved. Amid the tiny stores is this brick house which John Hancock inherited from his uncle. Courtesy, Boston Redevelopment Authority

The Massachusetts State House, designed by Charles Bulfinch in 1796, is an outstanding example of Federal style architecture. The location of the State House in the sparsely populated fields near the Common led to the subsequent real estate development of Beacon Hill and the shift of the institutional and residential center of Boston to the west, away from the waterfront. Courtesy, Boston Redevelopment Authority

Homes built in Boston suburbs for the wealthy commuter of 1880 now provide homes for new residents who are attracted to the convenience of city life and the quality of the older homes. This Victorian masterpiece is in Dorchester. Courtesy, Boston Redevelopment Authority

Far left: When the navy left the Charlestown Navy Yard in the 1970s, they left behind a variety of buildings now occupied by the Boston Urban National Park. Courtesy, Boston Redevelopment Authority

Left: A problem with gentrification is the availability of housing for those pushed out by rising rents and higher land values accompanying renovation. During the 1970s rows of houses like these were purchased and renovated by a neighborhood group. Courtesy, Boston Redevelopment Authority

Left: The triple decker was an architectural style that encouraged middle class home ownership by providing space for the owner and for renters on three floors. Courtesy, Boston Redevelopment Authority

Above: Since 1960 many South End rowhouses have been purchased by middle and upper class individuals and have been renovated to capture the original beauty of the buildings. Courtesy, Boston Redevelopment Authority

Right: This beacon, erected after the Revolutionary War, symbolized Bostonians belief that they were a perfect commonwealth, a "city upon a hill." The State House dome is visible behind the hill. This 1858 lithograph by J.H. Bufford was taken from a watercolor painted by J.R. Smith in 1811/12. (TBS)

Far right: This statue of Samuel Adams—Revolutionary War patriot, signer of the Declaration of Independence, and a member of the first and second Continental Congresses—stands before Faneuil Hall. Courtesy, Boston Redevelopment Authority

Below: Boston University, one of the largest universities in this education-rich city, was originally located in a variety of buildings throughout the Back Bay. Founded in 1869, the campus now stretches along Commonwealth Avenue between the trolley line and the Charles River.

Courtesy, Boston Redevelopment Authority

Top left: Bunker Hill Monument stands atop Breed's Hill. Courtesy, Boston Redevelopment Authority

Top right: The John F. Kennedy Library, designed by I.M. Pei, opened in 1978 on the edge of Dorchester Bay. Courtesy, Jeffrey Howe

Middle: The Massachusetts Institute of Technology, one of the premier science and engineering schools in the country, sits quietly on the Cambridge side of the Charles River. Courtesy, Jeffrey Howe

Bottom: The Science Museum, in this building on the Charles River, has its roots in the Boston Natural History Society which was incorporated in 1831. Courtesy, Jeffrey Howe

*Boston's diversity is one
of its strengths—the
many faces of Boston
are captured here.*

Above: The U.S.S. Constitution *was built in Edmund Hartt's shipyard and launched in 1797. Nicknamed "Old Ironsides" because it appeared impervious to enemy gunfire, the ship is still a commissioned flagship berthed at the Boston Naval Shipyard in Charlestown. All its copper and brass parts, including the rolled copper sheathing, were made by Paul Revere. Courtesy, Boston Redevelopment Authority*

Right: *Boston celebrated America's Bicentennial with a visit from the Tall Ships, a collection of sailing vessels from around the world. The scene was a vivid reminder of the glories of an earlier time when the harbor was filled with vessels of all sorts and sizes. Courtesy, Boston Redevelopment Authority*

Left: This view of the harbor is seen from a south Boston street. Courtesy, Boston Redevelopment Authority

Above: This is a view of the harbor and commercial district, looking southwest across the city. In the foreground is a dock in South Boston. The twin towers to the right are Harbor Towers condominiums; to the left is part of the commercial high-rise spine of modern Boston. Courtesy, Boston Redevelopment Authority

Right: The old and new Hancock Insurance buildings form a backdrop for the Park Street Church spire in this 1980 photograph. Courtesy, Boston Redevelopment Authority

Below: Three periods are captured in this view of the Christian Science Church. The Gothic stone building was the original church, founded in Boston by Mary Baker Eddy in the 1880s. A new church was built in 1913 in classical style with a mammoth dome. By 1965 the church was one of the largest private enterprises to take part in Boston's urban renewal, owning over 30 acres of land on the boundary between the South End and the Fenway. Designed by I.M. Pei, the church built a reflecting pool, underground parking, several buildings for the church center, and a variety of apartment units on surrounding streets. Courtesy, Boston Redevelopment Authority

serious, sober, and devoid for the most part of humorous quips and clever phrases. The new mayor carefully planned his inaugural ceremony to reflect his commitment to Boston's neighborhoods and a city government accessible and responsive to Boston's grassroots constituency. Symphony Hall and Fanueil Hall, traditional inaugural sites, were discarded in favor of the spacious Wang Center for the Performing Arts for what would be the largest number of people ever invited to an inauguration in Boston's history. Flynn invited 4,200 guests, many neighborhood residents who had never before attended a mayoral inauguration. Other precedents were dispensed with: dress was semi-formal rather than black tie, and guests were not expected to pay for their tickets. The entire event was paid for by the Committee to Elect Ray Flynn.

The new mayor's schedule of events for inaugural day reflected his ambitious resolve to personally make Bostonians "feel good about themselves and their city." The day began early with the Flynn family arriving in the familiar and by now symbolic 1975 rust-gutted Dodge station wagon Flynn had driven throughout his campaign, for eight o'clock Mass at Don Bosco Technical High School Chapel in downtown Boston where 15 year-old Edward Flynn attended school.

A light snow was falling by the time the inauguration was about to begin. Flynn's 19-minute address, a simple and dignified reaffirmation of his campaign promises, was interrupted 23 times by applause from his ebullient audience, with the retiring Mayor White seated on stage to the right of Flynn one of the most enthusiastic cheerers. By far the most emotional moment of this otherwise low-keyed, straightforward address came when Flynn described his parents, his father, a longshoreman who "left the house each morning on cold winter days just like this, not knowing whether he would find work," and his mother who "worked as a cleaning lady in downtown

Left: A work crew cleans the "99 Steps" in the Wilderness area of Franklin Park. The crew, made up of high school students recruited and hired by the Franklin Park Coalition for summer work, is helping give the park new life after decades of neglect. Courtesy, Franklin Park Coalition

office buildings from 11 at night until seven in the morning." His voice momentarily breaking, Flynn recalled that more than anything else his parents had taught him the importance of dignity and respect for others, "no matter what the cut of coat or color of the skin."

Pledging a city open to all, Flynn made clear his opposition to "Reaganomics" announcing "Our theory of government will be trickle up, not trickle down." In a

Below: The annual Kite Festival at Franklin Park brings together hundreds of people each April for a day of celebration. Courtesy, Franklin Park Coalition

manner reminiscent of another Irish working class mayor, James Curley, Flynn promised: "This will also be an administration that listens. Should you ever feel the need, know that there will be a welcome sign at the office of the mayor, where you will be received with respect." Flynn also called for safeguards for Boston tenants, attention to Boston's neighborhoods, improved educational facilities, and the streamlining of city services. Without doubt the strongest statement made by the new mayor was his commitment to creating racial harmony within the city: "The full weight of city government will be brought down," Flynn declared, "on all those who seek, because of race or color, to deny anyone from any street, any school, any park, any home, any job, in any neighborhood in the city."

Flynn had candidly admitted to reporters prior to the inauguration: "I'm not one of those people who can write those clever phrases," and indeed he had relied on sincerity and plain talk to move his Boston audience. He told reporters that when he sat down to write his first draft of the speech, "two words immediately flashed into my mind: 'You

count.' I wrote them down right away and underlined them and those are the words I want the people of Boston to remember from my speech."

If Flynn's sentiment was not enough, his itinerary for the remaining portion of the day embodied his inaugural pledge to the people of Boston: "You will count during this administration." Following the ceremony, Flynn stopped briefly at city hall to look over his new offices. While he posed for pictures with his daughter on the Queen Anne sofa in the mayor's outer office, Flynn got word that a fire had driven occupants out of the recently completed New Westin hotel in Copley Place. In typical Fiorella La Guardia style, Flynn chased the fire engines to the hotel where he spoke with firemen and guests who had been evacuated. Later in the afternoon the new mayor attended a performance at the D Street housing project in South Boston. Speaking briefly to the audience, which included about 100 persons bused in from public housing projects in Dorchester, Charlestown, and the South End, Flynn reassured them that he would not forget his roots now that he was mayor. "The name is still Ray, and I'm going to come to D Street

Dignitaries gather at the beginning of the annual Walk for Hunger, a project that raises hundreds of dollars for Boston's homeless and hungry residents. Governor Michael Dukakis and his wife, Kitty, join two of Boston's newest leaders: Archbishop Bernard Law, spiritual leader of Boston's two million Catholics; and Ray Flynn, who took office as mayor in January 1984. Law and Flynn have each begun their term with energy, high visibility, and a commitment to speak for individual needs and concerns, leading many people to consider this a new era for Boston. Courtesy, Photo Service, City Hall

to play basketball." Following the suggestion of mayoral opponent Mel King, Flynn also visited the Franklin Hill Housing project in Dorchester where tenants handed him a list of more than 100 complaints concerning sanitary code violations in the project.

The evening's inaugural festivities, which was headlined by the *Globe*, "FLYNN'S INAUGURAL BALL SHOWS THAT MONEY ISN'T EVERYTHING," likewise emphasized Flynn's sensitivity to economic hardship within the city and his promise to trim city spending and focus attention on the people of Boston. For the over 8,000 supporters who packed the Plaza Hotel, this properly downscale celebration, costing a mere $13,000, epitomized the kind of change they had sought for the city when they chose to back Ray Flynn. Missing was the White penchant for show and lavishness. Flynn held no gala cocktail parties and the ball itself was conducted in the most frugal manner possible. For those participating, this in itself was cause for celebration. Jubilant, although somewhat awed, Flynn arrived at 9:00 p.m. and spoke briefly to the throng of well-wishers: "Tonight is the time for celebration."

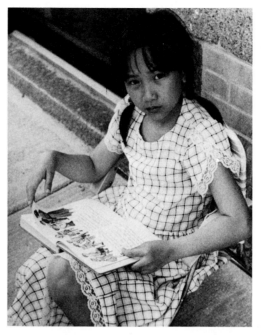

Boston's newest immigrants are hispanics from Puerto Rico, Cuba, and Central America, and Asians, especially from Vietnam and Cambodia. These groups are experiencing the same kinds of prejudice, crowded conditions, and difficulties finding work that other groups in Boston's past experienced. Courtesy, East Boston Community News

Ray Flynn is the 46th mayor of Boston. His style is different than his predecessors, but his commitment "to the idea that government is more than merely a broker among narrow, special interests, but is instead the highest expression of common values and goals which we all share," is at once a familiar and noble theme for the people of the city on a hill.

Mayor Flynn, addressing a group of constituents, describes his plans for Boston's elderly residents. Known as a Populist, with concern for the ethnic, age, and class divisions within the city, Flynn's campaign and early months in office raised the hopes of many that their needs will be addressed by a responsive city administration. Courtesy, Photo Service, City Hall

XI
Partners in Progress
by Mary M. Whelan

Fortunes have been made in Boston. They have been made in the basic economic function of sea-borne commerce—in the trading of rum, indigo, molasses, codfish, tea, furs, and glass. They have been made in the China trade; in textiles and in leather and in wool; in insurance, investments, and banking; and now they are being made in silicon and wire, in computers and high technology. And each generation of enterprise has left something behind for the welfare and civilization of those who followed. Virtually every institution that is claimed as part of our quality of life, or our culture in Boston, came from benefactors who made their fortunes in business. As they grew, they shared their growth and success with the city. So it grew and succeeded as well.

Business in Boston—right from the settlement of the colony in 1630—has changed and grown as the old city on the hill changed and grew.

Before the hills of the peninsula vanished and the encroachment of land upon water that has marked the history of Boston began, the golden age of the clipper ships saw the spars and rigging of gallant vessels making a crazy network in the harbor; and the waterfront, along what is now Atlantic Avenue, teemed with shipping traffic even as the borsprits of Boston crafts were poking into faraway ports from Liverpool to the Java Straits. Alert Yankee merchants solved the riddle of the China trade, and along the wharves at the bottom of State (then King) Street, men like Thomas Hancock, Peter Faneuil, and Thomas Boylston transacted their business and accumulated their fortunes, giving proof of the persevering industry of the Massachusetts Bay colonists.

The mercantile capital of John Winthrop and his companies demonstrated its capabilities when, following the War of 1812, as it alternately prospered and suffered, Yankee resources were diverted to the more economically viable business of manufacturing and Boston and its communities fostered a wide assortment of industry. Adding new dimension to commerce through these generations were the colorful cast of immigrants arriving by steamships at the docks of Jeffries Point. They would, in an era of large-scale industrialization, assist in revitalizing the city's economy.

When in the 20th century the textile mills and the leather tanneries faced decline, Boston, pursuing its course along the pathway of prosperity, turned to electronics and experienced new growth. And post-World War II brought a shift to a service- and finance-specialized city in a more diversified economy.

Such change has been the hallmark of Boston. The '50s growth of high-technology, defense-related companies and the explosive boom of the computer industry, combined with the '60s renaissance of Boston's central city, accelerated new commerce, success, and prosperity.

To appreciate its future, we must know of its past. The organizations whose histories are detailed on the following pages have chosen to support this important literary and civic project. They illustrate the variety of ways in which individuals and their businesses have contributed to the growth and development of Boston.

The civic involvement of the city's businesses, learning institutions, and local government, in partnership with its citizens, has made Boston an exceptional place to live and work.

Opposite: These businesses were located on Washington Street, in Roxbury, before the elevated train was built. The site is near the John Shelburne Recreation Complex at Washington Park. Photograph by Henry Hadcock. (SPNEA)

GREATER BOSTON CHAMBER OF COMMERCE

Boston has never been an uninterested spectator of public movement in any portion of the continent, and its Chamber of Commerce reflects a historic participation in the development of the capital city from where many of the earliest American ideas sprung. The organization exists today under the same mandate of its original charter: "To Forward in a Business Way the Public Good." Consistent with the communal consciousness of that mandate, the association has moved forward effectively to preserve and promote the business and public interests of its community. Indeed, in paraphrasing James L. Sullivan, its president since 1981, "The reason for the Chamber's being is to interface between the private and public sectors, to be a convener in the collaborative efforts of a public/private partnership."

The Greater Boston Chamber of Commerce is the fourth in line of descent from one that was organized as a Grain Exchange (its 1,000 members represented the grain and produce trade especially), somewhere in the years between 1793 and 1804, before Boston became a city. In 1885, for the general advantage of Boston, now both a city and a port, a 500-member Boston Produce Exchange and a 300-member Boston Commercial Exchange consolidated to form a new Chamber to be the principal trading body of a city three times its original size, and making its living from the sea. The progressive and influential group held their formal meetings at the new Quincy Market Rotunda until January 21, 1892, when, replete with incandescent lighting, the pink granite, Romanesque-style, seven-story Grain Exchange Building, which still stands at

India and Milk streets, was dedicated for its interests.

In 1909 the preeminent concerns of the 670,000 people living in Mayor George A. Hibbard's metropolis were property taxation, the handling of coal fuels, education for its youth, extension of its streets, and rail and steamship transport problems. On June 15, by charter of the Massachusetts Legislature, a new organization called the Boston Chamber of Commerce was formed by the merging of the old Chamber and a reorganized Boston Merchants Association; its objective was to have a unified effective voice in the public interest of just and equitable principles of trade. In common tributary concern 100 "sustaining members" adopted bylaws and contributed dues of $200.

Complexities of a modern society enlarged the scope of issues affecting business and the local economy, thus broadening the Chamber's role as catalyst and coordinator in such concerns as environmental protection, governmental regulation of business, state, and municipal fiscal policy, development of new energy resources, expanded transportation services, educational needs, development and renewal issues, inner-city needs, health care, and aid to the nonprofit sector.

In 1952 members and directors of the city's largest business organization changed its name to Greater Boston Chamber of Commerce, thereby extending its area of corporate representation.

The dawning of the 1980s saw a new confident Boston, its modern skyscrapers rising over the harbor as a beacon to commerce guarding the public legacy of more than 350 years of Boston enterprise. The members, officers, directors, professional staff, and committees

of the Chamber, from offices at 125 High Street, continue to mediate and implement, in a cooperative spirit, those goals of community-wide interest that affect the economic, political, and social well-being of all that greater Boston is and will be. Today nearly 2,000 members are participants in programs initiated and administered by the Greater Boston Chamber of Commerce, united in their efforts to enhance the quality of life for all who live and work in the greater Boston area.

Boston's Grain Exchange Building, at 177 Milk Street, was constructed in 1892 for the Greater Boston Chamber of Commerce. The landmark facility is now owned and managed by the Beal Companies.

BANK OF BOSTON

The Manufacturing House at Long Acre (now Tremont Street) near the Granary Burying Ground was the first headquarters building of what is now Bank of Boston.

Two centuries of world history and accommodating change to evolutionary developments have brought Bank of Boston to its present character and scope in the regional, domestic, and international marketplace. One of the largest U.S. banking companies in the world, its family of banks now spans 39 countries in which operations are conducted through 160 overseas offices.

The saga of the first bank to serve Boston began in 1784, when Governor John Hancock's signature authorized its charter. The Constitution of the United States had yet to be adopted; George Washington would not become President until five years later; and Boston, one of the three largest communities in America, was a thriving seaport of 17,000 people and a center for international trade. Its shrewd merchants were seeking wider horizons for Boston's ships and new avenues of trade with the Far East. In the common interest of facilitating use of credit and aiding in the growth of commerce as a part of the colonial economy, the Massachusetts Bank, its beginning capital set at $300,000, opened its doors for business on July 5, and thus commercial banking in New England began.

The local bank's phenomenal growth is a story of changing times and how the bank was restructured at different intervals to conform to those changes. Through waves of national development and economic uncertainty, through 10 wars, and, since 1792, 20 major periods of depression, each generation of bankers built upon existing strengths and played active roles in the numerous trends that have shaped and continue to shape the world of banking and finance. In 1865 the bank joined the National Banking System. Consolidations and mergers followed, each of which amplified its resources, and the bank grew and prospered until by the early 20th century New England's oldest supplier of banking services was its largest.

In 1903 the bank acquired The First National Bank of Boston and took its name. Consolidations followed; new products and new services in substantially expanded branches evolved. In 1914 the bank joined the newly formed Federal Reserve System. One of the first U.S. banks to establish an overseas presence—in Argentina in 1917—the bank organized the following year an Edge Act office in New York which remained for 50 years the sole operation facilitating customers' international financing. Succeeding decades were years of assimilation, adjustment, and preparation for further change in a new era.

Modern history began in the '70s when amendments to the Bank Holding Company Act and movement toward deregulation enabled banks to serve their markets in ways not previously permitted. In September 1971 a newly organized First National Boston Corporation and its principal subsidiary, The First National Bank of Boston, took up

residence in a new and uniquely constructed world headquarters, and the concept of a bank holding company as a full-line financial services institution was formulated and directed by board chairman Richard D. Hill and president William L. Brown. Brown today serves as chairman. To create a common identity for its whole operation, a formal name change to Bank of Boston Corporation occurred in 1983.

Mindful of its local heritage and firm in its commitment to community, Bank of Boston continues in its tradition of shared programs with public- and private-sector agencies in a common concern for the work force of tomorrow and in its interest of the furtherance of history.

One Hundred Federal Street, in the heart of Boston's financial district, is the site of Bank of Boston Corporation and its flagship subsidiary, The First National Bank of Boston.

THE BOSTON HERALD

Just as Boston businesses close for the day and the sun sets somewhere beyond Fenway's Green Monster, the pace at *The Boston Herald* begins to accelerate.

Being a morning newspaper and the fastest-growing in America, *The Boston Herald* operates 24 hours a day, 365 days a year. With more than 600 employees representing a dozen unions, a fleet of 60 blazing red and yellow delivery trucks, 2,000 new tab-size news racks, and a complex Atex computer system, the *Herald* works its daily miracle.

Says president and publisher Patrick J. Purcell, "Today's *Herald* represents the newspaper of the future. It's concise, convenient, entertaining, and informative. We offer something for everyone. Exceptionally strong in local coverage, we're a newspaper of the people."

While sales, accounting, and administrative departments of the *Herald* operate on the dayside, much like any other corporation, it is the teamwork between editorial and production that sets this industry apart with the creation of a new product every night.

By 4 p.m. most graphic and feature copy is in hand. From this point on, the newsroom comes alive, with reporters and editors

In 1979 the entire Boston Herald *photography staff received a Pulitzer prize for their coverage of the Blizzard of '78. This is one of the prize-winning photos.*

Newspaper carriers have always been essential to the daily distribution of the product. Pictured here are carriers on an outing in 1933.

scrambling to consolidate the most timely material for that night's edition. Simultaneously, the display desk is processing late-coming ads to complete the page layouts designed by make up. Modern typesetting equipment produces up to 1,000 lines a minute. Engravers are preparing photos for reproduction and are making plates of the completed pages on three state-of-the-art plate-making machines. By 10:30 p.m. the paper is "locked up."

For every page in the paper, eight to 12 plates are required to accommodate the *Herald's* six multiunit presses. In the course of a night, these presses are totally replated at least two times to include late sports scores and current news. Starting with an ear-piercing bell, each hulking press begins to roll, thundering out at a capacity of 50,000 papers an hour. In the course of a year, *Herald* presses consume 40,000 tons of newsprint, 1.5 million pounds of black ink, and 150,000 pounds of color.

Once off the presses, folded stacks of *Herald*s are conveyed to the mailers for bundling and sorting. From the loading dock they are distributed to seven states, Canada, and Washington, D.C. With an audited daily paid circulation of 325,086, *The Boston Herald* reaches nearly one million

readers every day.

Priding itself in aggressive journalism, the *Herald* has broken political, social, and sports stories. The *Herald* scooped the competition in reporting the death of Yuri Andropov and the strength of Gary Hart among Democratic voters in the Northeast. It broke major local stories including a Boston College grade scandal involving a basketball star and a back-tax bill owed by the mayor's new tax collector. The *Herald* also produced special supplements on short notice, covering such important events as the installation of a new archbishop and the biggest blizzard in years.

The Boston Herald has also put its energy behind diverse community projects such as Concerts on the Common, The Genesis Fund, Bank of Boston Golf Classic, and the U.S. Olympic Torch Relay. On October 12, 1983, the *Herald* was the first to conduct a mayoral debate immediately following a preliminary election. The *Herald* also held a senatorial forum on April 4, 1984.

The posture of *The Boston Herald* wasn't always as clearly defined as it is today. Before the December 1982 purchase of the property by Rupert Murdoch's News America and his initial $16-million investment under the leadership of president and publisher Robert E. Page, the

The Boston Herald *presses in 1983.*

Herald went through a series of evolutions.

Emerging from two newspaper lines—that of *The Daily Advertiser* and that of *The Boston Traveler*—today's *Boston Herald* combines a unique blend of conservative editorial policy and vibrant editorial style.

The *Ayer Directory of Publications* identifies *The Boston Herald* as being founded in 1825 based on the first publication date of *The Boston Traveler*, although the (original) *Herald* wasn't established until 1846. It boasted of two sides of a single sheet of paper and sold for one cent. In 1861, with the advent of the Civil War and increased demand for news, *The Sunday Herald* was added. Near an area that is now Government Center, Newspaper Row evolved until it was swept by the Great Fire of 1872. Forty years later the *Herald* purchased the *Traveler,* publishing morning and evening editions until 1967 when the papers merged as *The Herald Traveler.* In 1972 *The Herald Traveler* was sold to the Hearst Corporation.

On March 3, 1813, in a substantial stone edifice near the Old State House, *The Daily Advertiser* was born. With the War of 1812 and a depression hovering near, newspaper entrepreneur Nathan Hale, cousin of the famed patriot, positioned this product to serve the wealthy and cultivated Republicans of Boston. In 1840 *The Daily Advertiser* took over five older papers including one of the nation's earliest publications, *The Independent Chronicle,* founded in 1768. In 1884 the *Advertiser* began printing *The Afternoon Record,* which was the first newspaper in New England to take the tabloid format. In 1904 William Randolph Hearst entered the market with *The American,* and in 1917 and

1921 purchased the *Advertiser* and *Record,* respectively. In 1938 their names were modified as *The Daily Record, Evening American,* and *Sunday Advertiser.* In 1961 the *Record* and *American* merged into an "all-day newspaper," and three years later *The Sunday Advertiser* converted to a tabloid. It wasn't until 1976 that the Hearst-owned *Record American/Herald Traveler* was named *The Boston Herald American.* In 1981 the product was converted from broadsheet to tabloid.

During this colorful history, *The Boston Herald* garnered nine

Pulitzer prizes, the most recent being awarded to the entire photography staff for exceptional coverage of the Blizzard of '78.

It is with competitive and enterprising spirit that today's *Boston Herald* has propelled itself to the 22nd-largest newspaper in the nation. Perhaps best summarized in a statement from the 1983 News Corporation annual report is the essence of this ideology: "We recognize the uncertainties associated with any . . . pioneering effort. We believe the potential rewards fully justify the risks."

Probe records dispute DA's denial

By GAYLE FEE and WARREN BROOKES

NORFOLK County District Attorney William Delahunt, who on Monday denied he was questioned in an investigation of a suspicious 1981 fire, was in fact interrogated extensively, documents obtained by The Herald reveal. Delahunt told The Herald on Monday he was "never questioned" about his personal knowledge of the case. But according to Boston Arson Squad records, he was interrogated on Oct. 17, 1983 about his relationship with a former Quincy Patriot Ledger reporter who died in the blaze.

Catherine Dwyer, who had covered Norfolk County courts for the Quincy daily, died in the suspicious early morning fire at her home at 11 Monson St. in Dorchester.

When informed yesterday The Herald had obtained a 12-page transcript of the interrogation, Delahunt backed off his earlier denial, saying he "assisted the Boston Arson Squad in investigations" whenever his help was requested.

Told that the documents did not detail a professional request for assistance, but rather an extensive inquiry regarding his personal knowledge of Dwyer, Delahunt replied "I made my statement, and you can print that.

"I am telling you that I have aided and assisted the Boston Arson Squad on a number of investigations, but it would be inappropriate for me to tell you what kind of aid and assistance I provided.

"It is a violation of criminal statutes and the canon of ethics we are bound by."

According to the documents, when arson squad investiga-

Turn to Page 2

NEW YORK ♥ FRITZ

By JOE SCIACCA

NEW YORK — Walter Mondale knocked the wind out of Gary Hart's campaign here yesterday, trouncing the Colorado senator in both the city and the suburbs to claim the biggest primary prize thus far in the campaign.

And Jesse Jackson captured more than 80 percent of the Democratic primary's Black vote, insuring that he will be a continuing force in the campaign for the nomination.

With near complete returns, Mondale was ahead of Hart by a 18 percent margin while Jackson followed closely on the heels of Hart.

"We had a very good day today in New York," Mondale said. "Apparently we did very well across the board."

Exit polls by ABC News of about 1,300 voters showed Mondale with a comfortable and growing 15 percent lead in the city and a clear edge in the suburbs.

The regionally-balanced polls revealed this combination for the former vice-president's success:

● The Jewish Vote — Mondale took 58 percent of this large voting block compared to 34 percent for Hart. Jackson, who was sharply criticized for his reference to New York City as "Hymietown," took only three percent of the Jewish vote.

● Endorsements — The support of New York Gov. Mario Cuomo and Mayor Ed Koch boosted Mondale's candidacy. About 19 percent of the

Turn to Page 4

Archbishop's in the driver's seat
Archbishop Bernard F. Law holds up his new license — plus a complimentary copy — he received at the Registry yesterday. Law plans to drive his own car. Story, Page 3.

Staff photo by Barry Chin

BOSTON GAS COMPANY

In 1822 Boston was chartered as a city; and that July, gas lights first glowed within the precincts of the newborn municipality. (The first user of gas, however, was Daniel Darby, a Devonshire Street bootmaker who lighted his shop in 1817.)

By an act of the Massachusetts General Court on January 11, 1823, a charter to lay pipes in the city's streets was granted to Boston Gas Light Company. Its maiden operating plant—which made gas from a compound of coal and resin—was established with the purchase in 1827 of an estate on Copps Hill in Boston's North End. The earliest public street lamps were lighted in Dock Square in 1829; 50 years later there were 10,000 gas lamps in use in the city.

Although rudimentary cooking with the fuel had been practiced for years, 80 percent of all gas sold was for lighting until electricity's competitiveness in the 1880s challenged this market. Still, by the early 1900s population growth and expanding industry had increased consumer needs; and Boston Gas Light, by developing new uses of gas as an efficient fuel for water heating and cooking, maintained uninterrupted growth. The firm merged with several local competing operations to become Boston Consolidated Gas Company, and in 1927 the largest gas-heated building in the world—at 13 stories and located at Arlington and Stuart streets—was dedicated in its name.

Beginning in the '30s the urban organization extended its franchise territory and began providing gas to suburbs north, west, and south of Boston, while new properties and facilities were added to meet increasing demands. In 1955 the corporate name was changed: The second-oldest chartered gas distributor in the United States, and the oldest and largest in New England, officially became Boston Gas Company.

Major changes followed. After supplying manufactured gas for 130 years, Boston Gas began distributing natural gas in 1959 when gas pipelines from southwestern states were completed. In the late '60s, to meet increasing demand, the company was the first to import liquefied natural gas (LNG) into the United States. The company's LNG storage facility, once the largest in the country, became a Boston landmark in 1971 when one of its storage tanks was adorned with the Boston Gas "Rainbow," the largest copyrighted work of art in the world. Today a network of 5,600 miles of distribution mains, utilizing gas in a variety of residential, industrial, and commercial applications, brings fuel to 500,000 customers who consume over 65 billion cubic feet of gas annually.

Company president John J. Bacon, reflecting on the firm's long history of service to the community, says, "The Boston Gas heritage is founded upon consistent dedication to providing our customers with safe, reliable, reasonably priced gas energy services, recognition of the contributions of employees, and the maintenance of our financial health for our investors. These same ideals guide us today and will in the future."

A gas company crew takes a break while the "sidewalk superintendents" check on progress. The photograph was taken at Broadway and L Street in South Boston on October 31, 1894.

The Boston Gas Liquefied Natural Gas (LNG) Plant at Commercial Point in the Dorchester section of Boston.

JORDAN MARSH COMPANY

On a frosty morning in 1841, Eben Dyer Jordan sold to one Louisa Bareiss a single yard of cherry-colored ribbon—thereby accomplishing the first transaction of Jordan Marsh Company, and setting into motion its journey to becoming a world-renowned mercantile establishment.

The innovative and daring 19-year-old Jordan, operating from a dry goods counter at 168 Hanover Street, envisioned and achieved steady growth. An essential and enormous line of credit from England allowed him to stock his shelves with articles strange to Boston: linens from Ireland, silks from China, rugs from Iran, and ivory from West Africa.

In 1851 Jordan went into partnership with Benjamin L. Marsh—linking the two names that now stand atop Jordan Marsh enterprises. As new properties were acquired, hoop-skirted ladies and top-hatted gentlemen came first to Milk Street, then to Pearl, on to Winthrop Square in 1859, and finally to 450 Washington Street to stock their New England homes. With the passage of years, clipper ships bringing home ever-new products from foreign worlds were replaced by steamships and rail cars, while trucks replaced wagon trains.

Upon Jordan's death in 1895 the felicitous merchandising team of Jordan Jr. and Edward J. Mitton took over the helm of the company. They sold to retail customers on credit, which jolted store owners from Boston to Berlin. Whatever was good and new they adapted to Jordan Marsh, and the store ventured into mechanized progress with the installation of telephones, glass showcases, electric lights, and elevators.

Mitton and Jordan Jr. passed on in 1913 and 1916, respectively; Mitton's son, George W., assumed the presidency until 1930, followed by his brother, Richard, and in 1937 by his son, Edward R. Under the visionary leadership of the Mitton family, Jordan Marsh became a full-line department store and a springboard in merchandising. Each descendant, by prescribing to the traditions of his forebears, initiated a move forward with the times, but retained a handclasp with the values of the old New England.

When the '50s and '60s brought demographic changes to the area, Jordan Marsh began an interrelationship with suburban growth to accommodate the alteration in residence patterns and the now auto-oriented consumer. Expansion to shopping centers in suburban areas commenced in 1951, and with the completion of its first Connecticut store in 1984 and its first New York State store in 1985, the company's branch operations throughout the Northeast will number 18 and encompass over four million square feet. Conversely, ambitious reconstruction of the downtown Boston landmark store was undertaken; when completed in 1977 it encompassed 825,000 square feet and dominated a full city block at the intersection of Washington and Summer streets. Computerized merchandising techniques and continual updating of all stores reflect a contemporary fashion image geared to today's two-income-family population.

Operations of Jordan Marsh, now the flagship division of Allied Stores, and its 8,000 employees are directed by president and chief executive officer Elliot J. Stone. Retail sales now exceed the half-billion-dollar mark—a growth record reflecting the continued strength and dedication of the company's personnel.

Jordan Marsh Company—situated on the corner of Avon and Washington streets, Boston, in 1880.

Quality merchandise designed for living in the 1980s is attractively presented in all Jordan Marsh department stores.

EASTERN GAS AND FUEL ASSOCIATES

Returning to its home port in Boston Harbor and passing the Custom House-landmarked skyline, the tugboat Cabot *carries on the work of the Boston Tow Boat Company, a marine division of Eastern Gas and Fuel Associates.*

A major force in Boston's business community for more than half a century, Eastern Gas and Fuel Associates is today a billion-dollar company and the parent of several major businesses that produce, transport, and distribute energy-related products. Eastern is a significant employer in Massachusetts, and counts more than 7,000 in its work force nationwide.

Serving major industry and energy consumers, the Boston-based company's principal subsidiaries are Eastern Associated Coal Corp., a leading Appalachian coal producer headquartered in Pittsburgh; Midland Affiliated Company, the largest barging operator on the nation's inland waterways, headquartered in Cincinnati; and Boston Gas Company, New England's oldest and largest distributor of natural gas.

Eastern was formed in 1929, through a merger of the Massachusetts Gas Companies with units of Koppers Company. The original concern principally engaged in coke production and production of gas manufactured from coke and coal mining. Primary markets for bituminous coal in those days were electric utilities and the steel, railroad, and shipping industries. Coke was sold to industry as a more efficient fuel than coal.

The early success enjoyed by Eastern gave way during the years of the Great Depression. These,

and the ensuing World War II years, were difficult for the company—as they were for all segments of industrialized America. Dramatic changes in markets were required when a renewed postwar economy surfaced. A rapid switch by railroads from coal-fired locomotives to diesels removed an enormous market, and the development of natural gas pipelines to the Northeast signaled the disappearance of coal for home heating. Meanwhile, cheap oil began to be imported from the Middle East, competing with coke in industrial markets.

During the '50s Eastern responded to these challenges and new business opportunities by participating in the construction of the New England Natural Gas pipeline in 1954. The natural gas now available in New England via pipeline was marketed by Boston Gas as home heating fuel. At the same time, Eastern Associated Coal aggressively mechanized its coal-mining operations. In 1951, in partnership with the U.S. Bureau of Mines, the coal company introduced highly productive longwall mining to this country. A merger with Midland Enterprises in 1961 accelerated Eastern's use of waterways to transport energy cargoes and brought the firm to its current focus on energy-related business.

Eastern experienced tremendous growth during the '60s and '70s. Its

Boston Gas subsidiary constructed a liquefied natural gas storage facility, acquired additional gas companies, and became the first utility to import overseas gas. Coal mines became even more highly mechanized, dramatically improving productivity. In the inland marine division, innovative techniques for towing and the acquisition of barge-building and -repair facilities increased the scope of Midland's services.

Today Eastern Gas and Fuel Associates looks forward to a future where the basic requirement for energy will provide ample opportunity for continued involvement in the development of natural resources.

The headquarters of Eastern Gas and Fuel Associates is now located in this modern office building in the heart of downtown Boston at One Beacon Street.

WARNER AND STACKPOLE

The *Directory of the City of Boston* in November 1874 recorded that Joseph B. Warner and James J. Myers commenced the practice of law at 39 Court Street, an area with a very different atmosphere from that which exists today. Their three fireplaced rooms overlooked the Courthouse in Court Square, a building that housed the Supreme Judicial Court, all sessions of the Municipal Court for Boston, offices of the sheriff, and, in the basement, a police station with cells. This site, in Boston's Suffolk County, is now occupied by City Hall Annex.

Economic uncertainty and inflation following the Civil War culminated in the Panic of 1873, and the times dictated the type of law to be practiced. Early cases involved financial default, breach of contract, personal injury, and property damage, the intricacies of which were carried out with the kind of machinery a more modern generation would find difficult to appreciate. Telephones, typewriters, and electric lighting were unknown

entities in the 1874 law office. All documentary work, pleadings, letters, and copies of same were handwritten; appointments were arranged by messenger or by mail; shelves holding papers and books constituted a library.

Having met as freshmen at Harvard College in the Class of 1869 and later at Harvard Law School, Warner and Myers continued in practice until the mid-1890s when Myers became a member and later the speaker of the Massachusetts House of Representatives. Following Myers' departure, Henry E. Warner joined his brother in the new firm of Warner and Warner with offices at the "new" 53 State Street building and remained a dominant partner until 1930.

The nature of law practice shifted according to the times and needs of clients. The large percentage of personal law cases in the courts and the exercise of the firm's customs practice diminished with the enactment of antitrust laws in 1915 and the federal income tax in 1913. Modern American law, with its emphasis on regulation and statutory law, began in the 1930s.

The small law practice maintained a continuity with the times and grew over the years in size and range of capabilities to become a recognized firm. Distinguished partners joining, who subsequently played an important part in its development and contributions, were Charles Stetson, E. Barton Chapin, and William J. Speers, Jr. Pierpont Stackpole's association began in 1900 and his administrative expertise added greatly to his prominence as a Boston attorney for many years. By 1960 the firm retained 30 attorneys.

Today Warner and Stackpole is a full-service general-practice law

firm. Its client base is local, regional, and national in scope, representing companies in both public and private sectors and in most major industries. A staff of approximately 75 attorneys, backed by a full complement of paralegal, administrative, and support personnel, provides counsel in seven principal areas of practice: business law, real estate/environmental law, litigation, tax, probate law, bankruptcy, and health care law.

A leading law firm and one of the city's oldest, Warner and Stackpole, following a 60-year residence at 84 State Street, now is located in offices at 28 State, which house its computer systems used for legal research and data collection. A significant amount of work is done by the firm on behalf of charitable and educational entities.

James Jefferson Myers co-founded Warner and Stackpole in 1874, and later became speaker of the House of Representatives of the Commonwealth of Massachusetts.

Joseph Bangs Warner, co-founder of Warner and Stackpole.

BOSTON COLLEGE

The history of Boston College and its founding surely is the history of the exodus of Irish Catholics from the political and economic climate of their native land and their subsequent immigration to America. Without the latter, the first would not have occurred as early as 1863.

Fleeing Ireland's Potato Famine in the mid-19th century, they came—130,000 strong—to Boston's English-flavored culture. Deprived by circumstances of the times, but with a yearning that their children might take their place in the democratic administration of this country, the immigrant population determined to prepare their sons for positions of trust and responsibility. Bound together by religion, ethnic background, and class, they were eager to contribute to the funding and support of a college that would accept their youth.

The human agent chiefly responsible for the creation of Boston's Jesuit college was the Reverend John McElroy, S.J. Experiencing more problems because of animosity between the Yankees and the Irish than because of finances, Father McElroy, after 16 years of courageous planning, overcame the opposition and was able to secure 65,000 square feet of property on Harrison Avenue and James Street in the South End and, in 1863, to obtain a charter for the school's incorporation. Three buildings were erected and, on September 5, 1864, with 22 students and three teachers, Boston College opened its doors.

A traditional classical curriculum common to the times and comparable to the program of the early American college was adopted. The goals of the Jesuit program of study, derived from the University of Paris, were to provide a broad liberal education, emphasizing intellectual achievement and

scholarly research and, as important, a development of moral, spiritual, and social values.

Enrollment remained small, surpassing 200 for the first time in 1899, and the college began to outgrow its urban facility. The recent extension of the trolley line to Lake Street along Commonwealth Avenue prompted the college's imaginative and daring new president, the Reverend Thomas Ignatius Gasson, to acquire four parcels of land in rural Chestnut Hill. Plans for a second era at a dramatic new university campus commenced. Promulgated by Father Gasson, a $10-million fund-raising effort and an architectural competition culminated on January 20, 1908, in the grounds dedication of "University Heights"—so-named by Father Gasson.

The move from the South End took place in 1913, with the completion of landmark Gasson Hall. By 1928 three additional buildings had been added—St. Mary's, Devlin, and Bapst. Together the four structures constituted one of the nation's outstanding clusters of Gothic architecture.

Enrollment had risen, passing 1,000 in 1925 and 1,500 during the

The campus, including war surplus building, in 1951.

Depression years. A classical-philosophical curriculum held sway and the emphasis remained on undergraduate education. But, as the physical setting of the college expanded, so too did the curriculum widen to offer greater numbers of programs and courses. In its second half-century, Boston College began to fill the dimensions of its university charter. The Summer Session was inaugurated in 1924; the Graduate School of Arts and Sciences in 1925; the Law School, 1929; the Evening College, 1929; the Graduate School of Social Work, 1936; the College of Business Administration, 1938. The latter, along with its Graduate School, established in 1957, is now known as the School of Management. The Schools of Nursing and Education were founded in 1947 and 1952, respectively. Weston Observatory was accepted as a department of Boston College in 1947, offering courses in geophysics and geology to graduate students. Thus, from a once-small liberal arts commuter college with an enrollment limited to only males living in the greater Boston area, the school eventually

The Rotunda, Gasson Hall.

evolved into one of the larger coeducational universities in the country conferring a variety of degrees.

The conclusion of World War II brought an avalanche of students to The Heights and enrollment passed 5,000 in 1948. Purchases of adjacent land and the filling in of the smaller of two reservoirs to accommodate student housing and athletic facilities doubled its property, and by the early '50s new buildings surrounded Gasson Hall to form the upper and lower campuses and centralize all schools.

Pressures from graduate and professional schools for specialized college preparation led to the modification of the school's former curriculum. Under the presidencies of the Reverends Joseph R.N. Maxwell (1951-1958), Michael P. Walsh (1958-1968), and W. Seavey Joyce (1968-1972), Boston College attracted a large and distinguished faculty, departments were strengthened in personnel and resources, new majors and honors programs were initiated, and graduate offerings were enlarged. Three doctoral programs were

authorized in 1952, eventually to grow to 14. The efforts of the faculty and administration in this period gave the institution its greatest forward thrust toward quality programs and a reputation for academic excellence. The maximum and balanced development of the individual is part of the Boston College educational tradition, and the pursuit of this objective was furthered by the scholarly and personal commitment of the expanded faculty.

Boston College, as an academic community, continued to grow in numbers and in attractiveness in the '70s. In 1972 the Reverend J. Donald Monan, Jesuit-philosopher, became its 24th president and reestablished the university following the difficult period of student unrest in higher education in America. Under his sound administration, the school gained new direction, streamlined fiscal management (which included the commissioning of a long-range financial planning body with its goal the most ambitious fund-raising program to date), broadened programs, and increased applications. In a decade of turmoil, the college grew in national recognition and influence.

The 1974 acquisition of the property and facilities of Newton College of the Sacred Heart expanded the physical plant by one-third, and its 15 Georgian buildings set on a parklike estate of 40 acres located one and one-half miles from the main campus now house the Law School. The early '80s saw the restoration of Gasson Hall and Bapst and the completion of a theater and a $28-million research library.

Meanwhile, the school's alumni had swelled to include fourth-generation graduates and

families with 25 BC graduates. Boston College can be proud of the leaders who have moved through its halls; they have more than justified the hopes of its founders and supporters born so long ago. Graduates have achieved positions of prominence in almost every form of professional and business endeavor, and there is pride among their number in the rise of their fellow sons—and an occasional daughter—to the heights of state and federal government. First among them is its silver-haired patriarch, Speaker of the U.S. House of Representatives Thomas P. "Tip" O'Neill, Jr., in whose name a university professorial chair has been endowed and for whom a new research library has been named.

Boston College was founded and preserved by men of vision, of courage, of faith, of perseverance; it happened they were men also of humility. The vision of a greater Boston College was realized through the ability of its leaders as well as the combined efforts of countless friends in every period, and the size of the present institution bears testimony to this devotion. The Boston College of today is the largest Catholic school in the nation and one of its leading universities. With full- and part-time enrollment of over 14,000 students attending 11 schools and institutes offering 13 degree programs, women comprise 57 percent. Some 40 states and 27 countries are represented in the freshman class. Of the 700 full-time equivalent faculty, 40 are Jesuits.

Certainly, the present has fulfilled the promises of the past, but what of the aspirations of the future? Father Monan explains: "Each stage of excellence we attain will be a stimulus to continue to reach."

THE BOSTON GLOBE

It's a wonder, with hindsight of more than a century, that *The Boston Globe*—the dominant news and advertising medium of New England, winner of 11 Pulitzer prizes, and a friend to hundreds of thousands of readers every day of the week and on Sunday—was ever started.

For one thing, none of the handful of wealthy men who originally financed *The Globe* had ever run a newspaper. For another, Boston in 1872 already had more newspapers than its population of 250,000 could support. Surely, had any of the seven prominent businessmen who gathered to incorporate *The Globe* on February 7, 1872, thought to consult his State Street broker, he would have been advised against so precarious a venture.

But the merchants listened instead to Maturin Ballou's promise of something new—"a superior commercial and business journal, of outspoken independence," offering eight pages to sell at four cents. Three of five floors in a building on Washington Street's "Newspaper Row," taken over for the new paper, would house *The Globe* for 86 years, though not long for Maturin Ballou's version.

The entrepreneurs of the new publication, intending to produce a better one and expecting it to be profitable, put up the hefty sum of $150,000; it would not be sufficient to cover costs. The new newspaper made little impact. In its first year, circulation never exceeded more than 5,000, as compared with *The Herald*'s 90,000, *The Advertiser*'s 17,000, and *The Journal*'s 35,000. Within 12 months the entire amount was gone, a deep depression had set in, and *The Globe* was near bankruptcy.

The proprietors turned to Chas. H. (General) Taylor, then

Gen. Chas. H. Taylor, publisher, 1873-1921.

publisher of *American Homes Magazine* and, at 27, an already experienced soldier, printer, journalist, publisher, and politician. Taylor, who had apprenticed at *The Traveler* as a staff reporter and also as a correspondent for Horace Greeley's *New York Tribune,* had become recognized as one of the leading newspapermen in Boston, and tentatively agreed, in 1873, to come on board as general manager for a few weeks. He never left.

The only one of the original incorporators to stay the course was Eben Jordan, self-made merchant prince and founder of Boston's largest department store. Sponsor Jordan backed a new financial arrangement and *The Globe* turned the corner to success under a new concept—quite different from Ballou's—of what a Boston newspaper should be. Chas. H. Taylor (he never used Charles) became nominal owner of the paper, without any capital in it; Jordan, nominally only a creditor, became in effect its owner. The joint ownership continued, through the heirs and estates of each, until the company became a public

William O. Taylor, publisher, 1921-1955.

corporation in 1973. On Eben's death in 1895, General Taylor, by agreement, purchased enough shares from his estate to gain one-half ownership in *The Boston Globe.*

Now his to make or break, he decided to make a radical breakthrough in newspaper methods by turning a losing morning newspaper into an all-day newspaper; changing *The Globe* from Republican to Independent Democrat and inaugurating a new policy (rare in that day of partisan journalism) to deal impartially with political news; giving the paper a family dimension by introducing material aimed at women and children; and reducing its price to two cents. He did all this at once, and launched his reorganized *Globe* on March 4, 1878. By 6 p.m. that day, with its Hoe press clanking overtime, 50,000 copies had been sold. The first evening edition was introduced on March 7; *The Sunday Globe* on March 10.

General Taylor had broken with tradition, assumed a new viewpoint in newspapering, and made *The Globe* the most innovative newspaper in Boston. In less than

William Davis Taylor, publisher, 1955-1977.

William O. Taylor II, current publisher, 1978-.

three years *Globe* circulation rose from 8,000 to 30,000; within 10 years it became the dominant newspaper of the region.

Introducing into American journalism a new note of tolerance and the objective point of view, he was one of the first to glimpse the possibilities of the 20th-century concept of newspapers as an instrument of social service.

The year 1921 brought the death of then editor and publisher Chas. Taylor. Since then, management of *The Globe* has continued in the hands of the Taylor family, first under his son, William O. Taylor (1921-1955), later under his grandson, William Davis Taylor (1955-1977), and currently under his great-grandson, William O. Taylor II. The Taylor tradition has been the unifying and progressive force behind *The Globe* that continues to this day.

Thus *The Globe* survived through depression, wartime restrictions, and competition. With innovation and promotion, the smallest member of the Boston press in 1872 became the leader in readership. By the turn of the century, in a Boston populace of

560,000, sales were 200,000 daily, more than 150,000 on Sunday. Circulation dominance continued until the mid-1930s when, in an over-newspapered city (there were nine), *The Globe* fell to third place, to regain by the end of the decade its present preeminence. Recognized by *Time* magazine as one of the nation's 10 best newspapers, *The Globe* is the 15th-largest daily and 8th-largest Sunday paper in the country. Currently, *The Globe* assumes advertising lineage supremacy as well; more than 80 percent of all advertising placed in Boston newspapers is carried in *The Globe.*

Since the 1950s much of the publication's gain has been owed to improvements in the product. Sophisticated research and expanded editorial coverage have combined to improve the depth of coverage in such areas as education, the economy, the arts, science and medicine, sports, and religion. More recently, several new once-a-week sections have been added to broaden the paper's appeal. The process of gathering and disseminating the news itself in an electronic information age

has meant dramatic change at *The Globe.* In the three-story, 11-acre, computerized Morrissey Boulevard plant that has been *The Globe's* home since 1958, video display terminals have replaced newsroom typewriters, and direct lithography and offset methods have superseded the traditional letterpress method of printing. And expansion of communications technology continues. In 1983 *The Globe* opened its $43-million satellite printing plant at Billerica, Massachusetts, to accommodate all of the paper's future needs for expanded printing capacity.

But bricks and mortar are by no means *The Globe's* only concern. The newspaper sponsors a variety of public-service programs that help enhance the academic, cultural, and social climate of its community. Among its efforts are an annual book festival, jazz festival, art and drama competitions for high school students, annual science fair and photography contests, high school journalism workshops, sports clinics, and Globe Santa. In addition, The Boston Globe Foundation, a nonprofit organization, was created in 1982 to give financial support to New England's worthy organizations and agencies.

A subsidiary of Affiliated Publications, Inc., *The Globe* is currently expanding its overseas commitment. In the past two years it has opened foreign bureaus in London and Tokyo, and plans to open a third bureau in the Middle East in January 1985.

As always, since the time of its founding in 1872, *The Boston Globe* continues to be committed to editorial excellence, circulation growth, the spirit of the First Amendment, and corporate responsibility to the community it serves.

BOSTON UNIVERSITY

Dr. John R. Silber, president of Boston University.

Boston University was founded at a convention of New England Friends of Improved Theological Training held in Boston in April 1839. For the next 28 years the school was located in northern New England, first in Newbury, Vermont, and later at Concord, New Hampshire. In 1867 it moved to Boston where it was called the Boston Theological Seminary. In May 1869 the Commonwealth of Massachusetts made seminary president Isaac Rich, vice-president Lee Claflin, and treasurer Jacob Sleeper and their associates and successors, a "body corporate forever" under the name of the Trustees of Boston University. In establishing the university as a means of promoting learning, virtue, and piety, the founders specifically sought to offer educational opportunities to men and women in "all departments of science and the arts."

During the university's first decade, five schools and colleges were added to the original Department of Theology, which became a school in 1871. These were Law, Medicine, Liberal Arts, Music, and the Graduate School. In the 20th

century, many other programs were slowly added. Boston University now offers degrees through 16 schools and colleges and two independent programs: Program in Artisanry, School for the Arts, College of Basic Studies, Goldman School of Graduate Dentistry, School of Education, College of Engineering, Graduate School, School of Law, College of Liberal Arts, School of Management, School of Medicine, Metropolitan College, School of Nursing, School of Public Communication, Sargent College of Allied Health Professions, School of Social Work, School of Theology, and the University Professors Program.

Boston University was first housed in a series of buildings around the top of Beacon Hill, Copley Square, and the South End. During the 1920s plans were developed to bring together the several schools and colleges in one location along the Charles River between Bay State Road and Commonwealth Avenue. The Great Depression set back these plans, however, and only the Charles Hayden Memorial (1938) had been completed when World War II broke out. After the war construction was resumed, and by 1966 all colleges and schools were located on the Charles River

Campus with the exception of the School of Medicine and the School of Graduate Dentistry, which remained in their original locations. The latter two schools, with the Massachusetts Memorial Hospital (renamed University Hospital in 1965), became the members of the Boston University Medical Center, established in 1959.

In the ten years from 1971 to 1981 the university acquired by purchase or gift a total of 96 new properties. Sixty-three were used to meet a growing demand for on-campus housing for students, faculty, and staff; the rest were put to academic and general use. During this era the Charles River Campus was transformed into a more beautiful and graceful place, with many mini-parks and tree-lined streets.

Early in 1982 Boston University began a major construction and renovation project to upgrade facilities for the sciences and engineering. The Center for the Sciences and Engineering features newly renovated buildings at

The skyline of Boston with Boston University's Charles River Campus in the foreground. Dominating the campus skyline is the 18-story School of Law Tower. The riverbank park was designed by Frederick Law Olmsted, designer of New York City's Central Park.

Before moving to its Charles River Campus following World War II, the schools and colleges of Boston University were scattered throughout Back Bay and Beacon Hill neighborhoods, such as this site at 20 Beacon Street.

586-596 Commonwealth Avenue, which provide over one-quarter of a million square feet for instructional and research activities in biology, chemistry, and physics. The project extends along Cummington Street, with facilities for a science library, computer sciences, mathematics and academic computing, and new and renovated buildings for the College of Engineering.

In 1983 Boston University opened the largest bookstore in New England. In the heart of Kenmore Square at the east end of the university's Charles River Campus, the new bookstore is a 70,000-square-foot, seven-floor vertical mall. Georgian and Regency motifs have been used throughout to suggest the architectural charm of neighboring Bay State Road brownstones. With 440,000 volumes of textbooks, reference books, general trade books, and children's books, and 18 specialty shops, the new Boston University Bookstore is a significant addition, not merely to the campus, but to the City of Boston

and the New England area.

The physical growth of Boston University has been more than matched by additions to its academic programs and by a growing recognition of its superior contributions to teaching and scholarship. In 1971 a new administration brought with it a comprehensive vision of the university's destiny. Its seventh president, John R. Silber, and its board of trustees undertook a sustained drive toward new levels of excellence and scholarship. Distinguished teachers and scholars from throughout the world were recruited to build upon the university's solid foundation in the arts and sciences and many professional fields and to develop new educational opportunities that combine specialized training with intellectual and professional breadth. Thirteen years later, with its multitude of resources and a faculty increased to number 2,600, Boston University has achieved distinction as an institution of academic excellence and transformed itself into a national university of international significance.

From its modest beginnings and after a century of slow growth, Boston University has emerged as the fourth-largest independent insti-

tution in the nation. Its student body of over 28,100 students (approximately 19,000 full-time and 9,100 part-time), come from every part of the nation and from more than 100 foreign countries.

Through its schools and colleges, the university offers 2 associate degrees, 3 certificate programs, 13 bachelor's degrees, 27 master's degrees, 4 certificates of advanced graduate study, 7 professional degrees, and 12 doctor's degrees.

In symbiotic relationship with the city of which it is a part, there is a mutually beneficial coexistence of Boston University and Boston. One of the city's largest employers, with 6,000 employees, its Commonwealth Avenue campus on the banks of the Charles River is a 10-minute trolley ride from downtown; the city is not a supplement to the student's education, but an essential part of it.

Supported by the confidence of all its constituencies and of the city of which it is a part, Boston University is equal to the task of the challenges of its next decades.

The stately brownstone town houses along Bay State Road in Boston's Back Bay exemplify dormitory life on an urban campus. These homes are part of Boston University's housing facilities.

GEORGE B.H. MACOMBER COMPANY

It requires the combination of technical expertise and years of experience for a builder to know the best way of transforming an architect's plan into a concrete, steel, brick, and glass reality. A successful building reflects a careful balancing of the aesthetic demands of the architect, the program needs and economic constraints of the owner, and the practical limitations of men and materials. For 80 years the George B.H. Macomber Company, a family-owned business in its third generation, has strived to achieve that balance for owners and architects throughout the greater New England area. During this time, the Macomber personnel have developed a wide range of imaginative, innovative construction and management capabilities, having successfully produced buildings that have won numerous architectural and construction awards.

The founder of the firm that bears his name began his lifelong career at the age of 11 as a water boy. His "super" was Charles Clark, whose daughter, Grace, he would later marry. By 1904, at age 36, having broadened his expertise and knowing he knew how to "Build It Right," George B.H. Macomber began a journey toward an eventual legacy of a tradition of shared growth with New England through the company's integral part in the development of some of America's greatest institutions.

The first project for the young enterprise was the construction of the 11-story Post Office Square Building at 79 Milk Street, one of the first structural steel buildings in the United States. Others quickly followed: the Gilchrest Building; Boston Edison Company; the Blake Building; the Paramount Theater; the Engineer's Club (now Emerson College); the Essex

Faneuil Hall Marketplace, Inc. Benjamin Thompson & Associates, Inc., Architects.

Building; and the Dexter Building.

C. Clark Macomber assumed the reins of the organization upon the death of his father in 1927. The former Harvard football All-American remained president for 32 years of

The Devonshire, Washington Street. Steffian. Bradley Associates, Inc., Architects.

continued growth in often difficult times. Remaining solvent through the severe Depression years and the complicated labor-management relationships of the times, Clark implemented "Construction Management," an imaginative and most effective way of satisfying an owner's building needs by treating the project planning, design, and construction phases as integrated tasks within a system.

The majority of Macomber's work continues to be done under the Construction Management Negotiated Contract Basis.

The aftermath of the war brought jobs in a wider area; school, office, and industrial buildings formed a large part of the company's work. Clark Macomber's tenure saw the completion, in 1951, of the country's first regional shopping mall—Shopper's World in Framingham, Massachusetts. Other highlights of these years included the building of such recreational facilities as the Skating Club of Boston on Soldiers Field Road, and the David S. Ingalls Hockey Rink at Yale University.

A new era commenced in 1959

when George Macomber, son of Clark, an MIT graduate, two-time U.S. Olympic skier ('48 and '52), and honored member of the National Ski Hall of Fame, became president. In the ensuing years technological advances and regulatory restrictions meant new interpretations of buildings, new innovations, and new challenges for one of the most respected construction firms in the country. Quality building in a modern age is a highly complex process involving coordination of efforts of many factions.

Under the leadership of George Macomber, the firm increased its participation in the construction and restoration of the area's built environment, while adhering to the same values and principles of service of its founder, his grandfather, and his father, and a continuity of growth was maintained.

Linking building design to building function, recognition for excellence began in the '60s with a succession of awards. Many of the buildings receiving these awards are familiar landmarks: C. Thurston Chase Learning Center at Eaglebrook School, Deerfield; Brandeis University, Brandeis Academic Quadrangle; First and Second Church, Boston; Faneuil Hall Marketplace, Boston; The Car

Massachusetts General Hospital, Cox Management Center. Perry, Dean Partners, Architects.

Barn, New Bedford; the Art & Architecture Building, Center for British Art, Yale University; and University Place, Cambridge, Massachusetts.

Leading American architects with whom Macomber has worked include I.M. Pei, Louis I. Kahn, Eero Saarinen, Paul Rudolph, Hugh Stubbins, The Architects Collaborative, Philip Johnson, Benjamin Thompson & Associates, and Skidmore, Owings & Merrill.

Church Court Condominiums. Graham Gund & Associates, Architects.
© Steve Rosenthal, photographer.

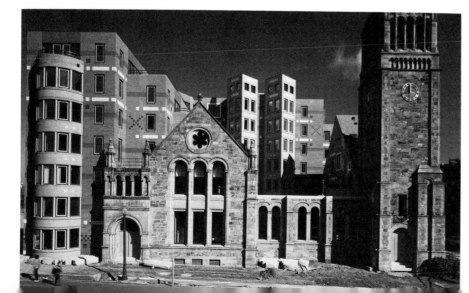

Macomber's guiding precept is to build "to specification, to schedule, and to budget." The firm's ability to do so has resulted in it being retained to perform repeat projects for many satisfied clients.

The Macomber Company progressed into the '70s, constructing thousands of multiple housing units, including extensive building to meet the special needs of the elderly. These years also brought the completion of the restoration of Boston's historically famous edifices: Faneuil Hall Marketplace; The Devonshire, on Washington Street in Boston; and University Place, in Harvard Square. The Four Seasons luxury hotel and condominium structure will be finished in early 1985.

Through its company history, the Macomber family has been proud to have had its important role in the preservation of New England's rich and varied architectural heritage. Today with a $100-million-volume operation, Macomber Company averages 20 percent minority employment company-wide and actively encourages the hiring of women in construction jobs. A fourth-generation Macomber is aboard—John D., son of George— and ensures that in the new Boston of the '80s and the decades beyond, George B.H. Macomber Company will continue to "Build It Right."

ARTHUR D. LITTLE, INC.

"Think tank with brains" said the headline of a recent *Barron's* article on Arthur D. Little, Inc., of Cambridge, Massachusetts.

The renowned worldwide technology and management consulting company prospers solving other people's problems, and proves that doing what others may deem impossible can be very possible if the right group of experts focus their efforts on the problem.

Arthur D. Little, Inc., was founded in 1886 to help industry utilize the technology beginning to emerge from universities. Today it helps industry, institutions, and governments adapt to and benefit from shifts in society, technology, and economics. The firm has a professional staff of specialists in several hundred disciplines and is unique in its ability to coordinate the interplay of the specific managerial, technological, and sociopolitical perspectives required to solve particular problems.

More simply, ADL is in the business of selling solutions and hands-on help. From its eight-building, 40-acre headquarters at Acorn Park, the oldest consulting firm in the world turns problems into profits. It deals with the effects of change—external and internal—on industrial and governmental clients in 60 countries on six continents. The 5,000 assignments it handles each year cover agribusiness, telecommunications, health care, economic development, energy, and new-product development.

The ADL professional staff handles megaprojects like setting up an advanced telecommunications system for Saudi Arabia and helping Third World countries with their economic and industrial development. It also focuses on straightforward issues like designing computer-assisted dispatch systems for police departments, corporate organization and development, and helping hospitals to cut their operating costs.

ADL was founded by Dr. Arthur Dehon Little, a 23-year-old chemist-businessman. He opened an analytic testing laboratory. The company's Memorial Drive building, now devoted to research in the life sciences and biotechnology, has been designated a national historical landmark as the birthplace of contract research.

Over the years a long list of "firsts" have emanated from ADL. In 1903 the firm wove the first commercial textile fiber from cellulose acetate, and in 1911 it helped General Motors plan and establish the first corporate research center. In 1925 ADL synthesized the iso-octane compound used for the first antiknock gasoline, and 14 years later it developed the Kleinschmidt Still, used for converting saltwater into fresh. Another first came in 1964 when it launched a program to train managers from developing countries. That program evolved into the Arthur D. Little Management Education Institute, a fully accredited academic institution, which grants a master's degree in management to students completing its 11-month intensive program.

More recently Arthur D. Little, Inc., has developed and patented the concept of generating electricity from solar-powered satellites, developed most of the thermal probes implanted in the lunar surface by the *Apollo 15* mission, and helped design the first interactive fiber-optic cable television system near Osaka, Japan. ADL has patented several thousand products and processes.

ADL has tripled in size in the last decade. Once chiefly in the business of rendering technological development and consulting, the company has evolved into a diverse full-service consulting firm with management counseling services as important as technology. John F. Magee, who began his career as a member of the consulting staff, is president and chief executive officer. Arthur D. Little is now a publicly traded company; the majority of its shares are held by the employees' retirement trust.

Whether researching complex cases with global implications or implementing more simple nuts-and-bolts projects, brain power is the major resource of Arthur D. Little, Inc. Diversity is its strength, its people and reputation are its assets, and a roomful of selected experts are its weapons.

The company attracts people from all over the world. Here John F. Magee, president and chief executive officer, chats with students attending the Arthur D. Little Management Education Institute, which grants a master's degree in management. Photographer, Lee Lockwood.

JOHN HANCOCK MUTUAL LIFE INSURANCE COMPANY

Under the best of circumstances, the beginning of any new enterprise carries with it elements of risk and uncertainty. In time of crisis, the odds rise steeply.

When the John Hancock Mutual Life Insurance Company was chartered in 1862, the Civil War was raging into its second year. Eleven states had seceded from the Union and more than two million men were under arms.

In retrospect, a nation torn by dissent and drained by debt now seems an unlikely proving ground for an untried business. Yet with only a handful of agents, and a one-room office in Boston's financial district, the fledgling organization reported that 287 policies had been written in its first full year of operation. And by the end of the decade assets reached two million dollars, with nearly 10 times that amount of insurance in force.

The financial Panic of 1873 and the long depression that followed

The first office of the John Hancock Mutual Life Insurance Company at 41 State Street in 1862.

was the first crucial test of strength. Twenty-one insurance firms had already failed, and thousands were jobless in the wake of widespread business failures.

The Hancock not only met all its obligations, but also emerged from the debacle with heightened awareness of the compelling need for insurance in helping to preserve the fabric of family life. In 1879 it became the first mutual company to introduce weekly premium policies for workers of limited means.

Scaling down premiums to an affordable level was clearly an idea right for the times. The ready market for smaller policies lent an impetus to corporate growth that extended well into the next century.

As the nation continued to prosper, funds invested on behalf of Hancock policyholders played a significant role in the development of both the public and private sectors. It was, in fact, this expertise—refined and honed for more than a hundred years—that prompted a major change in the company's strategic plans.

Alert to the growing sophistication of the American investors, management determined to build on demonstrated strengths by integrating traditional lines of individual and group insurance with a full spectrum of financial products and services. The success of its entry into the mutual fund market in 1968 led to the formation or acquisition of 14 more subsidiaries over the next decade.

Collectively known as the John Hancock Companies, they offer a diversified range of investment vehicles, money management, administrative, brokerage, pension, and advisory services to individuals, corporations, and institutional clients.

The award-winning John Hancock mirrored glass tower took its place in the skyline at Copley Square in 1976.

For nearly a century and a quarter the Hancock's underlying purpose has remained constant. The foundation stone is insurance protection in all its forms, domestic and worldwide. As one of the leading organizations of its kind in the nation, the new family of companies also intends to be a major provider of investor-related instruments for financial appreciation and security.

Generations of policyholders have placed their confidence in the John Hancock Mutual Life Insurance Company. Continuing to fulfill that responsibility by serving the financial needs of present and future generations is both a commitment and a valued trust.

ARTHUR ANDERSEN & CO.

Arthur Andersen & Co. is a worldwide, multidimensional organization engaged in the broad business of accounting and auditing, tax consulting, and management information consulting. Clients numbering in the tens of thousands cover a broad spectrum—from high-net-worth individuals to the world's best-known business, industrial, governmental, and institutional organizations. Headquartered in Chicago and Geneva, the firm has offices in 70 U.S. cities and in 41 countries abroad. Approximately 25,000 people form the Arthur Andersen global community.

A decision to serve New England clients in an environ closer than New York prompted the firm's entrance on the Boston business scene following the Great Depression. In 1937 Harry I. Prankard II opened the office, and in the '40s Paul Swantee became

William F. Meagher, managing partner, Arthur Andersen-Boston.

manager-in-charge. George W. Pierce, now a retired partner who was important to the early development of the office, was loaned to Boston from New York in 1939. Returning permanently in 1941, he directed the office from 1943 until 1953.

When the firm entered the Boston business scene in the late '30s, it was virtually unknown. Its clients came from the New York office and included paper mills, boat yards, a dairy company, and several woolen mills. Expansion began in earnest during the '50s and continued into the '60s with the emergence of high technology and electronics as growth industries. A number of financial clients were added and utility work also increased.

Walter J. Oliphant transferred from Chicago to Boston, arriving as managing partner in 1953. He returned to Chicago in 1959 and John March became managing partner. Thomas A. Sampson, who was admitted to the partnership in 1962, took over the Boston office in 1965 when John March transferred to Chicago and remained managing partner until 1982. Sampson became one of the city's leaders when, during the '70s, he assumed the chairmanship of the board of directors of Boston 200, presidency of the Greater Boston Chamber of Commerce, chairmanship of the 1978 United Way of Massachusetts Bay campaign, and presidency of Jobs for Massachusetts.

Arthur Andersen-Boston doubled in size between 1960 and 1965, and again between 1965 and 1970 as the high-technology and service industries of the area continued to expand and the practice reacted to the growth of the specialized industry segments. In need of qualified personnel to meet its demands, the Boston office is

Thomas A. Sampson, area manager for Arthur Andersen & Co.

fortunate in its ability to draw from the many highly regarded colleges and universities located nearby. Today the firm's Boston office, located in the heart of the city's financial district, offers to its 500 personnel tremendous opportunity for quality training and professional development.

William F. Meagher, managing partner since 1982, believes the future is bright in Boston for a firm like Arthur Andersen & Co. that is willing to make the commitment of resource and involvement with the community. As Boston and its surrounding communities continue to grow and prosper, Arthur Andersen will, as it has in the past 45 years, play a significant role in the city's future, with a highly skilled staff of professionals committed to superior service and innovation.

BOSTON EDISON COMPANY

It was Victorian Boston and the setting was the gala opening of the spectacular Bijou Theatre on Washington Street. John L. Sullivan, the great boxer, and Hugh O'Brien, the first immigrant mayor, ruled the city that President Grover Cleveland would visit in this year of 1886. Liberated ladies, wearing pants for the first time, were breaking loose on bicycles. The filling in of the Back Bay neared completion, Copley Square with its new Trinity Church was the city's cultural center, and the North End was becoming Italian when, on the evening of February 20, Boston Edison—then the Edison Electric Illuminating Co.—started lighting its city. Rooftop lines were extended from its Head Place Station, and a 200-horsepower boiler and a 90-horsepower engine driving two Edison K-type dynamos started pumping direct current to the stage of the first theater in America to be so illuminated.

Electric lighting had crept into the city's world of gas as early as 1875; the radical novelty first appeared at Barnum's Circus on Boston Common and later on Scollay Square's sidewalks. But it wasn't until October 21, 1879, at Menlo Park, New Jersey, when Thomas Alva Edison perfected his gift to humanity that the remarkable contribution to the advancement of civilization was created in the form of an electric incandescent lamp for commercial use.

With capital of $100,000 and control of the patents of Thomas Edison, the Edison Electric Illuminating Co. was organized on December 26, 1885, despite apprehension that the competitive source of lighting would attract a limited market. By first-year's end the company owned new miles of

Thomas Alva Edison (left) and Charles L. Edgar, president of Boston Edison Company (then Edison Electric Illuminating Co.), circa 1930.

overhead lines extending to 70 acres and was servicing 260 customers.

The postwar Hub expanded to 30 times its original size by the end of the century, growing in population and accelerating in industrialization, and the new company became an integral part of the growth, its name synonymous with a unified central system providing light and power to 40 communities. In 1900 Charles Leavitt Edgar, electrical engineer and protege of the prolific inventor, became president, and for the next 32 years directed tremendous changes in the complex art of producing and distributing dependable electrical service as it revolutionized economic and material progress. These years saw underground transmission of power

by cable, circuit breakers, advanced engines, and the world's first high-pressure turbine generating current from the new L Street and Edgar stations.

The Edison Electric Illuminating Co. became Boston Edison Company and in 1941 James V. Toner its chief operating officer. Mystic Station opened to accommodate a larger capacity for war industries and postwar growth years. Coincidental with increased demands were benchmarks of technological progress and vast improvements in consumer service and energy use. The '50s brought Route 128, its research firms and industrial parks, and a new challenge, under president Thomas G. Dignan, to provide generation as well as transmission for the electronic highway.

By 1961 Boston Edison was servicing 487,500 customers and was continuing to build generation to meet a downtown building boom and a new electric home heating market. The 30-year sustained growth continued into the '70s with the building of Pilgrim Station, the firm's nuclear power plant. But the oil embargo of 1973 created a climate of change and a need for a more efficient use of energy. In 1982 Boston Edison introduced IMPACT 2000, an energy plan for developing and implementing programs into the next century to reduce dependence on foreign oil, to minimize the need for new capacity, and to secure the area's energy supply.

In an industry that changed the life and landscape of America, Boston Edison Company, under chairman Thomas J. Galligan, Jr., approaches its 100th year of anticipating and servicing the needs of the now two million industrial, residential, and commercial consumers of its community.

PRUDENTIAL INSURANCE COMPANY OF AMERICA

The post-World War II building boom that hit many American cities bypassed Boston. The aftermath of an economical, political, and class struggle dominating the city in the first half of the 20th century had created a climate of stagnation, and the business and financial communities were convinced that Boston was a hopelessly antibusiness environment. Construction of office buildings in the city was an incalculable risk; few had been built in the '30s, '40s, and '50s.

Prudential Insurance Company of America was a pioneer in the revival of downtown Boston as a center of commerce when in 1965 it built Prudential Center—the city's first modern skyscraper. Erected on the site of the blighted railroad yards of the Back Bay, the $250-million Prudential Center sparked urban renewal and Boston stood taller. The structure would remain a major presence during the physical transformation and resurgence of the city of the later '60s and '70s.

Prudential Center is a uniquely conceived complex of civic, business, and residential housing. The heart of the superstructure and grandparent of today's skyline is its 52-story tower. Rising 750 feet above a landscaped plaza, the tower is set in a wide moat spanned at four points by access bridges, and contains one million feet of office space. The window glass wall of its 50th-floor public skywalk offers a 360-degree panoramic view of the old—and now the new—Boston.

The 32-acre site today houses 12 modern structures, including the 1,400-room Sheraton-Boston Hotel, four low-rise commercial buildings, another 25-story office tower, the Massachusett's Convention Center Authority's John B. Hynes Civic Auditorium, 34 retail stores, including Lord and Taylor and Saks Fifth Avenue, and three 28-story apartment buildings. Five acres of landscaped plazas and parks surround the base of the complex. Remaining space is devoted to enclosed shopping pavilions, an outdoor exhibition arcade, and a three-level parking facility with a 3,000-car capacity.

For the thousands of Bostonians working and living in the city, as well as countless numbers of visiting tourists, the Prudential Center has become a major focal point of city life. Accommodating over 35,000 visitors every day, it is the hub of many of the community's civic and cultural events, with a year-round program of public activities, many of which have become seasonal Boston traditions for guests and neighbors. Springtime officially comes to the Prudential with the April celebration of Patriot's Day and the internationally famous Boston Marathon. Prudential Center provides the finish line for the 26-mile, 385-yard course from Hopkinton, first run in 1897.

A more recent Boston tradition is the annual Christmas tree lighting and carol singing by more than 10,000 Bostonians who gather in front of the Prudential Tower Building every year to officially open the holiday season the first week of December. This Christmas tradition began with the late Arthur Fiedler, conductor of the world-famous Boston Pops Concerts, and a gift of a 60-foot Christmas tree sent to the people of Boston from the people of Nova Scotia, Canada. It is decorated with more than 15,000 multicolored lights and is the official City of Boston Christmas Tree.

Prudential's Northeast headquarters remained the center's prime tenant until January 1, 1984, when the insurance company consolidated eight regional offices in four U.S. locations. Now managed and operated by the R.M. Bradley Real Estate Company, the successful complex—one of Prudential's largest single real estate investments—will continue as a major asset to the company and to the Boston community.

A view from the Cambridge bank of the Charles River of the Prudential's 52-story tower and complex in Boston's Back Bay.

PEAT, MARWICK, MITCHELL & CO.

To commemorate its 75th anniversary, the Boston office of Peat Marwick has taken a lead role in launching a fund-raising effort by the business community for the much-needed refurbishing of the McKim Building of the Boston Public Library—which was designated a national historic landmark in 1973.

"The Boston Public Library is a vital component and symbol of the city's rich architectural, cultural, and educational heritage," says Herbert E. Morse, managing partner of the Boston office of Peat Marwick and a member of the firm's board of directors. "The library is not only a world-renowned treasure house of book collections and artwork but also a living example of the city's historic commitment to the advancement of learning and culture. We want to contribute to the renovation project so that we can give to the city something of what we have gained, to thank Boston for being such a good home to business."

Public accounting was new to North America when Scotsmen James Marwick and Simpson Roger Mitchell crossed the Atlantic in 1897 and established their New York practice. The partnership was soon reinforced by the merger with Sir William Peat of London's W.B. Peat & Co. In the intervening years the firm has opened 100 offices in the United States and, through Peat Marwick International, operates more than 200 offices in 81 other countries. One of the world's foremost accounting firms, Peat Marwick provides auditing and accounting, tax, and management consulting services to more than 50,000 clients worldwide.

The Boston office of Peat Marwick was opened in 1910. Over the years it has diversified to serve the full spectrum of Boston business, developing special competencies in retailing, manufacturing, banking, insurance, health care, higher education, municipalities, and high technology.

Today the Boston office's practice includes such prestigious Boston-area clients as Gillette, Polaroid, Tufts University, Stop & Shop, the Boston Bruins, Liberty Mutual, BayBanks, the Children's Hospital Medical Center, and the City of Boston. The scope of services has also expanded to meet the needs of clients. The office has specialists in data processing, employee benefits, executive compensation, executive search, manufacturing controls, government contracting, and many of the other specialized areas required by today's demanding and complex business environment.

Underscoring its commitment to specialized industries, Peat Marwick-Boston in 1983 became the first major accounting firm to bring a full-service suburban office to the area surrounding Route 128, "America's Technology Highway." A complement of 50 professionals proficient in those services required by growth-oriented, high-technology industries assist clients to identify and analyze business alternatives from a new Burlington, Massachusetts, office.

Peat Marwick's commitment to help in the Boston Public Library project is preceded by a long tradition of community service among the Boston and Burlington office partners, who actively support and participate in scores of civic and professional organizations. These include the Salvation Army, the Greater Boston Chamber of Commerce, the New England Aquarium, the Dana Farber Cancer Institute, the Boston Symphony Orchestra, the New England Council, the Institute of Contemporary Art, the French Library in Boston, the Beth Israel Hospital, the Boy Scouts, and the International Business Center of New England.

Boston Mayor Raymond Flynn and Peat Marwick's Herbert E. Morse, in the courtyard of the Boston Public Library, discuss the upcoming renovation of the McKim Building, which will be sponsored in part by a major corporate fund drive.

ERNST & WHINNEY

With capital of $500, a skill in managing figures, and an ambitious concept of accounting as a potentially vital force in assisting the success of an enterprise by producing information that could interpret and control its operations, brothers Alwin C. and Theodore C. Ernst launched a general accounting practice in Cleveland in 1903. Their venture began in an era when the scope of accounting in this country was, by and large, no more than the scope of bookkeeping. For most companies at the turn of the century, a condensed balance sheet and summarized income statement sufficed; "systems" were a recent thing and suspect. But, as the nation's business entered a period of unparalleled vigor, the times took their character from a burgeoning economy and from the great industrial mergers of the early 1900s, creating a new climate and stimulant for change in the discipline. There came not only examination of the accounts of the companies involved, but also closer attention to their accounting techniques.

The British influence on American accounting was dominant then. Industrial England had long been of age, and its firms were far advanced beyond their American counterparts. The creative principles of total information as interpreted by Ernst & Ernst had little precedent and were in contrast to the conservative English attitudes.

In 1906 Theodore Ernst asked for the return of his investment to take advantage of an opportunity in a more established line of business. A.C., less reserved about the future of the profession, continued to define his ideas and build his practice with determined interest in auditing and in the practical application of accounting theory. His convictions of what his profession should offer put him a length ahead of both business and accounting as they were then known and hastened the growth of his firm. Eventually, Ernst's vision would transform the small Cleveland practice into a prominent worldwide organization comprising 22,000 employees in more than 300 offices in 75 countries. By this time the firm name would be Ernst & Whinney—the year, 1984.

In 1917 Ernst & Ernst's annual volume surpassed one million dollars and the firm opened its ninth office in the stately old-new Boston of James Michael Curley. The city was home also to Alvin T. Wilkinson, a dentist with a desire to be of service to industry. A change of his professional career brought Dr. Wilkinson to Ernst & Ernst-Boston as managing partner, a position he would retain until his retirement in 1953.

The 16th Amendment to the Constitution allowing Congress to impose taxes on income became effective in 1913. Demands of

---

In 1903 Alwin C. Ernst, with his brother Theodore, founded the firm that would become today's Ernst & Whinney.

wartime 1917-1918 followed and the need for improved accounting procedures was clear and immediate. The profession found new areas to make financial reporting more useful in the second decade of accelerated growth for the Ernst firm.

The time-honored secret of success of the pioneer founder of modern accounting was hard work. A.C.'s exacting tradition of long hours and top-quality service was observed by Boston's staff of accounting technicians and business advisers. Ten hours per day they worked; six, sometimes seven, days per week, 52 weeks per year, representing the firm in client contact work and public service projects, as a local reputation grew and a client roster expanded to include a large amount of bank examinations and tax work. Success was gratifying. Ernst & Ernst-Boston flourished and was an important impetus in a network of what became, by 1922, the largest fully national accounting firm in the United States, enjoying vigorous growth commensurate with the growth of the economy.

By the late 1920s accounting had established its professional identity but still had to prove itself as a working partner of business. Its greatest growth in maturity was about to begin.

Federal regulations multiplied, in keeping with a philosophy of increased control being formulated in the federal government. In 1933 the Securities Act requiring that the annual statements of all listed corporations be accompanied by certificates of opinion from independent accountants was established; in 1934 the Securities Exchange Act was passed to regulate trade in the stock exchanges; in 1935 Social Security was enacted. A nation financially unnerved was suddenly much in need of the independence and reliability the accounting profession had long been building. But the flood of new accounting problems in the 1930s would not mean profitable business. Times were hard as a shadow fell across a financial scene that had just begun to brighten. For Ernst & Ernst, these were years of entrenchment and growth in depth rather than breadth.

However, changes in the profession followed World War II when accounting took on a new dimension in the framework of free enterprise. A growing business climate recognized the vital role of the accountant. The Boston firm tailored tax planning to meet the business or personal needs of owner/manager, evaluated and selected financial alternatives, assisted with inventory management, and helped prepare business plans for such diverse industries as banking, insurance,

Paul G. Smith, vice chairman and regional managing partner.

James G. Maguire, managing partner.

investment companies, sports, health care, printing, and publishing concerns. Its business doubled in the 1940s. It would again double by the end of the next decade.

In 1953 Eugene R. Halloran became managing partner, at the same time the small, scientifically oriented plants that now line Route 128 on the city's rim were beginning to appear on the New England landscape. If Boston is the site of much of America's historical past, it is also the location of her business future—specifically, the many high-technology companies that are now headquartered here. The firm became a significant presence in serving the needs of these new enterprises, many of them emerging companies or privately held ventures, and presently serves as business adviser for companies in defense/aerospace; communications; technological controls; medical technology; electronic instruments/testing equipment/robotics; semiconductors/electronic parts, peripherals, and software; and computer manufacturing.

By the 1970s the Ernst & Ernst organization had expanded to all parts of the world. A principal association of more than 50 years with Whinney, Murray & Co., one of the United Kingdom's leading accounting firms, culminated in 1979 in a name change for the 76-year-old firm. Ernst & Ernst became Ernst & Whinney in the formation of a single unified worldwide firm—in one organization under one name. The new structure allowed the acknowledged international leader of public accounting to strengthen identification and more effectively communicate its depth and quality of professional and technological resources to help meet the challenges and opportunities in today's international business arena.

The well-respected name of Ernst & Whinney, tracing its lineage to the infancy of American industry, has grown to become an integral part of its community, identifying with the old and the new businesses of Boston. With a continued commitment to timely personalized client service, Ernst & Whinney-Boston offers a full range of accounting and auditing, tax planning and compliance, and management consulting disciplines. The list of clients it serves gives quick insight into a thriving Boston that combines tradition and modernity.

The headquarters for the Northeast Region of the firm is located on the 46th floor of the soaring John Hancock Tower, a visible symbol of the new Boston, overlooking yesterday's rooftop chimney pots of the Back Bay in a confident city of commerce. Operations are directed by Paul G. Smith, vice chairman and regional managing partner, and James G. Maguire, managing partner.

ZAYRE CORP.

It was 1956 when the Max and Morris Feldberg family, owners of a chain of ladies' apparel stores since 1919, concluded that discounting—a then-untested form of retail distribution—was the growth direction of the future. That year Zayre opened the country's first-of-its-type neighborhood, self-service, general merchandise discount department store, launching a new concept in retailing.

Barely more than 25 years later, the sagacity of this foresight has been validated. Today one of the largest discount store chains in the United States, the $2.5-billion, 35,000-associate Zayre Corp. owns and operates more than 800 stores in the suburban centers and inner cities of states throughout the Northeast, Southeast, and Midwest.

Massachusetts-based, with headquarters in Framingham, the corporation represents three separate retail businesses, each with a distinctive character and individual mission based on its own set of dynamics. The Zayre Stores are 300 classic, full-line discount department stores. Among the top four of the industry leaders, the Zayre Stores are the firm's largest division. T.J. Maxx is a chain of 150 off-price, brand-name family apparel "supermarts." Started in 1977, it is today the country's second-largest off-price retailer. Hit or Miss is a chain of 400 women's specialty shops. Acquired in 1969, it offers current, high-fashion, high-quality merchandise to the style-conscious career woman at low retail prices. Chadwick's is a direct-mail operation featuring merchandise found in Hit or Miss stores.

The Zayre accomplishments are significant beyond growth numbers. The company, from its small, experimental-store origins, saw meteoric growth in the '50s and '60s. A broad-based and all-encompassing market development program was initiated in the late '70s and was responsible for greater productivity. With a focus on the three existing businesses in major markets, a combination of extensive refurbishment and expansion spurred sales and earnings.

One of the largest discount store chains in the United States, Zayre Corp. represents three separate retail businesses: (below) Zayre Stores, 300 full-line discount department stores; (bottom left) T.J. Maxx, 150 off-price, brand-name family apparel "supermarts"; and (bottom right) Hit or Miss, 400 women's specialty shops, offering current, high-quality merchandise at low retail prices.

Zayre Corp.'s newest division, B.J.'s Wholesale Club, is a membership wholesale warehouse price club that will serve small business and club members. During 1986-1987 Zayre will see a doubling of volume to approximately $5 billion, generated by the opening of over two million square feet of retail space to accommodate 1,200 stores.

The company credo, "Zayre Cares," has been reflected in its principles of satisfaction and service to its customers. The Zayre effort, directed by its 13-year-old Office of Consumer and Community Affairs, has been recognized by the White House Office of Consumer Affairs and by other governmental agencies and institutions for its significant nationwide contributions.

MARR COMPANIES

The building of New England has, since 1898, been the professional mission of Daniel F. Marr and his descendants. For more than 85 years and continuing through five generations, the privately owned construction services business of the Marr family has been in the forefront in helping to provide the necessary construction support for this area's, commercial, industrial, and government building progress.

Helping the builders to build, the Marr name has traditionally been associated with the erection and restoration of structures of all types from high-rise office buildings to educational facilities, from scientific and industrial plants to hospitals and hotels, from the hoisting of the irreplaceable steeple bells of the Old North Church, to the recovery from icy waters of several jumbo jets, to the renovation of a floating dry dock, to the erection of a Papal pavilion on Boston Common.

With the help of the men from Marr, the Braves Field of 1915 was constructed, the Park Square Building of 1922 built, and the Boston Garden of 1928 erected. The Commonwealth Armory and Fenway Park, the Hartford and Worcester civic centers, the Seabrook Nuclear Power Plant, John F. Kennedy Memorial Library, Foxboro's Schaefer Stadium, Boston's Westin and Marriott Long Wharf hotels, and the New England Aquarium are other architectural landmarks to which Marr has contributed.

Corporate offices are at One D Street in South Boston; branches are at Springfield, Massachusetts, and Providence, Rhode Island. And here, too, longevity prevails. Management's relationships with a professional staff of long tenure emphasizes the firm's successful commitment to investment in its

Marr contributed its expertise to the construction of the Seabrook Nuclear Power Plant in New Hampshire.

people, and to a tradition of teamwork. Up to 200 field personnel are employed at peak periods, contributing to the architectural and engineering challenges of the Marr Companies' vast projects.

Since 1915, when the first Daniel Marr became an owner of the original Boston Braves baseball franchise, the Marr family has enjoyed affiliations with professional sports teams. Colonel Dan Marr in 1960 was one of 10 co-founders and a director of the Boston Patriots Football Club. Upon his death in 1969, sons Dan and Bob assumed his board seat; Bob Marr, as team president, directed the New England Patriots through their 1974-1975 seasons.

From Colonel Dan Marr and his ancestors evolved a legacy of community leadership and involvement, fostered by a successive generation. Inaugurated in 1969 by Dan and Bob Marr, in memory of their father, the Colonel Daniel Marr Boys' and Girls' Club today provides recreational, educational, and vocational services to more

than 1,000 boys and girls of the Dorchester community.

Assuring a new chapter in a new century of contributions by the Marr Companies to progress in its industry is a new Marr generation. Already on board are Daniel III, Stephen, Jeffrey, and David Marr, all sons of Dan Jr. These young men look to the future with a sense of a job well done in the past by an enterprise begun in a pioneer's spirit—five generations and eight decades of construction activity ago.

A scaffold project in Boston's Copley Plaza was designed and erected by Marr craftsmen.

NORTHEASTERN UNIVERSITY

Northeastern University, from its very beginnings, focused on being of service to the city of which it is a part.

It began, and for its first 40 years remained, an outreach of the Boston YMCA. Today the largest private university in the nation, Northeastern continues to respond to the changing needs of its community. In addition to its approximate 60-acre campus on Huntington Avenue, Northeastern operates 12 suburban educational sites, and serves a population of 21,000 full-time and 35,000 part-time students.

The late 1880s through the 1890s was a time of rapid immigration to the United States. Boston's population almost doubled in these years and was accompanied by growth in commercial and industrial enterprise. The city was viewed as the "Athens of America," a center for education. Yet college was available only to those who could afford the luxury of an education. In 1896 the Boston Young Men's Christian Association (YMCA)

The first World Series baseball game, 1903. Northeastern's Cabot Physical Education Center now occupies this area.

established an "Evening Institute for Young Men," which in 1909 became the Northeastern College of the YMCA, located at the corner of Boylston and Berkeley streets. "A good education possible to every young man" was its promise.

The Department of Law was the first to be established, in 1898. It provided evening law courses to train the working men of Boston for the increasing number of legal opportunities available. Tuition was $30 per year, including a five-dollar YMCA membership. The deans of Harvard and Boston University Law Schools sat in on the first night of class to endorse the new concept of part-time evening education for adults. Thus began Northeastern's long tradition of reaching out to satisfy the urban needs of the community. Similar programs of evening education were later launched in the areas of business and technical training.

Frank Palmer Speare, who served as director of the Evening Institute, became the first president of Northeastern and had one of the longest tenures in the history of American education (1909-1940). In addition to initiating day programs, Speare was responsible for establishing a sense of direction

and commitment for the institution.

Under Speare's creative leadership Northeastern became the only school in the nation founded under the principal theme of the "Cooperative Plan of Education." Speare had heard of an experiment conducted by the University of Cincinnati's School of Engineering that utilized the plan and decided it made sense to organize a school based on this method. The plan linked paid employment to traditional college study so that children of immigrant laboring families could work their way through college. The Cooperative Plan was initiated with the College of Engineering in 1909 and subsequently adopted by the colleges of Business Administration in 1922 and Arts and Sciences in 1935. The plan has since been applied to all of the colleges, both day and evening programs, within the university. Students spend one-half year in school and one-half year working in their field of study. It affords both financial assistance and career experience and is recognized today as a superior form of education. In addition, many Boston-area employers have grown to rely upon the constant labor supply of Northeastern students.

Three of the four presidents of Northeastern University. From left, they are Dr. Carl S. Ell (1940-1959), Dr. Asa S. Knowles (1959-1975), and Kenneth G. Ryder (1975-).

In 1922 the name of the college was officially changed to Northeastern University and a number of new schools were founded, including the School of Business Administration. By this time Northeastern had already received authorization to grant bachelor's degrees in areas such as commercial science, law, commerce, and finance, as well as civil, mechanical, chemical, and electrical engineering. With the rapid growth and expansion of Northeastern, the official separation from the YMCA was planned in 1936. Carl S. Ell, who served as Northeastern's second president, was responsible for the construction of the new Huntington Avenue campus.

Construction of the campus was completed by Dr. Ell's successor, Asa Knowles. President Knowles was also known for his innovative programming and was responsible for establishing the first doctoral programs at Northeastern. Under

his administration, the university was brought into the modern age as a mature, multifaceted institution of higher learning.

Throughout its history, Northeastern has been remarkably flexible in attending to the changing needs of its community. Female students were admitted to the day colleges in 1943. Following World War II the College of Education was established to provide teachers for the rising tide of new students. When the Harvard Teaching Hospital came with a plea for nurses, Northeastern established its School of Nursing. In 1953 the Law School was shut down because there was so little demand for lawyers. During the 1960s dissatisfaction within the legal community arose because young lawyers were not equipped with appropriate courtroom preparation. Northeastern's new School of Law then opened and addressed itself to the problem through its Cooperative Plan of Education.

Most recently, under the leadership of president Kenneth Ryder, Northeastern's College of

Business Administration has been particularly creative in developing programs to meet the needs of industry. Northeastern is the only school in the country to establish a High-Tech MBA, designed to provide a master's degree directly relating to problems of high-technology industry. In 1983 the university inaugurated its Graduate Engineering Live Television Education Program into corporate facilities on Route 128, Massachusetts' Technology Highway. Under this most innovative system, engineers who are enrolled as part-time students leave their desks during the work day to take part in a class via live broadcast with direct telephone lines to the instructor at Northeastern.

President Ryder, a former history professor at Northeastern, has also maintained the university's continued partnership with the Boston community and promoted the importance of the arts in education. He hopes to create a balance between scholarship in the arts and the pragmatic thrust of the university. Student-exchange programs have been established with a number of arts institutions including Boston's Conservatory of Music and its Museum of Fine Arts.

Today the student body represents a cross section of American society, and confirms that the Cooperative Plan is appealing to all types of individuals. Students come from all over the United States as well as from many foreign countries. Hundreds of students are working under the plan in Washington, D.C., and abroad. Northeastern University now serves as a model throughout the world as the pioneer of the Cooperative Plan of Education.

TUCKER, ANTHONY AND R.L. DAY, INC.

Tucker, Anthony & Company became a banking and brokerage business on the first Monday in May 1892, when William A. Tucker and S. Reed Anthony began their partnership at 50 State Street in the center of Boston's financial district.

They were an unlikely pair: Tucker, who had begun his career at age 18 as a clerk at James Tucker & Co., where his father was a partner, was, at 42, a dignified and formidable gentleman whose bold personality became quickly evident in his willingness to take the risks that came with speculation. Anthony, on the other hand, at 28 years old, was cautious and conservative. Perhaps their ancestry had created a bond between the two. Anthony was a direct descendant of both Miles Standish and John Alden. On his mother's side he numbered among his progenitors the colonial governor of the Commonwealth. Tucker was a descendant of Robert Tucker, who came to America in 1635 and established the town of Milton, Massachusetts.

Nevertheless, the early years

Tucker and S. Reed Anthony's main office at 50 State Street in 1892.

brought modest prosperity to Tucker and S. Reed Anthony. A still-held seat on the Boston Stock Exchange was assumed during the first year and, in celebration of the firm's seventh year, it was announced that Philip L. Saltonstall and Nathan Anthony, brother of S. Reed, were joining the partnership. The four bought and sold "all classes of stocks, bonds, and securities" and, as the new century began, Tucker, Anthony found a specialty. As Americans were enjoying the novel convenience of streetcars, the firm was financing and representing nearly all of the electric street railway mileage in Massachusetts and venturing forth to the plains of the Midwest to develop further opportunities, simultaneously helping to invest the fortunes of many New England families. By this time the gas light had all but disappeared in favor of the incandescent bulb powered by the companies that Tucker, Anthony underwrote. An identity with public utilities, which was to span 30 years, was established.

In 1902 S. Reed Anthony bought a seat on the New York Stock Exchange, a seat that would remain unoccupied for some years. Boston was Tucker, Anthony's birthplace and there was no reason to leave home. But in 1908 William Tucker opened a small branch of the company in New York's financial district. Eventually, Tucker, Anthony's main office would be in New York City; its home office would continue to remain in Boston.

The year 1914 brought the death of S. Reed Anthony. The family name and conservative approach continued through Nathan Anthony and later Reed P. Anthony, son of S. Reed Anthony, who would become a partner in 1933. Others

would follow him.

The Dow Industrials broke 100 in 1919. A great deal of money was to be made in the decade when the nation was rebounding from the war and enjoying an unprecedented industrial expansion and growing popularity of consumer credit. Beginning in 1922, Wall Street enjoyed uninterrupted bull markets. And, as America prospered, so too did Tucker, Anthony. The firm celebrated its birthday in 1922 with a partnership of 12 and new branches in New Bedford, Massachusetts; Manchester, New Hampshire; and Providence, Rhode Island.

In 1924 William A. Tucker retired from the firm he founded and had led. The Calvin Coolidge bull market was under way when Tucker, Anthony took to upgrading its entire range of underwritings, turning away from speculative ventures, and redefining its family of partners as a group of bankers and brokers who distributed only high-quality securities with issues originated by the most reputable banks.

The partners who were responsible for the redirection of the firm's business were John Maxwell, Rodney Williams, George Saltonstall West, Clement R. Ford, William H. Claflin, Jr., and Frederick B. Payne, who would be on board to help guide Tucker, Anthony through Wall Street's darkest hours and to play an enduring role in the firm's history. It became a conservative, first-line, well-run house whose prudent standards would remain constant with a spirit so strong as to guide its partnership until incorporation one-half century later.

Tucker, Anthony had reached the apex of its 37-year existence by October 19, 1929. A staff of more than 300 were conducting business

The Boston headquarters of Tucker, Anthony & R.L. Day, Inc., at One Beacon Street in 1984.

from Wall Street, State Street, and 10 branch offices; activities spanned four states and two continents. The firm was on the move on that hysterical day that became legend on Wall Street when 16 million shares changed hands and millionaires became paupers. The stock market crash and relentless Depression that followed five months later left their indelible mark on the firm's character and instituted a milestone of change for Tucker, Anthony—from growth, to preservation, and finally to retrenchment. In 1930 some 1,350 banks closed; by 1935, 10 company branches were closed. The experience defined the firm as it is today: The secret of survival would be control.

Investor confidence was bolstered during Franklin D. Roosevelt's National Recovery Administration; later by the Securities Act of 1933, and the ethical standards of the securities business greatly improved. By 1938 Tucker, Anthony had six general partners in New York: John Maxwell, Robert Haydock, Ramon Williams, Reed P. Anthony, Frederick Payne, Page Chapman; three in Boston: William Hackett, Horace Frost, and Gilbert Steward; and branches in New Bedford and in Rochester, New York. For the next 18 years the partnership would remain substantially the same; the list of offices, identical.

In 1942 the firm absorbed the old-line State Street firm of Burr Gannett & Co. Larger and more complex mergers were to come. In 1956 a merger with the highly respected Boston banking firm of R.L. Day & Co. would change its size, scope, and even its masthead. Tucker, Anthony and R.L. Day in 1958 acquired the Boston investment house of Elmer H. Bright & Co; in 1964 Davis & Davis of Providence. As its household expanded, the firm kept doing what it had always done well: giving its customers attentive service and controlling costs.

In 1949, riding the crest of America's postwar renewed economy, the bull market, from a low of 161, began a slow ascent, to continue to climb for 16 years. Tucker, Anthony, continuing to absorb small, profitable firms, entered the most successful period the firm had known to become a major regional investment house. By the early '60s the firm had 19 general and 8 limited partners and had expanded to 13 offices. Fitzhugh Gordon, Ernest Borkland, John C. Newsome, Gilbert Steward, Horace Frost, William Hackett,

William Claflin III, and David O'Leary were now partners. Men and tradition from the past mixed with a vibrant group of younger people making their mark at Tucker, Anthony and R.L. Day.

In January 1973 the market reached a top of 1,051, then plunged. For a period of seven years the brokerage industry was jolted successively by the paper crunch, the Bear Market of 1973-1974, and the May Day switch to negotiated commissions. A seat on the New York Stock Exchange that sold for $505,000 in 1969 was selling for $70,000 five years later. Tucker, Anthony survived these difficult years while the concern's leadership underwent major changes. In September 1975 the partners of Tucker, Anthony, under the leadership of William Claflin and Robert Hoguet, signed incorporation papers. Partners became officers and directors, the firm name became Tucker, Anthony and R.L. Day, Inc., and a partnership of 83 years became a corporation. In 1978 W. Ward Carey, formerly of Blyth Eastman Dillon, became its president.

The 1980s brought about significant structural changes in the rapidly developing financial-services industry. In 1982 the stockholders of Tucker, Anthony voted to sell their company to the John Hancock Mutual Life Insurance Company of Boston for $47 million. The arrangement ensured the future of Tucker, Anthony's name, independence, and business style. In 1984 Ward Carey succeeded R. Willis Leith as chairman of the board, Leith becoming chairman of the executive committee. Gerald Segel, formerly national sales manager, became president.

Tucker, Anthony looks forward to a gala 1992, when it will celebrate its 100th anniversary.

MOSELEY, HALLGARTEN, ESTABROOK & WEEDEN INC.

Moseley, Hallgarten, Estabrook & Weeden Inc. is one of the largest regional brokerage firms in the United States, and the cornerstone of the publicly owned parent financial services firm, Moseley, Hallgarten, Estabrook & Weeden Holding Corporation. Engaged in securities brokerage, trading, investment banking, investment management, and other activities, the diversified Moseley is a full-service New York Stock Exchange member firm, with 400 investment brokers and a combined staff of 800 serving over 75,000 individual and institutional customer accounts through 38 branches in 12 northeast and central states, as well as the District of Columbia. An international client base, creating approximately 10 percent of the firm's annual revenues, is represented through corporate offices in four European countries.

Tracing its origins to 1850, the company is the successor to the business of F.S. Moseley & Co., Hallgarten & Co., and Estabrook & Co., all of which were founded in the 19th century, and Weeden Holding Corp., parent of Weeden & Co., founded in 1933.

Frederick S. Moseley, a "note broker," founded in 1879 the company that bore his name and built an extensive business handling the paper of various industrial and commercial concerns in New England. Within a few years the venture became one of the principal factors in financing the short-term requirements of a large part of American industry. Such firms as American Telephone and Telegraph, R.J. Reynolds, Procter and Gamble, Edison Electric Illuminating Company, and Armour and Company used the services of F.S. Moseley & Co. as brokers.

Frederick S. Moseley III, chairman.

In 1905 the firm became a member of the New York Stock Exchange. A New York office was established to develop a substantial investment business. F.S. Moseley & Co. took over substantially the entire eastern division of Chase Harris Forbes Corp., investment affiliate of the Chase National Bank of New York. This unit made the business one of the major investment organizations in the Midwest. In the next decades F.S. Moseley & Co. became an active participant in many rail, public utility, industrial, and municipal issues. Over the years F.S. Moseley & Co. acquired several securities firms, including Arthur Perry & Co. in 1945, Whiting, Weeks & Stubbs in 1953, and Charles W. Scranton in 1970.

The house of Hallgarten & Co. was established in New York in 1850 when Lazarus Hallgarten commenced business as a foreign exchange dealer, exchanging immigrants' money into United States currency. The firm became an important channel for the building of the New World with the surplus investment funds of the old, and in the '60s attained prominence as one of the country's largest dealers in gold bullion. In later decades trading in stocks and bonds, and particularly in the securities of the nation's major railroads which they helped to reorganize, became another important endeavor.

Activities expanded to include numerous foreign government, state, and municipal issues. Hallgarten was one of the leaders in the purchasing and marketing of securities of the insular possessions of the United States, while acting as fiscal agent for many foreign governments. The scope and character of the firm's services changed to meet the needs of its clientele, and by 1930 was rendering services in the underwriting field and general brokerage business. By the late 1960s it was active in all phases of the investment banking business.

Estabrook & Co., under its original name, Brewster, Sweet & Co., opened its doors in 1851 and quickly became an important commodity in a young American investment banking community.

Jon A. Bulkley, president.

Today Moseley, Hallgarten, Estabrook & Weeden Inc. is completely computerized and one of the largest regional brokerage firms in the United States.

Following its appointment as fiscal agent for the sale of U.S. government bonds in New England, its growth was rapid. In those early days, men from Estabrook helped to provide the capital that built electric power plants, railroads, and a growing network of other industries. Continuing to seek and develop investment capital for business opportunities in this country and abroad, Estabrook & Co.'s traditional position in the leading national underwriting syndicates and its reputation for securities as long-term investments became widely known and respected in 20th-century New England.

Weeden & Co., founded in San Francisco in 1922, was, in the late '70s, the principal operating entity of Weeden Holding Corp., a publicly owned concern. Weeden engaged in the single line of business of buying and selling securities both as principal and agent. A major market maker in municipal and corporate bonds, U.S. government and government agency bonds, municipal notes, certificates of deposit, and preferred stocks, the firm, with beginnings in municipal bonds, entered OTC trading in listed preferred and utility stocks in the '30s and '40s, and third-market activity in the '50s. With San Francisco remaining its home office, Weeden & Co. expanded to New York and Los Angeles in 1927, to Chicago and Boston in the late '30s. By 1977 its offices numbered 15 nationally and internationally.

In 1973 F.S. Moseley & Co. combined its business with

Estabrook & Co. to form F.S. Moseley, Estabrook Inc. In 1974 that venture combined its business with the partners of Hallgarten & Co. to form Moseley, Hallgarten & Estabrook Holding Corp. as the holding company. In 1976 the firm acquired C.B. Richard, Ellis & Co., and in 1979 it merged with Weeden Holding Corp. Weeden, the broker-dealer subsidiary of Weeden Holding, merged into Moseley, Hallgarten & Estabrook Inc. to form the firm's sales and financial services subsidiary.

Moseley today is engaged primarily in providing individual and institutional investors with a broad array of professionally managed financial products and services. The firm also provides corporate and municipal clients with investment banking services, including new issues, private placements, and financial advisory service.

Moseley's investment brokers are equipped to provide individual investors with virtually every product and service available in the marketplace—stocks, bonds, mutual funds, and unit trusts.

Moseley investment bankers are organized as the Corporate Finance and Public Finance departments, and as Moseley Associates, whose primary activity is raising partnership equity capital, usually tax-advantaged investments, for the real estate and oil and gas industries.

Moseley, Hallgarten, Estabrook & Weeden Inc. is headed by Frederick S. Moseley III, chairman, at the organization's regional offices at 60 State Street, and by Jon A. Bulkley, president, in New York.

The F.S. Moseley office around 1890 provides great contrast to today's operations.

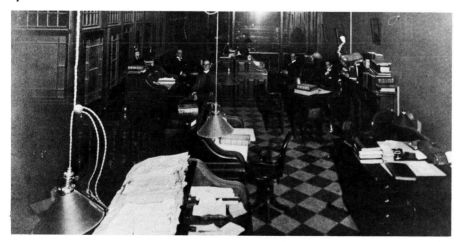

BLUE CROSS AND BLUE SHIELD OF MASSACHUSETTS

In the fall of 1937, a Williams College soccer player, Fordyce Turner Blake, Jr., of Worcester, raced an Army player for a loose ball at midfield. Neither man would relent. As athletes will, both men kicked vigorously at the ball and collided. Both suffered triple fractures of the right leg.

Fortunately for Fordyce Blake, Jr., his father had a few days earlier enrolled the family in the new group hospitalization plan called the Associated Hospital Service Corporation. As he recovered from his injury at Massachusetts General Hospital, young Fordyce knew neither he nor his family would be burdened by undue hardship because of medical bills. He was covered by what is now known as Blue Cross of Massachusetts.

Families who had suffered through the Great Depression latched onto the concept of prepayment as a means of securing health care without fear of being financially overburdened. For an established fee per month, they were protected from the risk of economic hardship that a catastrophic illness could create.

The Boston Herald headline of September 10, 1937, said it best: "Sickness Need No Longer Wreck Budget."

The Massachusetts Blue Cross plan enacted by the state legislature was the 26th created in the nation, but it was the first to offer protection to subscribers statewide.

Physicians also became interested in the prepayment concept of financing health care, and in 1941 the state legislature, at the urging of the Massachusetts Medical Society, established Blue Shield of Massachusetts. The plan was unique in that it paid for covered services only with participating physicians, producing widespread physician participation and establishing freedom of choice of physicians for subscribers.

The protection that subscribers enjoy today is significantly more comprehensive than coverage provided to young Fordyce Blake, Jr. Although they are separate corporations, Blue Cross and Blue Shield of Massachusetts have maintained a close and productive relationship over the decades. Together they serve more than 60 percent of health care consumers in Massachusetts. Blue Cross and Blue Shield have continued to grow and adapt to the needs of consumers, offering ever-increasing comprehensive coverages. Today they play a unique role in the health care system in Massachusetts. What started out as a hospital insurance plan in 1937 has evolved into a multifaceted health care organization involved in health insurance, health education, and the provision of low-cost alternative health care facilities and programs.

The Corporations, which in their formative stages could offer coverage only to groups, added non-group coverage in the 1940s.

A new "experience-rating" system, in which a group's rates were tied to its actual insurance-need experience, was introduced in the 1950s. Membership soared.

In the mid-1950s Blue Cross and Blue Shield introduced its "Master Medical" coverage, which became a household name for comprehensive benefits. Master Medical members felt secure that they held the most comprehensive private health care coverage in Massachusetts.

The unique role of the Corporations was further enhanced in the 1960s, when they were appointed as Medicare carrier for Massachusetts. Blue Cross and Blue Shield evolved from being an underwriter of financial risk to administrators of health programs underwritten by the federal government.

In 1966 the Medex supplemental insurance program for Medicare recipients over age 65 was established. Medex has remained the most comprehensive supplemental program available to senior citizens. As the federal government has reduced its Medicare coverage, Medex has increased its coverage, providing an important safety net of protection for the elderly.

In further service to the elderly, Blue Cross and Blue Shield in 1983 became the first health insurer in the nation to establish a network of health care for senior citizens at health maintenance organizations (HMOs). Combining the benefits of Medicare and Medex and stressing preventive medicine and regularly

After breaking his leg in a soccer match while a student at Williams College in 1937, Fordyce Turner Blake, Jr., became the first Massachusetts resident admitted to a hospital under the Associated Hospital Service Plan, now known as Blue Cross. Fordyce is still protected against unexpected medical expenses as a subscriber to nationally acclaimed Medex supplemental insurance program for individuals over 65 years of age.

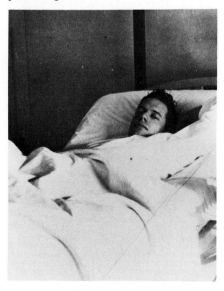

scheduled care, the "Senior Plan" provides total medical care at significantly less cost than traditional insurance programs. Senior Plan has been characterized as the plan of the future for providing quality health care for the state's elderly citizens, and will embrace hundreds of thousands of their population in years to come.

Blue Cross and Blue Shield have long recognized the need to maintain high-quality health care services while containing costs so that health care can be readily accessible and affordable to every consumer.

Involvement in the creation, promotion, and financing of HMOs in Massachusetts is one of the many efforts of Blue Cross and Blue Shield to reduce health care costs while maintaining quality care. HMO subscribers are cared for by an established group of physicians and other health care practitioners. HMOs emphasize outpatient care, reducing the need for costly hospitalization. By stressing disease prevention and health education, as well as regularly scheduled medical care, HMOs have had significant success in preventing and discovering illnesses before they become more serious and costly to treat.

In the 1970s Blue Cross and Blue Shield provided the technical assistance necessary to develop the first HMO in Massachusetts. Today Blue Cross and Blue Shield own or are affiliated with eight HMOs and plans are in progress to expand

A young member of Blue Cross and Blue Shield's Medical East Health Maintenance Organization has his height and weight checked by a staff nurse. The Corporations have been at the forefront of the development of HMOs, which stress preventive medicine, health education, and outpatient treatment of illnesses.

the Blue Cross and Blue Shield HMO system of health care statewide by the end of the decade.

Blue Cross and Blue Shield have continued to work with local, state, and federal officials to improve the health care system and to protect consumers from unwarranted health care costs. In 1982 landmark legislation, Chapter 372, was enacted in Massachusetts, redefining the way hospitals are reimbursed by insurers for services provided. Under the legislation, hospitals must operate within a predetermined budget. If a hospital exceeds its budget, the excess cannot be passed along to consumers through third party payors. If a hospital operates under or within its budget, it is allowed to retain the savings and apply them to improving its services. The cost-containment legislation was based upon a model hospital agreement formulated by Blue Cross and, as a result, health care consumers are receiving more protection than ever before against spiraling health care costs.

Blue Shield broadened a vital protection for consumers by expanding in 1968 its ban against balance billing by physicians to include all subscribers. Physicians who had signed a participating agreement with Blue Shield agreed to accept Blue Shield's Usual and Customary allowance as full payment for services rendered. The agreement constitutes significant savings to the state's health care consumers.

An important part of Boston's rising skyline, Blue Cross and Blue Shield's headquarters at 100 Summer Street illustrates the dramatic growth and popularity of the Plans, which now serve more than 3.4 million subscribers.

The Blue Cross and Blue Shield plans have acted as a cornerstone to the growth and development of one of the world's most highly regarded health care systems by providing the financial stability needed to make it work.

The accelerating rate of change within our health care system demands, however, that health insurance coverage keep pace with the changing needs and preferences of health care consumers.

In the past half century, Blue Cross and Blue Shield have insured and provided quality health care in Massachusetts and have served as a catalyst of much positive change in helping to make the state's health care system one of the most sophisticated in the nation.

But some things never change. Five decades after he became the first resident of Massachusetts to have his hospital insurance pay his medical expenses to repair his broken leg, Fordyce Turner Blake, Jr., was still insured by Blue Cross and Blue Shield through their Medex program.

SHREVE, CRUMP & LOW, INC.

The American Revolution was over. The Colonies had succeeded in winning their independence from Britain and a season of peace prevailed in the young independent country; a brilliant time of growth and prosperity it was, as a confident people responded to their condition in their attitudes, their way of life. By the 1790s Boston, with her near-20,000 inhabitants, was the most flourishing community on the North American continent, engaged in numerous trading pursuits centered around the 80 wharves and quays at the bottom of State Street.

Such was the atmosphere when in 1796, as Napoleon's bride, Josephine, from her court in Paris, was influencing dress and jewel fashion throughout the entire western world, it was noted that a John McFarlane, watchmaker and contemporary of Paul Revere, was "keeping a shop" at No. 51 Marlborough Street—the Washington Street of today—and carrying a stock of watches, silver spoons, and gold beads. This enterprise was the origin of what was to become one of the world's most respected jewelry houses and one of Boston's best-known and beloved landmarks, the Shreve, Crump & Low Company.

The Parisian authority soon affected the fashionable ladies of the peninsula of Boston. Jewels were worn in quantity: Diamonds and precious stones adorned necks, wrists, and waists, gowns were embroidered with jewels, and John McFarlane expanded accordingly. Ensuing years brought several name changes to the firm, to include in 1819 John J. Low, in 1852 Benjamin Shreve, and two decades later Charles J. Crump, whose entire career was identified with the firm. By 1888 Shreve, Crump & Low was incorporated with Benjamin Shreve as president.

Even as the firm name evolved, its operation changed to accommodate new purchasing habits. Discriminating customers of 1850 bought fobs and cuff links, jeweled fans, gold-mounted opera glasses, and ropes of pearls at a new location at Summer and Washington until the 1889 fire. In 1891, after several temporary locations, a move to Tremont and West allowed for a greatly diversified collection of fine giftware of sterling, ivory, crystal, and china, in addition to the ever-present gems. A final and fitting home was created in the 300th anniversary year of the founding of its home city by architect William Aldrich. Presidents, generations of families, organizations, and the carriage trade came, beginning in 1930, to the corner of Boylston and Arlington at the Public Gardens to view two floors of elegant merchandise and to take home a little bit of Shreve's. A now-internationally famous antiques gallery and exclusive Steuben glass room were added, as well as a bridal and baby gift registry and stationery department. Today Shreve's boasts of one of the finest displays of sterling, china, and crystal.

Over these years commissioned commemorative reproduction pieces designed and executed by Shreve

The present home of Shreve, Crump & Low, Registered Jewelers and Certified Gemologists.

craftsmen have included the Daniel Webster Vase, the Paul Revere and the Boston bowls, pottery of historic Boston landmarks, the 1900 Davis Cup, the Ted Williams Trophy, and a sterling silver replica of the *Mayflower*.

From the inaugural epoch of John McFarlane through the eras of Benjamin Shreve and his descendants, to a merger in 1979 with Henry Birks and Sons Ltd. of Montreal, Canada, and expansion to two full-line satellite locations, a jewelry house of uncompromising quality in products and in service has been the legacy of Shreve, Crump & Low to its distinguished clientele.

This etching depicts the Elizabethan-style interior of the Shreve, Crump & Low Jewelry House in the mid-1800s.

CABOT, CABOT & FORBES

In many ways the postwar history of Cabot, Cabot & Forbes parallels the postwar history of the country itself, which should come as no surprise for the company has been the leading industrial commercial property developer in the nation over the past 40 years.

Founded in 1904 as a financial management firm, CC&F had a relatively static growth pattern until the 1950s. As the nation embarked upon a postwar industrial boom, the concern evolved into the pioneer developer of "the business and industrial park," an innovative concept in commercial construction at that time. One of CC&F's first development ventures, the New England Industrial Park in Needham, became a focal point for future activity, as the firm developed 18 industrial parks in the Route 128 area over the next 20 years. Today, fueled by CC&F's continuing projects, the area has become one of the nation's capitals of high-technology industry.

After establishing itself as one of the premier industrial developers in Massachusetts throughout the 1950s, CC&F began to expand its projects across the country in the early 1960s. The firm developed King of Prussia Park in Pennsylvania and later opened a 500-acre joint development with Bethlehem Steel in San Francisco. In 1968 CC&F developed several industrial parks in Phoenix and completed a 500-acre park in Compton, east of Los Angeles.

Also in the 1960s the company entered into ownership of a number of properties nationwide, in addition to its development

National in scope, Cabot, Cabot & Forbes blends architecture and landscaping into each locale as exhibited in this 1-90 Office Center in the Bellevue (Washington) Business Park.

activities. CC&F accumulated assets of $150 million by 1971; that amount skyrocketed to $800 million by 1976.

In the 1970s, as America turned from an industrial "smokestack" economy to a high-technology service economy, CC&F became a leader in commercial high-rise development and suburban business parks. The firm's first high-rise office project was Technology Square, a four-building, 700,000-square-foot complex constructed in Cambridge in the late 1960s. Later projects included the Marine Midland Center in Buffalo, the Blue Cross/Blue Shield Building in Boston, the United Engineers Building in Philadelphia, and One American Place in Baton Rouge. Recent developments in the East include CC&F's headquarters at 60 State Street in Boston, Burlington Business Center on Route 128, and 1010 Market Street in St. Louis.

In the 1980s much of the firm's activities have concentrated in the Los Angeles area—high-rise office buildings on Wilshire Boulevard downtown; in suburban Glendale, the International Jewelry Center, which features the finest state-of-the-art security systems; and the Anaheim Stadium Center, a unique, multipurpose complex that will one day encompass six

A Cabot, Cabot & Forbes development, the 60 State Street high rise in Boston houses the firm's headquarters.

million square feet in a variety of building types.

Regardless of the project or location, Cabot, Cabot & Forbes incorporates high-quality standards in its development philosophy: expert architectural design and landscaping that blend well with the surrounding community, varied and complementary business functions within a specific complex, and—with its experienced management and construction subsidiaries—a full-service approach for all real estate needs.

ROPES & GRAY

The law firm of Ropes & Gray, a Boston patriarch of its profession, was established in 1865 when John Codman Ropes and John Chipman Gray, Jr., entered upon a partnership at a 20 State Street office, the rental fee for which included costs for "gas-stove, fire-place, and window-shades." Their young lives had paralleled; both descended from Salem ancestors in the days of merchant adventurers, both were Phi Beta Kappa graduates of Harvard College and of the Law School in 1861, and both had inherited the traditions and character only the Boston of their times could offer. Partners not only at the Bar, but in a lifetime of friendship, Ropes became a prolific amateur historian of the Civil War; Gray, a professor at Harvard Law School, widely known for his treatises on jurisprudence and the rule against perpetuities. The two lawyers built their practice from modest beginnings to fame and honor through 34 years of joint labor and for 15 more at the hand of Gray.

With the advent in 1878 of William Caleb Loring, who had distinguished himself as an assistant attorney general of the Commonwealth, the name of the partnership became Ropes, Gray & Loring. Early books of account were largely a roster of conveyance and title-examinations, then a valued factor in law offices. But the firm steadily expanded its activities and adapted to a tide of change; by 1894 its family had increased to 12—one of the largest law offices in Boston.

Following the death of John Ropes in 1899 and the appointment of Loring to the Supreme Judicial Court the same year, the firm name changed to Ropes, Gray & Gorham. A further change in 1914 brought the designation Ropes,

John C. Ropes, Esq.

Gray, Boyden & Perkins, to remain as such for 26 years.

These decades brought a trend toward a more modern character of legal activity due to the general change in the industrial world of the day. Bankers negotiated at home and abroad for the utility, industrial, and public security issues to satisfy the great investment market of New England; new statutes were passed in an endeavor to regulate the Industrial Revolution as corporations consolidated, railroads grew, public utilities expanded, and the new field of municipal bonds increased. Ropes & Gray's part in these activities consisted largely of action on behalf of banks and investment bankers. Demand for specialized legal services grew, and addition of personnel was frequent.

By 1940, 75 years following its founding, attorneys Ropes, Gray, Loring, Gorham, Boyden, and

Perkins were deceased. This illustrious succession of men who, by their industry and tradition established and maintained a law firm that sustained and increased its contribution to the community and to its profession, left a heritage of inspiration to their successors. In this year the firm became Ropes, Gray, Best, Coolidge & Rugg. In 1961 the firm resumed its original name of Ropes & Gray.

The modern firm of Ropes & Gray comprises 197 lawyers and a total nonlegal staff of 386 people. Engaged in the general practice of law at offices at 225 Franklin Street and in Washington, D.C., the firm represents the complex legal needs of more than 2,000 diversified, often multinational clients in the areas of corporate and business law, health law, litigation, taxation, labor law, antitrust, estate planning, trusts, public financing, and real estate.

John C. Gray, Jr., Esq.

JIMMY'S HARBORSIDE RESTAURANT

On Boston's bustling Fish Pier at the historic harbor's edge, where rugged fishing trawlers and wheeling seagulls have refuged since the early days of the colonists, is the home of Jimmy's Harborside Restaurant.

The landmark waterfront restaurant is as familiar a site as there is in this once provincial capital and as synonymous with Boston as Boston is with seafood. For 60 years the internationally acclaimed Jimmy's has been preparing a veritable feast of the sea for native New Englanders and visitors from around the world. Here, hospitality prevails and friendship abounds as lobster, shrimp, scallops, sole, Boston scrod, Jimmy's famous finnan haddie (a Harborside specialty), prime beef and poultry entrees, and steaming tureens of stews and creamy chowders are presented amidst an ambience of nautical artifacts and memorabilia Americana.

Boston was a mecca for immigrants early in the 20th century when 15-year-old Demetrios Efstratios Chistodoulos, his rightful birth name, of the Aegean island of Mytilene, arrived. He came by boat with a vision of opportunity, zeal, enthusiasm, a dedication to work, and $13 in his pocket. It would be enough. Jimmy Doulos, his adopted Amercian name, would eventually contribute to the achievements that shaped a part of the worldwide image of Boston and become, in the process, one of the nation's most successful restaurateurs.

An apprenticeship which brought him to the rank of chef at the Bromfield Street Cafe concluded in 1924 when Jimmy embarked upon his first entrepreneurial venture, a nine-stool cafe named the Liberty adjacent to Boston's Fish Pier. The name "Liberty" was chosen because of his love of America, the cradle of

liberty. The waterfront was a barren and desolate area then with few lights and no public transportation to it, but the nine stools of the Liberty were seldom empty. Each morning, Jimmy would go to the Fish Pier and personally select all his fish for his customers who were, in those days, the dock workers and hardy fishermen whose industry brought them to this edge of the sea. Returning to his kitchen, he would prepare the "catch of the day" and his robust chowders. The word spread, lines formed, and soon the nine-stool cafeteria burst into a full-fledged restaurant. It was 1955 when Jimmy's Harborside ceremoniously opened its main dining room established on the site of the old Liberty Cafe kitchen. The first restaurant in the nation to form a profit-sharing system for its employees, Jimmy's evolved into a rambling 550-seat, two-story structure with two dining rooms, a lounge, and a "Jimmy Jr." boat bar, all boasting magnificent views of the historic harbor. Jimmy's fame was now in place.

To be welcomed at the Harborside in the Doulos tradition by Jimmy, his gracious family and staff, was to be welcomed, indeed, and the proprietor was, until his death in 1981, host extraordinaire.

With this rich legacy in hand, a

second generation took the helm. Charles James Doulos, otherwise known as Charlie or "Jimmy Jr.," began acquiring his credentials at the age of eight. Subscribing to traditions engendered by his father, Charlie worked seven days a week learning every facet of the business and in 1956, after graduating from Harvard College, became president of the Harborside and its chief executive officer.

With Jimmy's as the parent organization, a satellite restaurant called Jimbo's Fish Shanty was opened in 1980 by Charlie Doulos. Located across the street from Jimmy's, Jimbo's features stick food or "kabobs," hobo fish stew, burgers, chicken, shrimp, and lobster in a casual atmosphere with a unique hobo character as its logo and reproductions of locomotives traveling along tracks suspended from the ceiling. The walls are punctuated with railroad artifacts and hobo, thematic memorabilia.

Together, the young Jimbo's and the venerable Jimmy's are intact under the stewardship of Charles Doulos, who is burnishing still brighter the accomplishments and fulfillment of his father's immigrant boy's dream.

Charles J. Doulos, known to his legion of regular patrons and guests as "Jimmy Jr.," oversees luncheon by harbor's edge.

BOSTON SAFE DEPOSIT AND TRUST COMPANY

Amidst the throes of postwar rebuilding that preceded Boston's Great Fire of 1872 and the financial Panic of 1873 with its drastic depression of values, was developed the history and the hopes of one of the first trust institutions in the region. Ulysses S. Grant was President and Boston's metropolitan population had grown from 140,000 to 341,000 in just one decade when, on June 1, 1875, the Boston Safe Deposit and Trust Company, with a subscribed capital of $400,000, a distinctive identity as a specialist organization dedicated to the management of capital for others, and a staff of eight, commenced business in the newly erected New England Life Insurance Company building at Post Office Square. It was the first such charter to be granted in the Commonwealth and, for the incorporators as well as the legislature, it was a venture into a new, unfamiliar field.

Trusteeship as we know it today got its start in Boston in the early days of the 19th century, when large fortunes were amassed by successful merchants and

The Boston Company building, One Boston Place.

The Boston Safe Deposit and Trust Company entrance at One Boston Place.

shipowners. At first, family attorneys managed these fortunes in connection with their other duties, but as wealth increased full-time managers were required, and the day of the Boston trustee arrived. Facilitated by Justice Putnam's significant "Prudent Man Rule" of 1830, Massachusetts trustees have been able ever since to exercise broad judgment in the fiduciary investing of assets placed in their care.

By 1884 Boston had 60 banks and the day of the merchant prince had passed. Increasing complexities of life brought a need for specialization and group judgment. Such departmental services as investment research, real estate, accounting, and taxation made trust companies well qualified for appointments as executor and trustee and the end of the century saw growth in the fields of trusteeship and investment management. Boston Safe Deposit and Trust, acting as trustee and investment advisor in the management of property for individuals, corporations and other business enterprises, institutions, and charitable organizations was by 1900 the largest trust company in New England.

In 1917 Boston Safe organized the Permanent Charity Fund of Boston, a pioneering step that would become a continuing

dominant force in strengthening and developing the entire range of the city's community services. Within 50 years the fund had distributed $16 million to deserving charitable organizations, and Boston Safe had become a leading administrator of charitable funds in New England. Among other principal trusts for which the bank acts as trustee or co-trustee are the Godfrey M. Hyams Fund, the Blanchard Foundation, the Permanent Science Fund, and the Permanent Diabetic Fund.

In most respects the company continued to carry out the objectives of its revolutionary charter by specializing in the "trust business" and its supporting services. As times changed, the demands upon the investment fiduciary changed and, in 1964, in order to facilitate diversification into broader investment activities and to serve new geographic markets, Boston Safe created its own holding company, The Boston Company, Inc., the first parent company of its kind in the country. In 1981 The Boston Company was acquired by Shearson Loeb Rhodes, the nation's second-largest securities broker. Shearson was later acquired by American Express to become Shearson

Lehman/American Express, forming a worldwide financial services network. The Boston Company today is one of the nation's largest organizations specializing in the management of corporate, institutional, and individual assets. The Pension and Endowment Services Division provides a wide range of financial products including master trust, defined contribution plan services, investment management, and alternative investments in real estate, oil, and gas to institutional clients and endowments. The Boston Company's Wholesale Banking Services Division markets banking services to such clients as thrift institutions, nonprofit and financial-services firms, government units, and the American Express Company and its subsidiaries.

Since entering the mutual funds services industry in 1976, The Boston Company has grown to become one of the very largest participants. The Mutual Funds Services Division provides investment advisory and subadvisory services, shareholder

Private banking is just one of a variety of financial services provided by The Boston Company.

An economic analysis prepared by The Boston Company.

servicing and administration, custodian, transfer agent, and marketing and distribution services to institutions and individuals.

Boston Safe, through the Private Banking and Investments Division, continues to specialize in providing highly personalized asset management and banking services to individuals and their families. Fiduciary responsibility has remained generation through generation the most enduring tradition at Boston Safe; that combined with innovative and personalized solutions to financial objectives form today the cornerstone of the individual client's relationship. The ability to anticipate and act on new investments opportunities in a changing environment of asset management is provided by the comprehensive resources of Boston Safe and The Boston Company.

In addition to asset management and related administrative services, Boston Safe offers a variety of financial services and products to meet the special needs of affluent and successful individuals, including private banking services (checking accounts, personal credit,

residential mortgages, and short-term investment alternatives) and trust, estate, and financial planning services.

As Boston has grown in the past century to become the second-largest financial center in the United States, so too has the Boston Safe Deposit and Trust Company grown. Currently its assets total more than $1.6 billion, and its Trust Department manages assets with a total book value in excess of $15 billion.

Clients from a broad range of professions, businesses, and backgrounds come to One Boston Place, headquarters for The Boston Company and Boston Safe Deposit and Trust Company—a single source for informed investment management and advice and other specialized financial services. Operations of the concern and its 1,300 employees are directed by chairman and chief executive officer George W. Phillips, vice-chairman and chief investment officer of Boston Safe Deposit and Trust Company and president of The Boston Company James N. von Germeten, and president of Boston Safe Deposit and Trust Company and executive vice-president of The Boston Company Michael W. Christian.

SHERATON BOSTON HOTEL AND TOWERS

When it officially opened its doors on April 18, 1965, at the southwest border of the Prudential Center, the Sheraton Boston Hotel and Towers deemed itself Boston's landmark of hospitality and promptly offered tours of its 29-story, 1,000-room property. Just as promptly, 2,000 visitors per day availed themselves of this welcome for the next six months. Today hospitality is an established tradition at the largest luxury hotel in New England—the 100th in the vast international Sheraton network.

Exactly 190 years to the day when New England patriots staged a revolution and started a new and independent world, Ernest Henderson and Robert L. Moore, founders in 1937 of the Sheraton empire, introduced the first modern hotel to be built in Boston in 50 years. The handsome 756,500-square-foot edifice, constructed at a cost of $28 million, was the icing on the cake for the new Prudential Center 32-acre complex, and an anchor in the launching of a major redevelopment program that would change the face of the Back Bay and reinforce Boston's historic role as a center for commerce.

An ambience of distinction and beauty greeted patrons of the stone and glass hotel and convention center. Its public rooms, its salons, and its saloons were a blend of the decor of many worlds joined together to give Boston a little more of something for everyone and to accommodate a local-to-international clientele in an environment of comfort, elegance, and luxury.

An innovator in the growth of the city's reputation as a major convention center, Sheraton Boston has exhausted the alphabetical range in the network of associations that have made the site their talking point. The largest convention staff in Boston provides expertise for its extensive business and function services and 41 technologically equipped meeting rooms allow for conferences of all sizes.

In 1965 the luxurious Sheraton Towers, an exclusive and intimate 150-room hotel-within-the-hotel was conceived at the four top levels to offer special amenities, including private registration and elevators. In 1975 the South Tower was added and now the twin-towered hotel boasts 1,385 guest rooms to accommodate the individual, the family, and the business traveler. Guest facilities include a variety of shops and a year-round, indoor/outdoor, near-Olympic-size swimming pool.

In its near-20-year history Sheraton Boston, now a recognized leader in accommodations, has been a home-away-from-home for presidents, kings, princes, and traveling families from around the globe, and—in keeping with its trademark of hospitality—a host for its community's medical, cultural, political, academic, and social functions.

The bold and striking new front entrance to the Sheraton Boston Hotel and Towers.

Automated electronic reservations, a verbal alarm system, teleconferencing and satellite programming facilities, and a sophisticated training program for 1,000 employees will be implemented by further modernization and expansion at the progressive hotel. Termed a "21st-century hotel" by vice-president and managing director Gary Sieland, the flagship division of the Boston-based headquarters of Sheraton Corp. plans to meet the increasing demands of Boston's growth and to remain an important factor in its economic life.

Apley's, the Sheraton Boston Hotel and Towers' signature restaurant, has earned a four-star rating and a national reputation for its contemporary American cuisine.

HUB MAIL ADVERTISING

It was an untimely career choice by Abraham Serber that prompted the founding almost 60 years ago of Hub Mail Advertising, today the largest full-service direct mail company in New England, its national reputation in the forefront of its industry.

The advent of Prohibition had brought an end to Abe's business in the spirits industry, and in 1927 he opened what was, in the truest sense, a letter shop. In its earliest days Abe, with a typewriter and a multigraph machine, produced and typed letters from a room at 194 Washington Street. During the 1930s Hub Mail earned its primary revenue by mailing bankruptcy letters for the federal courts.

By the late '30s Bill Bernheimer, Abe's son-in-law, was on board with new and farsighted visions for the potential of direct mail. Assuming ownership upon Abe's death in 1943, Bill directed operations of the five-employee company from new offices at Federal Street and initiated zestful advertising strategies for its promotion. A spectator at Fenway Park could not miss the airplane overhead or its tagline advertising Hub Mail, and Bill's purchase of the Chrysler Company's first postwar nine-passenger DeSoto brought to New England the first-ever mobile telephone-operated delivery vehicle and to the firm, new business. A Dial Hub Mail promotion, which allowed a caller to reach the company by dialing its name, became well known in the area and, by 1946, Hub Mail was already winning awards for its advertising efforts. A move to Bowdoin Square was made to accommodate a

$150,000 volume and 25 employees.

The '50s brought a growing reputation to Hub in the direct mail marketing areas of mail order catalogs and fund raising. Its unique delivery truck, built to the likeness of a mailbox, brought additional publicity. By 1955 the organization was occupying space at 1000 Washington Street, where it would remain for 25 years.

The age of total direct mail marketing arrived when Wally and Lenny Bernheimer, sons of Bill, joined the firm in 1961 and 1965, respectively. Computerized mailing, list processing, and creative functions were added to the existing production facilities at Hub Mail, and a complete package of mail marketing was formed to provide clients with a versatile and unprecedented range of successful applications for conceiving and implementing varying types of marketing situations. Greater printing capabilities were developed when the concern acquired the House of Offset in 1971. Ten years later Regal Lithograph was acquired and merged with the House of Offset to form today's United Lithograph Company, a wholly owned subsidiary of Hub Mail whose operations are directed by Lenny Bernheimer. Wally Bernheimer had assumed the overall presidency of the privately held enterprise in 1972, and the third generation maintains

continuity today at the 500-employee operation.

In 1980 Hub Mail moved to its present 35 Morrissey Boulevard headquarters, which allowed for expansion of both creative activities and technical functions. Business continued to grow; from 1978 to 1984 sales volume tripled for the now-major supplier of direct marketing ideas. A third plant was added in 1984, on Summer Street in South Boston.

From conception to delivery, Hub's full-service group of specialists assist client organizations in using mail to individualize their message in offering products and services, in maximizing fund raising, in promoting memberships, in creating attendance, and in making sales. They select mailing lists and customize mail programs, print pieces, and manage and coordinate marketing programs, as well as computerize lists and manage data bases. Hub is a leading source of mail fund raising and marketing counsel for public television and for the activities of the U.S. Olympic Committee.

And that is Hub Mail Advertising today. Once a company that mechanically produced mailings, it is now a full-service direct marketing corporation creatively producing ideas and concepts and implementing result-producing communications.

Hub Mail Advertising's mailbox delivery truck is a familiar sight on Boston's streets and in area parades.

HALE AND DORR

Hale and Dorr, Boston's largest law firm with 215 attorneys, maintains a tradition of energy and innovation in its practice of law. Partners at the firm have included Reginald Heber Smith, one of the nation's founders of legal aid and an early expert in law office management; Joseph N. Welch, the distinguished litigator who opposed Senator Joseph McCarthy in the historic Army-McCarthy Senate hearings of 1954; James D. St. Clair, one of the country's most respected litigators who was assistant to Welch in the McCarthy hearings and who later represented President Nixon in the Watergate controversy; and Paul P. Brountas, nationally recognized as a pioneer in the legal representation of developing high-technology businesses.

In the heart of the downtown financial district next to Faneuil Hall, the firm occupies six and one-half floors of modern office space at the new 60 State Street office tower, built on the same site occupied by Hale and Dorr from 1919 to 1969. Hale and Dorr has a branch office in Washington, D.C., which was opened in 1981, and its total staff of 650 is linked by an internal computer network.

Hale and Dorr traces its legacy to the early 19th century, when Josiah Parsons Cooke opened a law practice in the Old State House on Boston's State Street. After a succession of partnerships, the firm commenced business under its present name on July 1, 1918, when Richard Hale enlarged his father's small practice to admit Dudley Dorr, a respected member of the Boston Bar who also followed his father in the practice of law. Messrs. Hale and Dorr served as partners of the firm until their deaths in 1943 and 1961, respectively.

Hale and Dorr's managing partner John D. Hamilton, Jr. (center), with Harry T. Daniels (left) and John M. Westott, Jr. (right), assistant managing partners.

In 1919 the partnership was reconstituted to include Reginald Heber Smith, who brought with him six legal aid lawyers. During more than 36 years as managing partner of the firm, Smith was active in furthering legal services for the poor and became the first recipient, in 1951, of the American Bar Association Gold Medal and, in 1957, of the Reginald Heber Smith Medal, now awarded annually for dedicated service to legal aid. Hale and Dorr has remained foremost among Boston firms in pro bono programs, maintaining at any one time 50 to 70 open pro bono files involving over 7,000 hours of services per year.

The "Smith System" formula for measuring attorney productivity and determining partner compensation was developed by Reginald Heber Smith and has been a model for numerous law firms and professional service firms in this country and abroad. A series of articles written by Smith and describing the system were published in the *American Bar Association Journal* in 1940 and have been republished many times in booklet form, most recently in 1984.

In 1954 Smith recommended to his partners that the firm assume the fees and expenses for a new client, the United States Army; and the firm's leading litigator, Joseph N. Welch, was appointed special counsel to the Army in the Army-McCarthy hearings. The courtly and scholarly Welch, a deft and erudite courtroom attorney, impressed himself upon the national consciousness when, in the televised Senate Committee proceedings, he brought the powerful Senator Joseph McCarthy to a standstill. The Senate Committee hearing culminated in McCarthy's censure, and Welch, long one of the most highly regarded members of

Massachusetts Trial Bar, received national respect for his determination in the face of an aggressive and formerly intimidating adversary.

Today the most extensive areas of practice at Hale and Dorr are litigation, corporate, and real estate, and its practice in the fields of tax, personal law, and commercial law continues to expand. The firm's litigation practice is the largest in New England and represents one of the most active courtroom practices in the country. In recent years the firm has been involved in a variety of significant cases, including representation of John Hancock Mutual Life Insurance Company in claims arising out of the construction of Hancock's glass skyscraper in Copley Place, Boston; defense of the town of Mashpee, Massachusetts, against land claims of Indian tribes; defense of Southern Pacific Company in a large antitrust case; and representation of the Boston Celtics in various basketball matters. Jerome Facher, chairman of the Litigation Department, also teaches a course in trial practice at Harvard Law School; James D. St. Clair taught another section of the same course for over 20 years.

Hale and Dorr's Corporation Department, under the chairmanship of Paul P. Brountas, has grown rapidly in the last decade and today represents a number of large public computer-related corporations which it helped found in the late 1960s and early 1970s. The firm continues to specialize in representation of both small, start-up enterprises and the venture capital investors which often

finance such businesses. More recently, the firm has developed a strong practice in the syndication area, representing public and private partnerships in real estate, research and development, and oil and gas, as well as a burgeoning practice in international transactions and representation of foreign investors in the United States.

Led by Herbert W. Vaughan, Hale and Dorr was one of the first large firms in the country to develop a significant real estate practice, playing a key role in representing both developers and lenders active in the commercial and industrial growth along Route 128 and the dramatic revitalization of Boston's downtown area. Now one of the nation's largest, the real estate department currently represents syndicators, developers, lenders, and investors throughout the United States. The firm's real estate expertise has also been instrumental in the related growth of its corporate and securities practice in the real estate syndication area.

Typical of its innovative style, Hale and Dorr is presently engaged in implementing a firm-wide

Joseph N. Welch and James D. St. Clair, counsel and assistant counsel to the United States Army during the Army-McCarthy hearings, relax on the Capitol lawn during a break in the proceedings.

computer network as extensive as any installed by a personal service organization. Each secretary, and also many attorneys and administrative personnel, has a desk-top computer terminal which provides word processing and other office automation functions (electronic mail, paperless files, litigation support, calendaring, mathematical spread sheet capabilities), as well as access to central information such as billing and time records. The firm's Washington, D.C., office is linked to the system, greatly enhancing communication and the sharing of resources. The system has greatly increased productivity for clients and will position Hale and Dorr to play a leading role in the development of computer applications which permit legal services to be delivered more efficiently in the future.

Reginald Heber Smith, partner from 1919 to 1966 and managing partner from 1919 to 1955.

THE BEAL COMPANIES

The Beal Companies, headed by Bruce A. Beal, partner, president, and treasurer of Beal & Company, Inc., and Robert L. Beal, partner and executive vice-president of Beal & Company, Inc., is a century-old, fourth-generation, closely held real estate corporation that offers professional services for selected clients while also developing and managing real estate for its own portfolio. The firm has extensive experience in the ownership, development, financing, construction, and management of real estate assets, comprising commercial, retail industrial, office buildings, multifamily housing, and land held for development throughout New England, concentrated along the Eastern Seaboard, and throughout the United States. The Beal Companies brings to its clients a broad range of services, including development and ownership; management; real estate counseling, evaluation and appraisal; real property taxation and assessment; financing and brokerage; and construction services.

Boston was the center of a complex metropolitan area and in an era of building when A.B. Beal founded the real estate firm in 1888. He was joined in the early 1900s by his sons, Julius and Benjamin Beal. The city burst with new institutions; Fort Hill had disappeared and with it the last trace of the colonial waterfront, and the tidal salt marsh known as the Back Bay was filled—the area reigned supreme as a residential district. Transportation by electricity was beyond imagination and traffic tangles were caused by horse-drawn vehicles. It was a transitional period for the first crude application of electricity serving as a bellwether for unprecedented social and industrial

progress. The Beal family became a significant part of this progress, as it purchased and operated real estate throughout the metropolitan area. One of the first firms to do appraisal and consulting work, the Beals became experts in the field of eminent domain and remained active until the mid-1960s.

Beginning in 1931, Alexander S. Beal, son of Julius, became involved in Beal & Company, Inc., specializing in real estate appraisal and tax valuation analysis of commercial, industrial, farm, waterfront, and residential real estate throughout eastern and southern United States. A lifetime honorary member of the Greater Boston Real Estate Board, he continues as a director of Beal & Company, Inc., and consultant to The Beal Companies.

Maintaining a conservative philosophy—a company tradition—toward its portfolio, one of Boston's oldest continuous real estate firms purchases properties as investment builders, acquiring distinctive landmark structures: The Old Corner Bookstore, Boston's first

brick building, which Beal owned at one time; the historic Grain Exchange Building, constructed in 1892; the Park Square Building, in 1922 the city's largest with a first-of-its-kind interior arcade; and Broad Street's 1929 block-long Batterymarch Building.

Through its principals and related entities, The Beal Companies is actively engaged in the development, ownership, and syndication of varying types of real estate and in the past five years has acquired and developed extensive commercial, industrial, and residential property. Illustrative is Technology Park/Southern New Hampshire, an office and industrial park that will contain approximately one million square feet of space, and the Ledgemont Research Center, the largest office park in Lexington, Massachusetts. The Beal Companies also participated in the acquisition and conversion to condominiums of the largest multifamily garden apartment complex in Boston.

The Beal Companies serves such clients as governmental agencies, corporations, communities, institutions, and individuals, and its principals continue a family tradition of personal involvement in the civic, educational, medical, and charitable affairs of its community.

The Batterymarch Building, 1929. This was Boston's first art deco skyscraper. Today it is owned and managed by The Beal Companies.

UNION WARREN SAVINGS BANK

It's no secret that there is spirit in Boston; it was founded in freedom long ago. While landlords sipped fine and fancy teas in the drawing rooms of England, the people of Boston gave spirit to a little tea party of their own. They struck a blow for freedom in 1776. And, when the time finally came to let their voices be heard, it would be from a thousand long rifles that echoed 'round the world. The message, loud and clear, was delivered from the unlikely podium of Bunker Hill.

General Joseph Warren had been there, displaying both a courage and a spirit that enshrined him in the hearts and minds of his countrymen as one of the heroes of Bunker Hill. Warren was truly a name for the ages.

Some 53 years later, a public-spirited man by the name of Major Timothy Walker paid tribute to the hero of Bunker Hill by naming a new bank The Warren Institution for Savings. Major Walker regarded the naming of the bank a fitting tribute for, like the man, the bank held a deep sense of civic responsibility. On the warm, sunny morning of June 3, 1829, The Warren Institution for Savings officially opened for business. It was an institution dedicated to serving the homogeneous Yankee population.

As with The Warren Institution for Savings, The Union Savings Bank had its historical roots in wartime as well. The year was 1865 and the Civil War had just ended. Although Boston was a far distance from the actual conflict, the city had suffered greatly as a result of it. The clipper ships with which Boston once led the world were fast disappearing and most of the steam vessels that replaced them sailed under a foreign flag. The cost of city government had been increased by relief measures for the poor and other necessary expenditures. For the previous four years a large percent of the wage earners had been withdrawn from their customary occupations and families had suffered.

During the 1800s the Most Reverend John B. Fitzpatrick, Roman Catholic Bishop of Boston, found it difficult to obtain loans from the savings banks of the city to build churches, schools, hospitals, orphanages, and other charitable enterprises. When the Reverend John McElroy, S.J., was building Boston College and the Church of the Immaculate Conception in the south end of the city, there was a possibility that the work would have to stop for want of money. It became apparent that a more liberal bank should be started to enable the large and increasing Catholic population to build their churches, institutions of learning, and to encourage "men of small means to build dwellings." Its primary aim would be to stimulate among its depositors those habits of foresight and reasonable economy that are the basis of national as well as private prosperity.

The cooperation of outside parties was solicited and, with the combined influence of such leading citizens as Moses A. Williams, William I. Bowditch, Joshua D. Ball, Robert H. Waters, and others, the act of incorporation was signed and approved by Governor John A. Andrew on February 8, 1865. On May 1, 1865, The Union Institution for Savings commenced business at 238 Washington Street under the leadership of its first president, John C. Crowley.

Over the years both banks grew and prospered along similar paths. Service to the community, promotion of home ownership, industrial enterprise, and aid in the operations of government through the ownership of national, state, and municipal bonds became the guiding forces for both banks. In 1968 The Warren Institution for Savings and The Union Savings Bank merged and became the Union Warren Savings Bank.

Today the bank relies on electronic technology to provide each customer with the latest financial services. Despite the fact that times have changed and banking has become a highly competitive business, Union Warren continues to retain a sense of the past through personalized banking service.

The past survives in what we think and do. Union Warren's sense of the future is based on its historic legacy of the past: People make the difference.

The Warren Institution for Savings was named for General Joseph Warren.

LEGGAT McCALL AND WERNER, INC.

At Leggat McCall and Werner, Inc., teamwork is more than a business slogan; it is the strength of the two-decade-old brokerage, appraisal, and consulting company, now among New England's largest real estate organizations. From penthouse headquarters at 60 State Street, president and director Bill McCall applies his partnership-like founding philosophy, encouraging group participation and cooperative problem-solving to all projects, with resultant compensation to the 70 members of the firm's team based on the success of the entire company.

Breaking tradition with the structure of conventional brokerage firms, specialists in research and financial analysis, marketing, and appraisal bring their respective knowledge to virtually every real estate problem, and work hand in hand with senior partners and brokers to analyze taxes, inflation, and long-term economic trends, assuring a comprehensive analysis of each project and efficient allocation of full company resources in meeting client needs.

With concentration in commercial and industrial real estate activities, the independent brokerage firm proves that shared expertise can achieve dramatic results. Handling at any given time in excess of 50 properties as exclusive leasing agent, Leggat McCall in the past five years has sold or leased over 17 million square feet and completed over 997 transactions with companies in every spectrum of business activity in greater Boston, eastern New England, and, with office expansion in 1979 to Washington, D.C., in its metropolitan area. Additionally, through ownership in the American Realty Services Group, Inc., the firm has become a significant force in servicing 40 supplemental markets nationwide.

A business of tangible assets controlled by intangible factors, today real estate is a business of information. In the years since 1965, when Leggat McCall was established, the focus of real estate has expanded from a primarily local perspective to be a macroeconomic influence, thus adding new

---

A company-wide sales meeting is conducted each Monday to share ideas, review user requirements, and discuss developments in the marketplace. This forum plays an important role in providing each client with the experience and attention of an entire team rather than an individual broker.

dimensions to the real estate decision process. The anticipatory and methodical application of the creative brokering practiced at Leggat McCall involves the assimilation of all possible factors that can affect a real estate decision. The firm has developed four separate support functions that act as resources to the brokerage team in harnessing, through specialization, a depth of knowledge: An in-house research department provides analyses of national market data by daily monitoring of market absorption statistics and development trend analysis and provides comprehensive rental rate, absorption acquisition, and sales data; real estate finance specialists, through a computer system, provide expertise in the widest range of financial issues; professionals in engineering, purchasing, design, and energy conservation provide support on questions ranging from estimating office build-out costs to feasibility analysis of major facilities renovation; and an appraisal division provides appraisal and consulting services relating to feasibility and best-use studies, acquisition and disposition, litigation, and ad valorem tax appeals for commercial and industrial properties and undeveloped land.

Currently the firm monitors the activity of 100 million square feet of property on a continuing basis and offers knowledge, experience, and abilities to corporations, developers, financial institutions, private investors, fiduciaries, associations, governmental agencies, and other real estate firms nationwide.

Its history is short, its accomplishments large. Leggat McCall and Werner has set itself apart in its capabilities of service.

NEW ENGLAND MUTUAL LIFE INSURANCE COMPANY

In 1835, when a young America lived at the edge of a limitless frontier, the Commonwealth of Massachusetts issued a charter for the nation's first mutual life insurance company. New England Life was born.

Today New England Life stands among the leaders in the insurance industry and is a growing force in the financial services marketplace.

For 150 years, New England Life has relied on innovative ideas and an adherence to the ideals of quality service and products for its policyholders and clients. Its history is tied closely to that of the nation which, during both good times and crises, provided the environment for the company's success.

New England Life sprang up from beginnings as modest as those of its founder, Judge Willard Phillips. A student of insurance and political economy, Judge Phillips

Judge Willard Phillips, founder of the nation's first mutual life insurance company.

early had a dream of establishing a mutual life insurance company, one steadfastly dedicated to serving the best interests of its policyholders.

His dream was transformed into reality in 1835 when the Massachusetts Legislature granted the charter for New England Life to him and four associates, with the stipulation that they raise a guaranty fund of $100,000—half in cash and half in notes—before conducting any business.

This was accomplished late in 1843, and Judge Phillips was elected the company's first president. Two rooms of office space were rented in a bank at 28 State Street, Boston. Two months later, on February 1, 1844, the first New England Life policy was issued.

Since that significant day in the firm's history, New England Life has written millions of policies, for the great orator Daniel Webster and champion golfer Bobby Jones, for Presidents Franklin Delano Roosevelt and Gerald Ford, and people in all walks of life throughout the nation.

New England Life attained its first million dollars in assets in 1857, its first $100 million in 1920, and its first billion dollars in 1949. Today its assets are approaching $10 billion, with assets under management, including subsidiaries and affiliates, of more than $22 billion.

While adhering to its heritage of quality and the ideal of superior policyholder service, New England Life brought change to the insurance industry when change was in the best interest of the public. Among its early "firsts" was the firm's guarantee of surrender values before they were required by law. More recently, it was the first to offer money market funds, the first to enter mutual funds, the first to establish discount

New England Life's home office at Post Office Square, Boston, where the company conducted its business from 1874 to 1941.

brokerage, and one of the first life insurance companies to establish a real estate subsidiary.

Growth, as well as excellence, is a part of the New England Life tradition. From an office staff of two persons who assisted Judge Willard Phillips when the company first opened its doors, New England Life now has a home office staff of more than 4,000 persons in Massachusetts. In addition, the firm has 274 agencies and offices located in 50 states and Puerto Rico.

New England Life continues to be a leader in the insurance and financial-services industries, serving an increasing number of Americans with its traditional emphasis on quality and comprehensive service.

FOLEY, HOAG & ELIOT

When Henry Foley and Garrett Hoag shook hands to begin their partnership in 1943, they didn't dream of its growth to nearly 100 lawyers today and thousands of clients ranging from individuals, small businesses, and local public bodies to major national and international corporations, Boston-based high-technology companies, most universities in the Boston area, medical organizations, public utilities, and trustees of numerous trust funds, and with recognition as a leader in labor and employment law practice.

High standards of scholarship, public service, and progressive outlook distinguished the firm from the outset. Foley had earned Harvard Law's highest degree of S.J.D., and was considered a brilliant maverick in the Boston legal community. At age 31 he had served as Boston's corporation counsel and later as acting dean and professor at Boston College Law School. Hoag was director of liquidation of closed banks in Massachusetts.

The two were soon joined by Thomas Eliot, a former congressman and Social Security Board general counsel, who later became chancellor of Washington University; and by Lewis Weinstein, fresh from Eisenhower's staff as liaison officer to DeGaulle, who later served as chairman of the State Board of Housing and president of numerous local and national welfare organizations.

Long before antidiscrimination became law, Foley determined that merit, not race or religion, would guide the firm's hiring. Quality of work continues as the most important factor in a lawyer's advancement in the firm, true for

both men and women.

Tradition of scholarship continues. One-half of today's partners served on their school law reviews and nearly as many were law clerks to judges of numerous courts, including the U.S. Supreme Court. A reputation for combining legal skills and dedication to public service results in the firm being called upon often in legal battles over major public issues.

In the early years the young firm was retained to advance the interests of the Port of Boston, and it successfully represented a fledgling Boston-based airline in its struggles before the Civil Aeronautics Board and courts to gain operating rights to Florida and California.

In a string of victories in the '50s and '60s, Foley, Hoag & Eliot upheld the legal foundation for public housing and urban-renewal programs in Massachusetts. After other proposals failed, the firm was a major participant in drafting and upholding legislation enabling the Prudential Center and other projects to be built in Boston and elsewhere.

Prominent in the area of real estate taxation, Foley, Hoag & Eliot won the landmark 1961 case striking down the widespread practice of disproportionate assessments and leading to major reform of the state's property tax system. More recently the firm, using a new technique for valuing a large industrial site, won a

multimillion-dollar tax abatement and then put together a financing agreement and new legislation to enable the municipality to undertake payment.

Foley, Hoag & Eliot's litigation and corporate law experts combined in 1981-1982 to thwart a hostile takeover of a major publicly held Boston-based client, through innovative applications of antiracketeering and federal and Massachusetts securities laws.

In 1982-1983 Weinstein served on the Ward Commission to investigate corruption in state and county building contracts; and in 1984, on behalf of the new mayor, the firm reviewed and made recommendations for strengthening Boston's contracting practices.

Known for its extensive pro bono program, the firm applies its talents and resources to cases having important public interest issues. Co-counsel in the suit that desegregated Boston public schools, Foley, Hoag & Eliot donated most of its court-awarded fee to a foundation to promote racial harmony in Boston. In 1981 the firm successfully participated in the Bob Jones University case before the U.S. Supreme Court, denying federal tax exemptions to racially discriminatory private schools.

When Paul Tsongas decided to leave the U.S. Senate at the end of his term and join a law firm in 1985, he chose Foley, Hoag & Eliot.

The headline "Youngsters of the Oldsters," remains apt for the city's ninth-largest law firm. From The Boston Globe, *1/13/1965.*

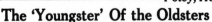

The 'Youngster' Of the Oldsters

By CAROL LISTON

ELIOT

The youngest of the city's "older" firms is Foley, Hoag & Eliot, now 21 years old.

The law office, with 30 attorneys, was founded by Henry E. Foley, after serving as Boston corporation counsel in the administration of Mayor Frederick W. Mansfield.

When he was sworn into office in 1934, at the age of 31, Foley was a political unknown, chosen purely on the recommendation of Dean Roscoe Pound of Harvard Law School.

Before serving as corporation counsel, Foley had been with Ropes & Gray, involved in corporate law. After retiring from public office, Foley started on his own in 1938.

He was joined shortly by Garrett S. Hoag, a Yale Law School graduate, and then by Thomas Eliot, in 1945. Eliot left the firm after a few years to begin an academic career. Today he is chancellor of Washington University in St. Louis.

Lewis H. Weinstein also joined the firm in 1945, dealing mostly in litigation and appellate work for the firm. However, as administrative law grew, Weinstein's activities extended into the area of urban renewal and housing law. Today he is one of the city's experts in these areas.

The firm handles a large amount of work before Federal regulatory agencies in Washington.

Over the years firm partners have taught in various law schools. Foley was acting dean and a professor at Boston College Law School.

Weinstein teaches a course in trial work at Harvard

University of California Law School at Berkley, at Harvard Law School and now teaches a course at M.I.T.

Among the firm's notable cases was the fight begun in 1948 against the then-proposed St. Lawrence Seaway. Foley was hired by a New England citizens group, financed by local railroad and utility companies, to fight the seaway proposal, because it was thought it would take commercial traffic away from the Port of Boston, Massachusetts and the other New England states. He travelled through the states arguing for his clients and made radio debates defending their position.

At that time he won the case and the seaway plans were shelved. Years later, with a strong push from Sen. John F. Kennedy, the seaway was approved by Congress.

The firm also handled Northeast Airline's successful case for a route from New England to Florida. That Federal grant of a temporary certificate to fly to Florida is now under litigation.

Probably the firm's most notable victory was getting the Massachusetts Port Authority equal rates with Philadelphia and Baltimore and other Southern ports for imports and exports going to and coming from the Middle West. Until the decision, upheld by the U.S. Supreme Court two years ago, Boston was assigned higher rates than the other

Foley, Hoag & Eliot

GARRETT HOAG, HENRY FOLEY AND LEWIS WEINSTEIN

firm, Laurence Fordham, won the first victory for taxpayers against tax assessors in Springfield. The case succeeded in

chairman of the Combined Jewish Appeal in Greater Boston; a trustee of the Beth Israel Hospital and overseer of the Florence Heller Graduate School at Brandeis University.

BOSTON'S BETH ISRAEL HOSPITAL

On February 4, 1917, in a converted 45-bed former estate on Townsend Street in Boston's Roxbury neighborhood, Beth Israel Hospital admitted its first patient, and a parade of 5,000 celebrated. The journey had been arduous.

Turn-of-the-century Boston had seen an influx of Jewish immigrants from eastern Europe, settling predominantly in the West End of the city, and a need became apparent for an inpatient facility to address the health-care needs of a poor and growing populace, in an environment where their special cultural, dietary, and language requirements could be attended.

It was the women of the Jewish community who pioneered the struggle. They were the visionaries who coordinated the Beth Israel Hospital Association, who sold miniature bricks and collected nickles and dimes door to door to fulfill their community's hopes for a Jewish-sponsored hospital "... for the purpose of affording medical care and nursing to sick or disabled persons of any creed or nationality." Beth Israel's doors opened to all.

In the succeeding decade the tireless association raised three million dollars to acquire land for the growing hospital on Boston's Brookline Avenue, near Harvard Medical School, and by 1928 a new 200-bed medical facility was completed. In time Beth Israel became a major Harvard teaching hospital.

Boston's Beth Israel has been a source of innovations and achievements in patient care,

The enthusiastic support of the women of Boston's Jewish community in the early 1900s helped in the struggle to establish a hospital "for the purpose of affording medical care and nursing to sick or disabled persons of any creed or nationality."

scholarship, and biomedical research over the years. History-making advances have included the development of an electronic cardiac pacemaker and cardiac defibrillator; studies of the mechanism of the action of heparin; publication of the first patients' bill of rights; a revolutionary system of primary nursing care established throughout the hospital; an alternative birth center; a hospital-based ambulatory care service that has become a national model; an innovative multidisciplinary rape crisis intervention program; development of techniques for dissolving life-threatening blood clots following heart attacks; successful clinical testing of medications to improve the functioning of impaired hearts; and the conception and delivery of the first baby in Massachusetts to be born as a result of in-vitro fertilization.

Today Beth Israel's modern medical center houses 460 adult inpatient beds in medicine, surgery, obstetrics and gynecology, orthopedics, psychiatry, neurosurgery, neuromedicine, and medical and surgical intensive-care units. Over 21,000 inpatients receive treatment each year. The hospital's 24-hour Berenson Emergency Unit is part of the Longwood Area Trauma

Two of the original buildings (foreground), dedicated in 1928, combine with striking new inpatient facilities to provide a gracious and contemporary setting for excellence in patient care.

Center, and responds to more than 33,000 patient visits annually.

Significant research is under way at Beth Israel's Charles A. Dana Research Institute and the famed Harvard-Thorndike Research Laboratory in the areas of nutrition and metabolism, endocrinology, hematology, oncology, cardiology, nephrology, obstetrics, surgery, and pulmonary disease. Computer technology has broadened potential for both research and direct medical care.

Service, scholarship, accountability, and origins have remained the fundamental elements of the internationally recognized Beth Israel Hospital. Its successful contributions to medicine and health and to the well-being of patients throughout the world reflect Beth Israel's concern for today's illness and tomorrow's health. In a city renowned for excellence in medical care, Boston's Beth Israel stands as a tribute to the vision of its founders and as a great resource to the constituencies it serves.

GASTON SNOW & ELY BARTLETT, ESQS.

The national firm of Gaston Snow & Ely Bartlett, Esqs., with roots established in the mid-19th century, lays legitimate claim to being the second-oldest law firm in Boston, among the oldest continuing practicing firms in New York City, and, consequently, one of the oldest law practices in the United States. Headquartered in Boston, with offices in New York, Palo Alto, San Francisco, and Coral Gables, its long heritage is a proud history of character and essence with the added proud prospect of being one of the nation's fastest-growing practices.

Gaston Snow & Ely Bartlett's first constituent began his practice in Boston in 1844. William Gaston, first president of the Boston Bar Association, mayor of Boston during the Great Fire of 1872, and later governor of Massachusetts, was joined by Frederick E. Snow and, in 1883, by his son William (Colonel) Gaston to form Gaston & Snow. The abilities of partners Snow, the superb lawyer, and Colonel Gaston, the rugged entrepreneur, proved an effective team and the new firm prospered and grew.

Shortly after the senior Gaston opened his office, a practice was founded in downtown New York City which, some decades later and until its merger in 1981 with GS&EB, bore the names Charles F. Beekman and Morton Bogue, Esqs. The Ely Bartlett element of the firm had related beginnings when, in 1872, shortly after the Civil War, General Charles W. Bartlett, a trial attorney, commenced practice in Boston and, contemporaneously, Henry Wilson Ely "read law" at his offices in Berkshire County. In 1935 Joseph B. Ely, son of Henry, and the retiring governor of the Massachusetts Commonwealth,

reopened his practice and specialized in the corporate reorganization cases of the times in three cities, including Boston. The Bartlett and Ely firms merged in 1946.

These many complementary threads tied together in 1974, when the 40-member Gaston, Snow, Motley & Holt merged with the 40-member Ely Bartlett, Brown & Proctor and in 1981 with Beekman and Bogue.

The offices of the law firm of Gaston, Snow & Saltonstall were located at 70 State Street in Boston. The portrait on the wall is of Governor William Gaston. Photo circa 1900.

While its predecessors have been practicing law for more than one-half of this country's period of constitutional government, tradition for GS&EB has not meant an entirely traditional approach to the practice of law. Its base has been in the areas of finance, banking, brokerage, real estate, taxes, corporate, litigation, and estate planning. But the firm of the 1980s has devoted significant resources to enlarging its expertise in developing areas of law. New methods of financing, under such labels as leveraged leasing and tax shelter syndication, have become a specialty, as have legal problems

involving natural resources, environmental issues, and hazardous wastes. The firm has added significant capabilities in health law. Additionally, advice on problems involving the development, financing, and protection of technology, particularly as related to computers, is provided. The multistate strategy adopted in recent years by GS&EB is relatively new to the United States and affords a variety of conveniences to multistate clients coast to coast, including representation of foreign corporations. With emphasis on personal service, over 200 lawyers in five cities now conduct a broad legal practice supported by a highly sophisticated legal research and communications capability.

Thus, clients of the firm include publicly held national and multinational industrial corporations, public utilities, banks and bank holding companies, oil companies, major investment banking houses, some 60 registered investment companies, securities and commodities brokers, insurance companies and other financial intermediaries, and large retail chains, in this country and abroad. GS&EB's quasi-governmental business includes representation of both offerors and purchasers in industrial revenue and pollution-control financings and in connection with offerings by governmental and quasi-governmental issuers in Massachusetts, Canada, and Puerto Rico.

The history of any institution is largely the history of the individuals who make it up and, historically, members of Gaston Snow & Ely Bartlett have combined private practice with public service. The firm's alumni include three governors of the Commonwealth of Massachusetts (including Robert Bradford) and one (Louis Brann) of the state of Maine. And tradition of service as citizens is carried forward to the present day. Partners at the firm include a former under secretary of the United States Department of Commerce, deputy assistant secretary of the Department of Health, Education and Welfare, general counsel of the Air Force, vice-president of the Federal Reserve Bank of Boston, a state court judge, chief assistant United States attorney, and a chairman of a Massachusetts regulatory agency.

Gaston Snow's practice in investment work dates from 1924, when a then-partner organized the first open-end investment company in the United States. In the 1940s the firm established itself as a specialist in investment and mutual funds when it helped draft federal legislation that ultimately became the Investment Company Act of 1940, without which mutual funds would not have become salable products. By the 1950s the firm of 19 active lawyers had developed a broad base of mutual fund clients including Massachusetts Investors Trust, Fidelity Group of Funds, Scudder Stevens and Clark Fund,

William A. Gaston, 1859-1927.

Henry W. Ely, 1853-1933.

Eaton & Howard Fund, and Vance-Sanders Fund. Representing investment trusts and investment companies is a strong tradition at GS&EB and today its 74-member corporate department includes a specialty group dealing with investment company mergers and acquisitions of private investment companies by mutual funds, sometimes serving as a nexus for venture capitalists and proposed startup companies. GS&EB's long experience as a full-service business firm brings other specialties to its clients, including real estate and equipment lease financings, real estate development and financing, proxy contests, and contested tender offers. A substantial practice exists in the regulatory area involving the entry of nonfinancial institutions into financial markets and the development of interstate banking relationships.

As law has evolved and expanded, the needs of clients have changed and multiplied. The traditional individual client needs that dominated legal services in the firm's early days are still the focus of vital legal functions today, and the continuing objective of Gaston Snow & Ely Bartlett is to function through the individual lawyer serving the client.

225

RYAN, ELLIOTT AND COMPANY, INC.

Boston's renaissance in the 1960s resulted in the development of the Back Bay's Prudential Center, an exceptional restoration of Quincy Market and Faneuil Hall Marketplace, the launching of the Government Center and City Hall Plaza, the beautifying of the waterfront, and the rebirth of downtown Boston. In a generation of development since that time, Boston has renewed its historic role as a center of commerce, and the Ryan, Elliott Companies have played a major role in implementing a recurrence of economic vitality to Boston's business district and environs.

On April 1, 1960, Ryan, Elliott and Company was the first commercial and industrial real estate agency in Boston to open for business in over 50 years. Founded by John Ryan, William G. Coughlin, and Graeme Elliott, three of the firm's original four employees, the privately owned Ryan, Elliott has made its mark by encouraging new development, while preserving and protecting Boston's unique past. Through its full-service capabilities, Ryan, Elliott specializes in the sale, leasing, and management of commercial, industrial, and investment properties, as well as arranging property syndications and limited partnerships, offering professional real estate consulting and property appraisals for downtown Boston buildings and high-technology identity properties on suburban Boston's Route 128 and Route 495.

The preservation of many Boston properties has been a landmark for Ryan, Elliott's leasing success, having included One and Ten Winthrop Square, Faneuil Hall Marketplace, the Sears Crescent and the Hudson Building, the former Salada Tea Building, now renamed Berkeley Place, and the Merchant's Building at 77 Summer Street, headquarters for the Ryan,

Founder John Ryan, chief executive officer and treasurer.

Elliott Companies.

In its quarter-century of real estate service, Ryan, Elliott has leased or sold over one billion dollars worth of Boston's office buildings, investment, hotel, and development properties; assembled large sites for developers; leased major office towers; inaugurated the sale and preservation of noted historical buildings; and conducted space searches exclusively for many major national corporations. Through many successful property syndications, Ryan, Elliott has provided Bostonians with a vehicle for individual investment in the city's real estate revitalization and has, as well, realized significant acquisitions for European, Middle Eastern, and Far Eastern clients.

Ryan, Elliott specializes in acquisitions and assemblages, having completed both for the Federal Reserve Bank of Boston, resulting in the development of the 32-story Federal Reserve Plaza tower. This specialization has also helped realize the development of

the Paine Webber Building at 265 Franklin Street, and, through a 10-parcel assemblage at Fort Hill Square, has helped implement the development of International Place, a mixed-use complex to be in excess of one million square feet of space.

In 1982 the largest lease transaction in the greater Boston area was negotiated by Ryan, Elliott at the State Street South Office Park in Quincy for a total of 182,000 square feet. To date, Ryan, Elliott has leased a total of 1,300,000 square feet at this suburban office park. In 1983 Ryan, Elliott again finalized the largest lease in the city with over 200,000 square feet signed with IBM at Copley Place. The Ryan, Elliott Companies are now introducing a thriving Boston and New England economy both nationally and internationally, attracting U.S. and foreign investment, and accommodating the increasing demand by individuals and institutions to invest in real estate.

Founder William G. Coughlin, chairman of the board.

PARKER HOUSE

Oliver Wendell Holmes, in his poem, "At the Saturday Club," wrote:

". . . Such guests! What famous names its record boasts, Whose owners wander in the mob of ghosts! . . ."

Indeed. Holmes had often gathered with Emerson, Lowell, Longfellow, Whittier, and Hawthorne, later with Parkman, Aldrich, and Howell, in the New Marble Building at the corner of School and Tremont streets, home to the literary Saturday Club of the 1860s and 1870s. Charles Dickens joined them for a time, taking up residence in Suite No. 338.

The Parker House, capturing the special essence of Boston, its dignity, its punctilious regard for form and manners, its grace and good taste, has remained open since October 5, 1855, the day Harvey D. Parker hung the simple sign "Parker's" atop his five-story, white-marble hotel. In an atmosphere of hospitality and elegant comfort, poets and philosophers gathered and politicians and visiting performers rendezvoused. Beacon Hill Brahmans, prim in their morning coats and boiled shirts, were at home here, as were long-whiskered "outlanders" from Maine and New Hampshire. Harvard blades and State Street merchants came in coaches across cobblestoned streets to drink Sherry Cobblers and dine on Scotch grouse and leg of mutton in Parker's dining room of distinction.

Of humble origins, the industrious and ambitious Harvey Parker built the original hotel to house his new and thriving restaurant. It was in Parker's kitchen that enduring contributions to gastronomy were produced. Such epicurean delights as Boston cream pie and Boston scrod originated here and, from the imagination of a German baker named Ward, the first of what would be known throughout the world as Parker House rolls were created.

Distinguished neighbors bordered the historic lot that Parker purchased from Joshua Steward for his enterprise. Adjoining on the east was Horticultural Hall, built in 1844 on the former site of America's oldest educational institution, Boston Latin School, from which the name School Street, laid out in 1640, derived.

The hotel prospered, continuing to host the city's most prestigious groups and enjoy the patronage of presidents and statesmen. Generals Grant, Sherman, Hancock, and Garfield came to stay, as did Sarah Bernhardt and Edwin Booth and his brother John Wilkes (just eight days prior to his unexpected appearance on the stage of Ford's Theater). Success led the enterprising and popular proprietor to acquire in 1860, then demolish, Horticultural Hall for expansion of the hotel. For the next quarter-century, up until his death in 1884, Parker continued to purchase, expand, and annex his property, a sprawling mix of buildings, elaborate and immense for its time.

In the 1890s the Joseph R. Whipple Corp. took over the vast complex, and in 1925 all but a small annex of the now-out-of-date marble palace of Harvey Parker was demolished to make way for a sleek and modern 1927 structure. A Parker House of steel and granite was constructed 14 stories above the corner of School and Tremont, and an 800-room hotel with a grand rooftop ballroom enjoyed a new burst of prosperity. But the hard times that followed the stock market crash of 1929 brought a mortgage foreclosure and a transfer of ownership to Glenwood Sherrard, who operated the property until his death in 1958.

In 1968 the hotel, which had fallen into disrepair in the past decade, was acquired by the Dunfey family, owners of hotels and restaurants throughout New England. The Dunfeys initiated a $12-million, long-range restoration program for their historic Boston property. In a spirit of tradition, elegant workmanship of another era combines with modern innovations and amenities to provide visitors from around the world 530 restored guest rooms and 14 function rooms, with names like Whittier, Longfellow, and Emerson, to accommodate gatherings of 10 to 400.

The oldest continuously operating hotel in the country, now the flagship of the worldwide Dunfey/Omni Classic Hotel Division, is once again a grand hotel. Gone now is the white facade. So are the echoes of the distinguished voices and the cobbled streets. But the ghosts still stalk the corridors of this Boston institution and, if fate is kind, will for many years to come.

The Parker House, circa 1880. The facility, which Harvey Parker initially built to house his new and thriving restaurant, has remained open since October 5, 1855.

FRANK B. HALL & CO. OF MASSACHUSETTS, INC.

A continuity of tradition prevails at Frank B. Hall & Co. of Massachusetts, Inc., where the primary mission for over a half-century has been to protect the human and business assets of its client community, in an effort to assure a secure environment for growth and prosperity. Under the leadership of Colby Hewitt, Jr., and Frederic C. Church, Jr., second-generation managers and namesakes of the firm's founders, the largest property and liability broker in New England provides full-service insurance brokerage and risk management for industry, commerce, finance, the professions, and government.

In 1933 Frederic C. Church and Charles Colby Hewitt consolidated several local agencies to establish the firm of Boit, Dalton and Church and affect competitive services and prices on the Boston insurance scene.

Over the next decades implementation of the process of protection changed dramatically. Initially offering essentially brokerage services, an expanded postwar society and global economy changed the nature of the industry. In a more vigorous marketplace, new exposures in new areas increased client liabilities and government regulations complicated business management. Responding to change, Hall created responsive new coverages and services such as exhausted value for older properties, errors and omissions for the Boston-founded mutual fund industry and for architects and engineers, as well as comprehensive self-insurance capabilities. Insulating business from a potential impact of loss became a permanent and integral function of financial management and resulted in the emergence of risk management, a new concept of insurance practice.

Frederic C. Church, Jr. (left), executive vice-president and chief operating officer, and Colby Hewitt, Jr., chairman of the board and chief executive officer of Frank B. Hall & Co. of Massachusetts, Inc.

In creative tradition the firm shifted from insurance brokerage to an insurance services firm, with concentration on risk analysis, loss control, claims management, self-insurance, and other specialized efforts. With a professional staff of translators and a team approach to defining risks and developing unique coverages for unique exposures, the firm prospered.

Boit, Dalton and Church was the largest broker in New England in 1971 when it merged with, and became the northeast regional headquarters of, the worldwide Frank B. Hall & Co. Inc. Combining and building on many years of pioneering enterprise, the concern later became 'one of the top three publicly held insurance service firms in the world. As Hall of Massachusetts, a self-contained unit autonomous in execution, the Boston operation is structured to the specific needs of its area, but, as part of the aggregate Hall team, has access to a global network of geographical and technical facilities and the resources of experts on six continents, as it serves growing and multinational clients in the United States and abroad. The firm's headquarters is at the same historic Batterymarch Building where its founders domiciled. Support branches are maintained at Manchester, New Hampshire, and Meriden, Connecticut.

Brokerage remains the central element at Hall of Massachusetts, providers of insurance and risk management to an ever-expanding business community. Comprehensive financial guarantee programs and dealing with exposures arising from the biotechnical industries, those caused by environmental hazard, and dealing with political risks and terrorism is the focus of the future for the firm's 225 staff members.

There is active participation among Hall of Massachusetts' personnel in civic, educational, and charitable endeavors, including directorships and trusteeships in the Chamber of Commerce, Junior Achievement, Deaconess Hospital, the New England Conservatory of Music, Wheelock College, Hampshire College, and Old Sturbridge Village. Frederic C. Church, Jr., currently serves as president of the Boys' and Girls' Clubs of Boston, following, in characteristic tradition, the footsteps of his father.

KEANE, INC.

Twenty short years ago a new technical revolution was taking place, and the world was indeed being transformed as the pace of innovation in high technology accelerated. New computers were flooding the marketplace. Few people really understood this growing technology; there were neither track records nor preset standards of performance for the required specialized skills that never before existed.

At the height of this revolution, armed with $7,000, a telephone, and a large amount of foresight, John F. Keane, consultant, opened a business over a doughnut shop in Hingham and entered the software services business—a totally unknown entity in 1965. That was 925 clients, $137 million in revenue, and thousands of person years of software services ago for Keane, Inc.

Founded to assist companies in overcoming the technical complexities associated with a new

John F. Keane, founder and president.

generation of hardware, the firm, in five years, had grown from modest beginnings to the Keane Associates, Inc., a publicly held company of 100 technical consultants, integrating many technologies and disciplines to service organizations representing every segment of business and industry in the design, development, and implementation of computer application projects. By 1970 Keane was New England's largest computer advisory services group. Its network of branch offices numbered five, and its range of services expanded to include management consulting.

To satisfy the requirements of multiple users, an approach to software development termed Productivity Management®, which utilized fundamental management principles and enabled the company to manage an environment in which change takes place, was adopted by Keane's team of specialists and became the foundation of the firm's operating methodology.

As market needs changed, Keane evaluated new services and products, and in 1974 acquired Innovations in Technology, Inc., a concern supplying data-processing services to the health-care industry. IIT became a division of Keane, known as KeaMed, which by 1979 had penetrated the New England marketplace, and watched its total hospital base grow sixfold. As the 1970s drew to a close, Keane Associates, Inc., became Keane, Inc., a full computer services firm, assisting the business community to adapt to the technologies essential for progress.

The Keane, Inc., of today is a 600-employee company, in the forefront of the software services industry, and is made up of two operating divisions. Its Information

Services Division supplies computer professionals to clients in every field of business and industry who provide continuing assistance in the design, implementation, modification, and management of the most advanced computer-based systems. The company's KeaMed Hospital Systems Division specializes in providing hospital financial management, patient-care and ancillary department applications, as well as computer hardware to an international health-care market.

Anticipated gross revenue for the firm in 1984 is over $30 million. Fourteen East Coast and Midwest branch offices now assist in solving client problems as Keane, Inc., headquartered at 210 Commercial Street on Boston's historic waterfront, postures itself for tomorrow's technologies, through the continued vision of its founder and president, John F. Keane.

The home office of Keane, Inc., is located at 210 Commercial Street.

BOSTON WHARF COMPANY

The birth of the Boston Wharf Company as a corporate entity took place with the granting of its charter on April 16, 1836, and the keen foresight of its small group of resolute subscribers who recognized in a vacant marshland a commercial opportunity. Their vision saw not an expanse of mud flats, but a road from Boston to the sea that was the source of the town's prosperity.

The original land, fronting on First and B streets, was purchased from the South Boston Association. A 12-foot-high seawall was erected. The area of Andrew Square was leveled, providing fill for the remaining acreage, and Boston Wharf Company's first real estate development venture commenced. The undertaking would prove, over the next decades, the wisdom of its founders.

For the next half-century the principal business of the Boston Wharf Company was the docking of vessels and the storage of their cargoes for the purchase and sale of products of trade. In 1856 the firm became exclusively engaged in the storage of sugar and molasses from vessels making regular passage between Boston and Cuba. Against a backdrop of the channel decorated with tall-masted ships, longshoremen unloaded troves of the products into 17 storing sheds for the merchants of the community who did a brisk business with the local distilleries and refineries.

By 1880 America's "Age of Big Business" was in full swing, and the country saw a technological revolution that dramatically changed its life and its landscape.

The Boston Wharf Company has been in existence since 1836, and today is a combination of the charm of the old and the spirit of the new.

Rising industrialism eventually designed the policy of the Boston Wharf Company. Its property became a highly regarded industrial real estate area with immense possibilities, as new enterprises required new facilities for expanding operations. Many of these facilities would be erected on Boston Wharf. The building era of the firm began in 1882 with an ambitious construction program that would see some 90 buildings erected for modern business.

By 1929 the bonded storage business at Boston Wharf had expired and the company had entered the field of management and development of industrial real estate. This "new" business grew by leaps and bounds, paralleling the eras of Boston's growth and prosperity. Gradually, the Boston

Wharf Company transformed what was into what would be. From the grass and mud flats of yesterday, the Boston Wharf of today is a combination of the charm of the old and the spirit of the new.

On 30 acres east of Fort Point Channel at the southern entrance to Boston's vibrant financial district is being created an integrated community, a revitalized hub of commerce and trade, art, and technology. Art galleries, restaurants, and specialty shops are beginning to appear on streets named after Boston's founding fathers. With an authentic backdrop of the past, 78 turn-of-the-century brick buildings are being restored and converted into showrooms and offices that support a wide variety of commercial activities, from software merchandising to kite-making. Some buildings have been converted to residential use, including condominium lofts and apartments, and others will follow. This comprehensive redevelopment project, now under way, will provide more than four million square feet of working and living space, maintaining a kinship with the past while infusing the conveniences of the present.

In partnership with respected development firms from both sides of the Atlantic, the company is committed to the continued renewal of Boston Wharf. From the United Kingdom, co-developer Town & City Properties, part of the Sterling Guarantee Trust Group, brings a long history of real estate development to bear on Boston Wharf. And Rose Associates, the United States partner, has more than 50 years' experience in the development, ownership, and management of commercial and residential properties along the eastern seaboard.

ROSE ASSOCIATES

When representatives of New York-based Rose Associates first started exploring the Boston real estate market in the late 1960s, local bankers and real estate professionals were curious about what they would do and just how long they would stay.

Today, many years, many millions of dollars, and many buildings later, they know that Rose Associates will be a major factor in the Boston real estate world for the foreseeable future.

With the 1.1-million-square-foot One Financial Center and the 728,000-square-foot Keystone Building already completed, with the rehabilitation and recycling of the 4,000,000-square-foot Boston Wharf properties already in progress, and with other major projects on the drawing boards, it is clear that the Rose commitment to Boston is real, is major, and is continuing.

Rose Associates is an organization that for over 50 years has been devoted to the successful development, ownership, and management of large-scale residential and commercial real estate projects along the Eastern Seaboard.

The hallmarks of the firm are competence and integrity, the Rose style is one of understated good taste, and the company perspective focuses on long-term relationships and the creation of long-term capital values.

In Boston, as in the other regions where Rose Associates is active, firm members work hard at being "good neighbors"—contributing to local causes, joining the boards of local civic and charitable groups, teaching and lecturing at local educational institutions and before local professional organizations.

Daniel Rose, Rose Associates' president, says: "Boston has been good to us and we try to return the compliment. It was a happy day when our British friends, who had just developed the State Street Bank Building, suggested that we join them in their proposed next Boston project, which eventually turned out to be the present Keystone Building. The years since then have been happy ones, and we look forward in high spirits to the future."

Two Rose Associates landmark buildings—the imposing Keystone Building (left) and the 1.1-million-square-foot One Financial Center (center).

HOUGHTON MIFFLIN COMPANY

An abiding sense of tradition is clear at the publishing house of Houghton Mifflin Company, as befits a company that can look back to having published Longfellow, Emerson, Whittier, Hawthorne, Dickens, Thackeray, Tennyson, Browning, Thoreau, and Twain, and a company primarily responsible for making Boston the nation's capital of both literature and publishing for many years.

Houghton Mifflin had its origins at the Old Corner Bookstore at Washington and School streets in the "Golden Age" of literary Boston. Built just after the Great Fire of 1711, the bookstore, for more than 50 years, was the literary center of Boston, headquarters for the famed Temple Club of 1829, the Tremont of 1851, and later the Somerset, the Union, and the Saturday clubs. In 1832 publishers William D. Ticknor and John Allen purchased the facility. Their partnership was short-lived, and soon thereafter Ticknor chose a partner who complemented his strengths, James T. Fields.

The history of Houghton Mifflin Company began more than a century and a half ago at the Old Corner Bookstore at School and Washington streets.

Together they assembled probably the most distinguished collection of writers ever associated with one American publishing house. They brought tact, discrimination, and generous royalties to their relationships with American and English authors, and the firm began to take its place as a leading publisher of the mid-19th century. To be published by Ticknor & Fields was a hallmark of success.

An association beginning in 1852 with Henry O. Houghton of the Riverside Press, and later with George H. Mifflin, culminated in 1880 in a merger of the two firms and the birth of the new partnership of Houghton, Mifflin and Company. By 1908 it would be a corporation.

Early on an Educational Department was established to publish books for a growing number of students. Today the educational publishing divisions are the backbone of the company. Houghton Mifflin is a leader in developing instructional techniques and educational materials. An extensive list of elementary, high school, and college textbooks, tests, software, and other educational materials, developed in Boston and by Chicago and Canadian subsidiaries, account for the largest segment of the business. Among the firm's best-selling educational publications are the *Houghton Mifflin Reading Program,* high school mathematics textbooks, college-level English and accounting programs, and standardized tests such as the *Iowa Tests of Basic Skills* and the *Stanford-Binet Intelligence Scale.*

Houghton Mifflin's general publishing activities have also remained important. Fine literature for adults and children is published under the Houghton Mifflin, Ticknor & Fields, and Clarion

Ticknor & Fields, forerunner of Houghton Mifflin Company, assembled one of the most distinguished collections of writers ever associated with one publisher. Here the founders, James T. Fields (left) and William D. Ticknor (right), are seen with one of their many authors, Nathaniel Hawthorne.

imprints. Through the years Houghton Mifflin authors have received numerous book awards, including a number of Pulitzer prizes and American book awards, as well as Caldecott and Newbery medals for children's books.

Publishing fine literary and educational works is Houghton Mifflin's heritage. For more than 150 years the company's objective has been to shape information, instruction, and entertainment into forms that provide unique features of value to its customers. The firm develops and manages ideas and intellectual properties with the help of an extensive collection of author relationships, a staff of experienced editorial talent, and a valuable storehouse of creative works.

Houghton Mifflin issues works representing a variety of viewpoints for a broad range of markets. Kate

Wiggins' *Rebecca of Sunnybrook Farm,* Edward Bellamy's *Looking Backward,* Henry James' *The Portrait of a Lady* and *The Bostonians,* Adolf Hitler's *Mein Kampf,* Winston Churchill's six-volume *The Second World War,* Esther Forbes' *Johnny Tremain,* and Rachel Carson's *Silent Spring* were all published by the firm as it built a list of distinguished as well as best-selling 20th-century authors. This list also included Woodrow Wilson, Margaret Deland, and Brooks Adams, and by mid-century added Henry Cabot Lodge, Theodore Roosevelt, Amy Lowell, Archibald MacLeish, General George Patton, and Field Marshal Bernard Montgomery. Its contemporary authors include Roger Tory Peterson, who began the popular Field Guide Series 50 years ago, and Stephen Birnbaum, well-known travel guide author, as

well as Louis Auchincloss, J.R.R. Tolkien, Howard Fast, John Kenneth Galbraith, Arthur Schlesinger, Paul Theroux, and Judith Rossner.

As society has moved into the information age, the firm now publishes materials in electronic as well as print formats. In 1964 Houghton Mifflin began work on a new dictionary, the first to establish a computerized word base derived from extensive word frequency research and to be typeset by computer. Introduced in 1969, *The American Heritage Dictionary* was acclaimed by literary critics, academics, and the public and remained on the *New York Times* Non-Fiction Bestseller List for 39 weeks. Other reference publications, including a variety of children's dictionaries, were derived from the extensive word base, which was also used in the development of sophisticated lexical software for word-processing applications. The firm continues to explore and develop new ways of

distributing information electronically.

A well-established firm moving with the times is the Houghton Mifflin Company of the 1980s. There is a blending of tradition and innovation even in its two separate downtown Boston offices. The firm's Trade Publishing Division occupies the handsome turn-of-the-century buildings at Two and Three Park Street, overlooking the Boston Common, where the company has been located since 1880. Corporate headquarters and other editorial offices are at the contemporary One Beacon Street high rise. Harold T. Miller, chief executive officer since 1973 and chairman since 1979, directs operations of Houghton Mifflin Company and its professional staff of more than 1,700.

Houghton Mifflin's extensive list of reference publications and lexical software are derived principally from the company's computerized American Heritage Dictionary *word base.*

Houghton Mifflin is a leading publisher of elementary, high school, and college textbooks and other educational material.

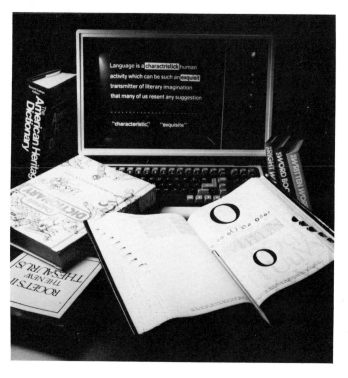

Patrons

The following individuals, companies, and organizations have made a valuable commitment to the quality of this publication. Windsor Publications and the Greater Boston Chamber of Commerce gratefully acknowledge their participation in *Boston: City on a Hill.*

Adia Personnel Services
Alexander & Alexander, Inc.
  OBrion, Russell & Co.
Arthur Andersen & Co.*
ARTS/Boston, Inc.
Bank of Boston*
Beacon Hill Travel Service
The Beal Companies*
Bentley College
Berman & Sons, Inc.
Ann Blackman & Company, Inc.
Blue Cross and Blue Shield of
  Massachusetts, Inc.*
Boston College*
Boston Edison Company*
Boston Gas Company*
*The Boston Globe**
*The Boston Herald**
Boston Insurance Center, Inc.
Boston Safe Deposit and Trust
  Company*
Boston School of Modern
  Languages, Inc.
Boston University*
Boston Wharf Company*
Boston's Beth Israel Hospital*
Vincent C. Bowhers, CLU
Harold Brown-Hamilton Realty Co.
Brown, Rudnick, Freed & Gesmer
Browning-Ferris Industries
Harold Cabot & Co., Inc.
Cabot, Cabot & Forbes*
The Chiofaro Company
John M. Corcoran & Company
Court Square Bank Note
Court Square Press Inc.
Hon. Lawrence S. Di Cara
Dun & Bradstreet Corporation
Eastern Gas and Fuel Associates*
Empire Cleaning, Inc.
Ernst & Whinney*
Faneuil Hall Travel Associates, Inc.
Fleet National Bank

Foley, Hoag & Eliot*
H. MacKenzie Freeman, M.D.
Frontier Capital Management Co., Inc.
Goldstein & Manello
Gaston Snow & Ely Bartlett, Esqs.*
Greater Boston YMCA
Ryna Greenbaum
Hale and Dorr*
Frank B. Hall & Co. of Massachusetts,
  Inc.*
Hall, Davison & Company
John Hancock Mutual Life Insurance
  Company*
Christos A. Hasiotis, M.D.
Haymarket Realty, Inc.
Hinds & Coon Co.
Hoffman Florist
Honeywell Information Systems
H.P. Hood Inc.
Houghton Mifflin Company*
Hub Mail Advertising*
Itzkan and Marchiel Real Estate
Jimmy's Harborside Restaurant*
Jordan Marsh Company*
Junior Achievement of Eastern Mass.
  Inc.
Karaian Limousine Corporation/
  Executive Service
Keane, Inc.*
Mirle A. Kellett, Jr., M.D.
William I. Kelly Associates, Inc.
John F. Kennedy Library
Robert T. Kennedy
Kinney Vacuum Company
Leggat McCall and Werner, Inc.*
Lincoln Property Company
Arthur D. Little, Inc.*
George B.H. Macomber Company*
B.L. Makepeace, Inc.
Manpower Temporary Service
Marr Companies*
Meredith & Grew, Incorporated
The MITRE Corporation
Moseley, Hallgarten, Estabrook &
  Weeden Inc.*
Lawrence A. Murray
Nathanson & Goldberg-Attorneys at
  Law
New England Mutual Life Insurance
  Company*
New England Sights
North Bennet Street School
North, North & Nelson Inc.

Northeastern University*
Olney Associates Inc.
Olympia & York Properties
Parker House*
Peat, Marwick, Mitchell & Co.*
Professional Designs Incorporated
Prudential Insurance Company of
  America*
Quincy Market Cold Storage and
  Warehouse Company
Retina Associates, Inc.
The Paul Revere House
Louis Rodier
Jaanus Roht
Ropes & Gray*
Rose Associates*
Ryan, Elliott and Company, Inc.*
Maurice H. Saval Insurance
Sheraton Boston Hotel and Towers*
Shreve, Crump & Low, Inc.*
Somerville Historical Commission
Harry M. Stevens, Inc.
Egil Stigum Associates
John J. Storm
Frank Sullivan Company
Texaco U.S.A.
The Thompson & Lichtner Company,
  Inc.
Trammell Crow Company
Trans World Airlines, Inc.
Trethewey Bros. Inc.
Tucker, Anthony and R.L. Day, Inc.*
Union Bookbinding Co., Inc.
Union Warren Savings Bank*
United Way of Massachusetts Bay
University of Massachusetts
George H. Wahn Co.
Warner and Stackpole*
Zayre Corp.*

*Partners in Progress of *Boston: City on a Hill.* The histories of these companies and organizations appear in Chapter 11, beginning on page 172.

Bibliography

Ainley, Leslie G., *Boston Mahatma* (Boston: Bruce Humphries, 1949).

Amory, Cleveland, *The Proper Bostonians* (New York: Dutton, 1947).

Antin, Mary, *The Promised Land* (Boston: Houghton-Mifflin, 1912).

Bailyn, Bernard, *The New England Merchants in the Seventeenth Century* (Cambridge: Harvard University Press, 1955).

Banner, James, *To the Hartford Convention* (New York: Knopf, 1970)

Bartlett, Irving, *Wendell Philips: Brahmin Radical* (Boston: Beacon Press, 1961).

Blodgett, Geoffrey, *The Gentle Reformers: Massachusetts Democrats in the Cleveland Era* (Cambridge: Harvard University Press, 1966).

Brooks, Van Wyck, *The Flowering of New England* (New York: Dutton, 1936).

Brown, Richard D., *Revolutionary Politics in Massachusetts* (Cambridge: Harvard University Press, 1970).

Brown, Thomas N., *Irish-American Nationalism* (Philadelphia: Lippincott, 1966).

Commanger, Henry Steele, *Theodore Parker: Yankee Crusader* (Boston: Little, Brown, 1936).

Curley, James Michael, *I'd Do It Again - A Record of All My Uproarious Years,* (Englewood Cliffs, New Jersey: Prentice-Hall, 1957).

Cutler, John Henry, *"Honey Fitz," Three Steps to the White House: The Life and Time of John F. "Honey Fitz" Fitzgerald* (New York: W. W. Norton, 1949).

De Marco, William, *Ethnics and Enclaves: Boston's Italian North End* (Ann Arbor: UMI Research Press, 1981).

Dever, Joseph, *Cushing of Boston: A Candid Biography* (Boston: Humphries, 1965).

Dinneen, Joseph F., *The Purple Shamrock: The Hon. James Michael Curley of Boston* (New York: W. W. Norton, 1949).

——————, *Ward Eight* (New York: Harper & Brothers, 1936).

Firey, Walter, *Land Use in Central Boston* (Cambridge: Arno Press, 1947).

Forbes, Esther, *Paul Revere and the World He Lived In* (Boston: Houghton Mifflin, 1943).

Fox, Stephen R., *The Guardian of Boston: William Monroe Trotter* (New York, Atheneum, 1950).

Gans, Herbert, *The Urban Villagers* (New York: Free Press, 1962).

Green, Martin, *The Problem of Boston: Some Readings in Cultural History* (New York: W. W. Norton, 1966).

Handlin, Oscar, *Boston's Immigrants* (Cambridge: Atheneum, 1941, 1968).

Horton, Jemes O. and Lois E., *Black Bostonians: Family Life and Community Struggle in the Intebellum North* (New York: Holmes and Meier Publishers, Inc., 1979).

King, Mel, *Autobiography* (Boston: South End Press, ?).

Kirker, Harold, *Bullfinch's Boston, 1787-1817* (New York: Oxford, 1964).

Knights, Peter, *The Plain People of Boston, 1830-1860* (New York: Oxford, 1971).

Kozal, Jonathan, *Death at an Early Age* (Boston: Houghton Mifflin, 1967).

Labaree, Benjamin, *The Boston Tea Party* (New York: Oxford, 1964).

Lane, Roger, *Policing the City: Boston 1822-1885* (Cambridge: Atheneum, 1967).

Lord, Robert H., *et.al., History of the Archdiocese of Boston,* 3 volumes (Boston: Pilot Publishing Co., 1945).

Lupo, Alan, *Liberty's Chosen Home* (Boston: Little, Brown, 1975).

Mann, Arthur, *Yankee Reformers in the Urban Age* (Cambridge: University of Chicago Press, 1954).

McCaughey, Robert, *Josiah Quincy: The Last Federalist* (Cambridge: Harvard University Press, 1974).

Merwick, Donna, *Boston's Priests, 1848-1910: A Study of Intellectual and Social Change* (Cambridge: Harvard University Press, 1973).

Middlekauf, Robert, *The Mathers* (New York: Oxford, 1971).

Morgan, Edmund, *The Puritan Dilemma: The Story of John Winthrop* (Boston: Little, Brown, 1958).

Morison, Samuel Eliot, *Builders of the Bay Colony* (Boston: Houghton Mifflin, 1930).

——————, *Harrison Gray Otis: Urbane Federalist* (Boston: Houghton Mifflin, 1969).

——————. *Maritime History of Massachusetts* (Boston: Houghton Mifflin, 1921).

——————, *One Boy's Boston, 1887-1901* (Boston: Houghton Mifflin, 1962).

O'Connor, Edwin, *The Last Hurrah* (Boston: Little, Brown, 1956).

O'Connor, Thomas H., *Bibles,*

Brahmins and Bosses (Boston: Boston Public Library, 1976).

Pleck, Elizabeth Hafkin, *Hunting for a City: Black Migration and Poverty in Boston, 1865-1900* (New York: Academic Press, 1979).

Russell, Francis, *A City in Terror - 1919 - The Boston Police Strike* (New York: Viking, 1975).

——————, *Tragedy at Dedham: The Story of the Sacco-Vanzetti Case* (New York: Mcgraw-Hill, 1962).

Ruttman, Darrett B., *Winthrop's Boston: Portrait of a Puritan Town* (Chapel Hill, North Carolina: University of North Carolina Press, 1965).

Schragg, Peter, *Village School Downtown* (Boston: Beacon Press, 1967).

Shannon, William V., *The American Irish* (New York: Macmillan, 1966).

Solomon, Barbara Miller, *Ancestors and Immigrants: A Changing New England Tradition* (Cambridge: McGraw-Hill, 1956).

Tharp, Louise Hall, *Mrs. Jack: A Biography of Isabella Stewart Gardner* (Boston: Little, Brown, 1965).

Thernstrom, Stephen, *The Other Bostonians: Poverty and Progress in the American Metropolis, 1880-1970* (Cambridge: Harvard University Press, 1973).

Thomas, John L., *The Liberator: William Lloyd Garrison* (Boston: Little, Brown, 1963).

Trout, Charles H., *Boston, the Great Depression and the New Deal* (New York: Oxford University Press, 1977).

Warden, Gerald B., *Boston, 1689-1776* (Boston: Little, Brown, 1970).

Warner, Sam Bass, *Street Car Suburbs* (Cambridge: Atheneum, 1962).

Wayman, Dorothy G., *Cardinal O'Connell of Boston* (New York: Farrar, Straus and Young, 1955).

Whitehill, Walter Muir, *Boston: A Topographical History* (Cambridge: Belknap Press, 1959, 1968).

——————. *Boston in the Age of John F. Kennedy* (Norman, OK: University of Oklahoma Press, 1966).

Whyte, William Foot, *Street Corner Society: The Social Structure of an Italian Slum* (Chicago: University of Chicago Press, 1943).

Winsor, Justin, ed., *The Memorial History of Boston. . .,* 4 volumes (Boston: Ticknor and Co., 1880).

Woods, Robert A., *Americans In Process* (Boston: Arno Press, 1903).

The City Wilderness, A Settlement House Study by Residents and Associates of the South End House (Boston: Arno Press, 1898).

Woods, Robert A. and Kennedy, A. J., *The Zone of Emergence: Observations of Lower Middle and Upper Working Class Communities in Boston, 1905-1914,* preface by Sam Bass Warner, Jr. (Cambridge: MIT Press, 1962).

Zobel, Hiller, *The Boston Massacre* (New York: W. W. Norton, 1970).

Index

Facing page: This mural of nine notable Boston women, commissioned by Workingmen's Co-operative Bank, depicts: Anne Hutchinson, who challenged the Puritan power structure; Phillis Wheatley, poet; Sister Ann Alexis, founder of the Nazareth Home; Lucy Stone, suffragist; Mary Baker Eddy, founder of the Christian Science Church; Ellen Richards, first woman to graduate from MIT; Mary Morton Kehew, leader in the Women's Educational and Industrial Union; Anne Sullivan, Helen Keller's teacher; and Melnea Cass, contemporary leader. Courtesy, Workingmen's Co-operative Bank

1983-84 BOSTON CELTICS

L to R (Front Row): Quinn Buckner, Cedric Maxwell, Paul R. Dupee, Don F. Gaston, Red Auerbach, K.C. Jones, Alan N. Cohen, Larry Bird, M.L. Carr.
L to R (Back Row): Dr. Thomas Silva, Jim Rodgers, Gerald Henderson, Scott Wedman, Greg Kite, Robert Parish, Kevin McHale, Dennis Johnson, Danny Ainge, Carlos Clark, Chris Ford, Ray Melchiorre.